Who to Release?

Who to Release?
Parole, fairness and criminal justice

Edited by Nicola Padfield

WILLAN
PUBLISHING

Published by

Willan Publishing
Culmcott House
Mill Street, Uffculme
Cullompton, Devon
EX15 3AT, UK
Tel: +44(0)1884 840337
Fax: +44(0)1884 840251
e-mail: info@willanpublishing.co.uk
website: www.willanpublishing.co.uk

Published simultaneously in the USA and Canada by

Willan Publishing
c/o ISBS, 920 NE 58th Ave, Suite 300,
Portland, Oregon 97213-3786, USA
Tel: +001(0)503 287 3093
Fax: +001(0)503 280 8832
e-mail: info@isbs.com
website: www.isbs.com

First published 2007

Hardback
ISBN: 978-1-84392-227-8

British Library Cataloguing-in-Publication Data

A catalogue record for this book is available from the British Library

Project managed by Deer Park Productions, Tavistock, Devon
Typeset by TW Typesetting, Plymouth, Devon
Printed and bound by TJ International Ltd, Trecerus Industrial Estate, Padstow, Cornwall

Contents

Index of cases

A v. Home Secretary [2004] UKHL 56, [2005] 2 AC 68 57n.68, 58, 60
Achour v. France (2005) 41 EHRR 36 175n.7
Ashingdane v. United Kingdom (1985) 7 EHRR 528 119
AT v. UK [1995] 20 EHRR CD 59 114–15
Attorney-General v. English [1983] 1 AC 116 141n.35

Bennett v. Superintendent, Rimutaka Prison [2002] 1 NZLR 616 (CA) 89
Blackstock v. UK (2006) 42 EHRR 2 50n.33, 51n.36, 76n.16, 119n.37
Bulger v. Home Secretary & Lord Chief Justice [2001] EWHC Admin 119
    110
Burgess v. Home Secretary [2001] 1WLR 93 50n.33

Campbell & Fell v. UK (1985) 7 EHRR 16 78, 116n.28
Coeme v. Belgium [2000] ECHR 250 81, 84

De Freitas v.Ministry of Agriculture, Fisheries, Lands and Housing
    [1999] 1 AC 69, p. 80 57n.67
De Wilde v. Belgium (1979–80) 1 EHRR 373, p. 407 47n.16, 49n.28
Dean v. New Zealand 1512/2006 89n.75

Finlay, In re [1985] 1 AC 318 132n.18
Flynn v. Her Majesty's Advocate [2004] SCCR 281 80, 81–2

Girling v. Home Secretary [2006] EWCA Civ 1779 130n.11, 140n.34
Grava v. Italy (10 July 2003) App No. 43522/98 120n.40
Gunnell v. Parole Board (*The Times*, 7 November 1984) 53n.43, 96, 111

H (minors), In re (Sexual abuse: standard of proof) [1996] AC 563 179n.17
Hirst v. Parole Board and another [2002] EWCA Civ 1329 56n.64, 104

Index of statutes

Notes on contributors

Hamish Arnott is a solicitor at Bhatt Murphy Solicitors. He specialises in public law with a particular focus on the rights of prisoners and other detainees. He is co-author of *Prisoners and the Law* (Tottel Publishing 2005) and *Parole Board Hearings: Law and Practice* (LAG 2006).

Gill Attrill is a Senior Principal Psychologist working for the Offending Behaviour Programmes Unit within HM Prison Service. Her work includes the design and implementation of programmes aimed at assessing and reducing risk. She specialises in work with violent and personality disordered offenders.

Helen Collins is a Senior Probation Officer in Durham. She previously worked for the Prison Service for eleven years and prior to this with young people in the care system. She currently manages a unit responsible for the resettlement of prisoners and has been nominated for a Butler Trust Award. She completed a Masters at the University of Durham in 2002 and graduated from the University of Cambridge in 2006 with an MSt in Criminology, Penology and Management.

Jackie Craissati is a consultant clinical and forensic psychologist and head of forensic psychology services with Oxleas NHS Foundation Trust in south-east London. She has a special interest in high-risk personality disordered sexual and violent offenders and manages a number of community projects in partnership with the Probation Service, Turning Point and First Step Trust. She has published widely in this area and is the author of *Managing High Risk Sex Offenders in the Community: A Psychological Approach* (2004).

Simon Creighton is a partner at Bhatt Murphy Solicitors and has practised in prison law since 1993 when he was appointed as the first solicitor to the Prisoners' Advice Service. He specialises in working with people serving life sentences. He is the co-author of *Prisoners and the Law* (Tottel 2004) and *The Parole Board: Law and Practice* (LAG 2006). He writes regular updates for LAG on prison law and is a contributor to Liberty's *Guide To Your Rights* and the *Prisons Handbook*.

Mark Elliott teaches Public Law at the University of Cambridge, where he is also a Fellow of St Catharine's College. A version of his PhD thesis was published in 2000 under the title *The Constitutional Foundations of Judicial Review* (Hart Publishing). He is also the author of the third edition of *Beatson, Matthews and Elliott's Text and Materials on Administrative Law* (Oxford University Press 2005). His research interests lie in constitutional and administrative law, and his recent publications include papers touching on (among other matters) parliamentary sovereignty, devolution and judicial review.

Tony Ellis is a leading New Zealand human rights barrister, with degrees in law from Australia, New Zealand and the UK. He is also President of the New Zealand Council for Civil Liberties. His caselaw approach is normally on an expansive international and comparative basis. He specialises in criminal appeals and judicial reviews which involve systemic issues. These have included *Taito v. R.*, a Privy Council case on unlawful appeals, *Rameka v. New Zealand* on preventive detention, the only successful case from New Zealand before the UN Human Rights Committee to date, and *Taunoa and Ors v. Attorney-General* on inhumane prison conditions at Auckland Prison.

Christine Glenn is a barrister and former Justices' Clerk and Justices' Chief Executive for the Inner London Magistrates' Courts. She was appointed Chief Executive of the Parole Board in December 2001. She also sits as an Immigration Judge and as a Parking and Traffic Adjudicator, teaches strategy on the Open University MBA Programme, is Deputy Chair of the London Region Courts' Service Audit and Risk Management Committee and is a member of the Courts Board in the Thames Valley.

Hazel Kemshall is currently Professor of Community and Criminal Justice at De Montfort University, Leicester. She has research interests in risk assessment and the management of offenders, effective work in multi-agency public protection and implementing effective practice with offenders. She has numerous publications on risk, including *Understanding Risk in Criminal Justice* (Open University Press 2003). She has recently completed an evaluation of multi-agency public protection panels for the Home Office (with Wood, Mackenzie, Bailey and Yates), and is currently investigating pathways into and out of crime for young people under an ESRC network (with Boeck and Fleming).

Alison Liebling is Professor of Criminology and Criminal Justice at the University of Cambridge and Director of the Institute of Criminology's Prisons Research Centre. She has published several books, including *Suicides in Prison* (Routledge 1992), *Prisons and Their Moral Performance: A Study of Values, Quality and Prison Life* (Oxford University Press 2004) and *The Effects of Imprisonment* with Shadd Maruna (Willan 2005). Her current research includes a detailed evaluation of the relationship between prison quality and prison suicide, an evaluation of the role of staff working with children in prison and a study of values, practices and outcomes in public and private sector corrections (with Ben Crewe).

Glenda Liell is a Senior Psychologist working for the Offending Behaviour Programmes Unit within HM Prison Service. Her work has involved the delivery of treatment to violent and sexual offenders, and she now specialises in violence risk assessment. She currently co-edits *Forensic Update*, a publication of the Division of Forensic Psychology of the British Psychological Society.

Terry McCarthy is currently Head of Casework at the Parole Board, where his duties include considering legal challenges to the Board's decisions and the associated training and policy implications that go with it. He has previously worked for (what is now known as) the Lifer Review and Recall Section in NOMS, setting up the first system of oral hearings by which lifers are considered for release by the Parole Board. Prior to this he was posted to the Category A section of the Prison Service, to the C3 division of the Home Office, investigating potential miscarriages of justice – now dealt with by the Criminal Cases Review Commission. He holds a degree in law from the University of Birmingham.

Sir Duncan Nichol CBE began his career in the Health Service and was Chief Executive of the NHS Management Executive for five years until 1994 and later became an Honorary Professor at the Manchester Centre for Healthcare Management, part of the University of Manchester. A former Commissioner for Judicial Appointments, he is currently Chairman of the Parole Board for England and Wales and Chairman of the Queen's Counsel Selection Panel. He is a Non-Executive Director of a number of private companies.

Nicola Padfield is a senior lecturer at the Law Faculty, University of Cambridge and a Fellow of Fitzwilliam College, Cambridge. A barrister by training, she has published widely on criminal law and sentencing, as well as on parole. Her books include *The Criminal Justice Process: Text and Materials* (OUP, 4th edition due 2007); *Criminal Law* (OUP, 5th edition, 2006); and *Beyond the Tariff: Human Rights and the Release of Life Sentence Prisoners* (Willan 2002). She sits as a Recorder in the Crown Court.

Stephen Shute is Professor of Criminal Law and Criminal Justice at the University of Birmingham and Director of the Institute of Judicial Administration. He has held Visiting Professorships at the University of South Carolina, USA, and the University of Bayreuth, Germany. His books and reports include: *Parole in Transition* (with Roger Hood, 1994); *Paroling with New Criteria* (with Roger Hood, 1995); *The Parole System at Work: A Study of Risk Based Decision-making* (with Roger Hood, 2000); *Criminal Law Theory: Doctrines of the General Part* (ed. with Andrew Simester, 2002); and *A Fair Hearing? Ethnic Minorities in the Criminal Courts* (with Roger Hood and Florence Seemungaal, 2005). He is a member of the International Penal and Penitentiary Foundation and is currently completing an evaluation of satellite tracking for the Home Office.

Hugh Southey is a barrister who specialises in public law in the fields of human rights, prison law, crime, mental health, immigration and election law. He has appeared in many of the leading cases regarding prison law and is the author of two books regarding judicial review.

Jo Thompson is a senior manager in the National Probation Service, and has been seconded from Nottinghamshire Probation Area as an Assistant Chief Officer to the Public Protection Unit within the Home Office. Since training as a Probation Officer in the 1970s she has worked in almost every field of probation practice as a practitioner or manager and has maintained an abiding interest in particular in dangerousness and the life sentence as it has developed from the mid-1970s. She also worked as an elected national officer in the Professional Association and Trade Union for Family Court and Probation Staff (NAPO) for four years in the 1990s.

Anthony Thornton is currently a circuit judge on the Technology and Construction Court (formally known as Official Referees). He was made Queen's Counsel in 1987, and was treasurer to the General Council of the Bar between 1990 and 1993. He was chairman of the Professional Conduct Committee of the General Council of the Bar in 1993, and was

Assistant Recorder and Recorder on the Midland Circuit. He is also currently a Bencher of the Middle Temple, is on the Executive Committee of the Middle Temple and is Chairman of the Fulham Legal Advice Centre and Law Centre. He has contributed a section on 'Building Contracts' in *Halsbury's Laws* (4th edition) and is author of *Human Rights and Construction Litigation* (forthcoming).

Chapter 1

Introduction

Nicola Padfield

The subject matter of this book could not be more topical. There is great public (or, at least, media) concern about the decision-making processes which result in the release of serious offenders back into the 'community'. Should we be concerned? Where, if anywhere, should the finger of blame be pointed? Are too many offenders being released, or is it a question of inadequate supervision on release? Or should we learn to live with the uncomfortable fact that some offenders will unpredictably reoffend? At the same time, the number of ex-prisoners in the community who are recalled to prison, very often simply because they are causing their supervisors significant concern and not because they have reoffended, is at a record high. Are those responsible for recall in fact being too cautious? Is the Parole Board unduly cautious? Or do many of the problems not lie with individual decision-makers but with the 'system'? These are some of the big questions discussed in this book.

The chapters were first prepared as conference papers. The conference took place at the Law Faculty at the University of Cambridge on 15–16 September 2006, and was co-hosted by the Centre for Public Law in Cambridge and by the Parole Board. The roots of the conference lie firmly in the context in which the Parole Board has to function. The recent past has seen extraordinary change: not least the Criminal Justice Act 2003, which fundamentally changed the ground rules for parole. But a growing prison population, court decisions, new assessment tools and a dramatic change in caseload also prompted many both within and outside the Parole Board to agree that an occasion in which to draw breath and to consider some fundamental questions would be useful.

The conference attracted a large number of people: Parole Board members, prison and probation staff, lawyers (both practitioners and academics), psychologists, psychiatrists and criminologists. It is to be hoped that the papers collected together as chapters in this book may prove useful to an even wider audience.

The Parole Board was created in 1967 and the recent changes were not the first major shake-up to it in its 40-year history. Most important, perhaps, was the Criminal Justice Act 1991. Parole eligibility for those sentenced to four years or more moved up to the half way point. Oral hearings were introduced for discretionary life sentence prisoners. Short-term prisoners could only be recalled by a court, which became a rather lengthy, drawn-out process. Long-termers could be recalled by the Home Secretary or by the Parole Board. Further significant changes were introduced throughout the 1990s and early 2000s, but the Criminal Justice Act 2003 has created the most radical change. Since determinate sentence prisoners are now eligible for automatic release at the half way point, discretionary early release for most is limited to Home Detention Curfew. The Parole Board now focuses on the release of lifers and other 'dangerous' indeterminate sentenced prisoners, with recall an executive process overseen by the Parole Board. It is only the Board who can order re-release.[1]

Setting the scene

This introductory chapter seeks to summarise the main arguments developed in the following chapters and to record some of the main themes arising from them. Sir Duncan Nichol, the Chairman of the Parole Board, divides his chapter (Chapter 2) into three parts: first he focuses on the 'reasonableness' of Parole Board decisions; secondly, he explores the Board's 'track record'; and thirdly he concludes with a discussion of their agenda for promoting 'safe' decisions. He makes clear that Parole Board decisions cannot be segmented or compartmentalised without a consideration of the wider context in which they are taken. A recurring theme throughout the book is the role that a human rights culture can play in improving the quality of decision-making. Human rights and due process may thus enhance public protection. On human rights, Sir Duncan points out that the Board has lost only seven of the 294 judicial reviews brought in the past five years. It is fascinating to note

---

[1] Participants at the conference were encouraged to read in advance Padfield (2006) and Padfield and Maruna (2006) by way of background. Both Shute and Thornton (this book) review the changes. The references listed at the back of this book will also provide readers with a detailed bibliography.

that the Chairman of the Parole Board leads the call for more institutional independence, suggesting that the Parole Board might be better 'sponsored' by the Department of Constitutional Affairs, rather than the Home Office, and that 'the most appropriate body for making appointments to the Parole Board could be the Independent Judicial Appointments Commission' (p. 18). Many of the audience at the conference was surprised to hear him argue thus (Simon Creighton felt the 'ground was taken from under his feet'!), but it is an issue that Sir Duncan has taken up both formally and informally with the government.

In Chapter 3, Stephen Shute, Professor of Criminal Law and Criminal Justice at the School of Law, University of Birmingham, argues that the Criminal Justice Act 2003 resolved some of the tensions in the parole system: it will 'will no longer be based on considerations of rehabilitation balanced against risk, grafted on to a largely retributive, "just deserts", sentencing structure, as was the case with the system introduced by the Criminal Justice Act 1991. Instead, in an approach that is plainly in tune with the public protection agenda that has driven criminal justice policy for the last ten to 15 years, the 2003 Act refocuses parole entirely on risk and risk assessment' (p. 22). Shute also identifies ways in which the parole system is much fairer now than it used to be. But the focus of his analysis is some recurrent problems. One is the difficulty involved in assessing risk (particularly when the type of reoffending that is of greatest concern, very serious violent or sexual reoffending, is that which is least likely to occur). He rehearses the swings and changes over the years in the use made by the Board of risk prediction tools. He questions the value of parole interviews, arguing that the better approach would be to offer personal hearings to all prisoners who request them. He concludes with a call for the ending of a separate system of recall for offenders aged 18–21 released under s. 65 of the Criminal Justice Act 1991.

Mark Elliott, constitutional and public lawyer at the University of Cambridge, in Chapter 4 gives a careful analysis of the changing face of public law over the decades since the creation of the Parole Board. He argues that there has been a shift of power away from the executive, and that both procedural rights and substantive rights have conditioned the options available to the Board. Pointing out that the legitimacy of judicial power lies in its independence, he explores the distinction between the punitive and the security phases of sentences. He explores the 'pivotal' role of Article 5 of the European Convention on Human Rights (ECHR), contrasting what he sees as the 'category-based approach of Article 5 with the 'the context-sensitivity of the common law' (p. 54). Thus while the common law afforded oral hearings only where necessary, once a case falls within one of the classes to which Article 5 applies, an oral hearing is automatically required. 'Article 5 has effected a major erosion of executive power over parole matters', which Elliott sees as an entirely positive development. He underlines the point that procedural fairness is quite compatible with protecting the public. As he puts it, 'one of the principal virtues of procedurally proper decision-making is that it is liable to yield more accurate outcomes – risk assessments, in the present context – by ensuring that decision-makers are in receipt of, and equipped fully to test, all relevant information' (pp. 55–56). He concludes with another fundamental point, that the ECHR 'is premised on the notion that the interests of the individual must yield where this is necessary in the interests of public safety. Properly understood, there is no inconsistency between due respect for human rights and a parole system which adequately protects the public' (p. 62).

Alison Liebling (in Chapter 5), Professor at the Institute of Criminology at the University of Cambridge, focuses on research into fairness in prisons to show why fairness matters. Looking at the way the Woolf Report (Home Office 1991a) was misunderstood in some prisons, she usefully points out that fairness should not be interpreted as laxity. Developing her own research, she explores the relationship between fairness, moral performance and outcomes. The link between fairness and well-being suggests that 'there are reasons to believe that a prison experience that is perceived as reasonably fair and respectful will be less painful and damaging than one that is unfair and hostile' (p. 70). Fairness matters for normative and instrumental reasons: 'being treated unfairly leads to negative consequences – non-compliance, and importantly, distress. We need just institutions of criminal justice if we are to avoid hypocrisy, disaffection and further damage' (p. 71). She ends with the valuable comment that criminal justice professionals need to be treated fairly too.

Finally, in the opening session Tony Ellis, a barrister from Wellington, New Zealand, gave a lively response from New Zealand. The conference organisers had decided that this conference was primarily for a domestic audience, and took an inter-disciplinary rather than comparative approach. Yet Ellis's critique of parole in New Zealand (Chapter 6) rang familiar bells with his largely English audience. Thus Ellis analyses the major changes introduced in New Zealand in 2002 and regretted another major review only four years later. As he says, 'trendy political amendments are no substitute for a principled approach' (p. 74). He raises some big questions: the impact of both the prison population and the public perception of increasing crime on parole.

Dealing with indeterminacy

The second part of the book moves from the general to the more specific, looking at the process for indeterminate (life) sentence prisoners. In

Chapter 7, Terry McCarthy, who is Head of Casework at the Parole Board, starts from the position that the Board's prime function is to protect the public, and moves on to discuss the sometimes competing demands for 'fairness' of the various parties affected by parole decisions. He identifies a 'quadrangle' of competing interests: prisoner, victim, witness and public. He reviews the recent case law on, for example, withholding information, on the use of hearsay evidence and on burdens of proof. His conclusions are clear-cut: 'The Board cannot countenance a situation whereby the public may be put at risk because the principle of fairness to the prisoner comes before that of fairness to the public' (p. 101), and that 'faced with an individual who has been proved capable of the most serious of offences, there is nothing unfair whatsoever in asking that the prisoner accept the burden of showing himself not to be dangerous before he is set free into the community' (p. 105). He points out, too, that fairness to the victim may apply even where issues of risk to the public do not arise (in the context of geographical licence conditions).

Simon Creighton, a practising solicitor with much experience of parole cases, explores, in Chapter 8, the nature of the Board as 'court'. He argues that the Board's hybrid role as both court and advisory body, while understandable in historical terms, is deeply problematic. 'Balancing the deference that must be shown to the executive on advice cases with the robust independence that is required on Article 5 cases is no easy task' (p. 115). The complexity of the task is well illustrated by his table (p. 117) of Parole Board decisions, which lists those to which Article 5 applies. He (like Mark Elliott) raises concerns about the relationship between the common law and Article 5, and is damning of the majority decision of the House of Lords in *R (Roberts)* v. *Parole Board* [2005] UKHL 45 to permit Special Advocates in parole hearings, when their role before criminal courts is limited to arguments on pre-trial issues of disclosure (see *Re H* [2004] UKHL 3). He concludes that the Board is 'central to the feasibility' of the current criminal justice system, with a central role in determining how long prisoners spend in custody. He would strip away the Board's advisory powers and urges a careful planned transfer of the Parole Board to the Tribunal Service and to the Department of Constitutional Affairs.

At this point in the conference on which this book is based, a paper was presented by Professor Andrew Rutherford, but unfortunately this does not appear in this volume. Pointing out the curiosity that the Parole Board is forced to focus only on the 'shallow-end' (for example, short-term recalls) and the 'deep-end' (lifers etc.) of the parole process, Andrew Rutherford himself focused on two features of the Parole Board's institutional environment: the 'powerful momentum towards release' and 'agency inertia'. The first means that the Board 'is hard pressed to apply cautionary brakes and may well get caught up in the momentum towards release'. Thus he, like the Chief Inspector of Probation in the much debated Rice report (Her Majesty's Inspectorate of Probation 2006b), explored the growing expectation by both prisoner and staff that release is only a matter of time. He explored, for example, the problematic ambiguity regarding the role of the open prison. He gave examples to illustrate his second theme of agency inertia, including that of a prisoner cited in the press who served more than three years as a recalled prisoner before he found a solicitor. He concluded that 'being stuck in the mud of NOMS is the fate of those individuals who have simply "got lost in the system" as well as persons who appear unable to progress with regards to offending behaviour courses or types of intervention'.

A response to these papers is given by Judge Anthony Thornton. In Chapter 9, he provides a detailed review of the law in relation to indeterminate sentences and the role of the Parole Board. He argues that the role of the Board as both executive advisory body and as tribunal is no longer tenable. He disputes whether the cost of an oral hearing is 'high', and rehearses numerous advantages of tribunal status: greater transparency and guideline judgments, for example. He would abolish the Home Secretary's gatekeeper role and change the 'very deficient' Parole Board Rules (targeting in particular Rule 20, which, he argues, seeks inappropriately to limit the Board's jurisdiction). He concludes that the Board 'should be transformed from an ENDPB to a Tribunal NDPB, should join the Tribunal Service once this has been fully established, should for the future be run and administered as a tribunal. It should also be provided with appropriate rule-making powers and procedural rules particularly now that it is no longer to be subject to the directions of the Home Secretary' (p. 143).

The particular challenges caused by recalls

The third part of the book focuses on the challenges posed by recalls, the number of which has more than trebled in the last five years. In Chapter 10, Jo Thompson presents the position from the perspective of the NOMS Pre and Post Release team at the Home Office. She suggested as she opened her talk that she felt like a 'lion in a den of Daniels', but her honest appraisal of the difficulties and challenges belies this. Her chapter sets out the use of recall as a 'flexible risk management tool' (see p. 149), and focuses on the reasons for the rise in recalls. She looks at the pressures, which have made practitioners and their managers much more risk averse. 'In a climate where staff are inclined to watch their backs rather than use judgment, more offenders are likely to be recalled'

(p. 153). She identifies some practical concerns, for example, that too many offenders are recalled without notification to NOMS and that on arrival in prison, reception staff often know little about the prisoner they are receiving. Interestingly, she comments that 'the Parole Board has not been re-releasing offenders in the numbers envisaged' (p. 150). Her paper refers to probation circulars: readers (particularly solicitors!) may well find the annexes to Probation Circular 76 of 2005 thought provoking – both the advice on 'dealing with difficult questioning' as well as the 'frequently asked questions'.

Some of the concerns raised by Jo Thompson are developed in Helen Collins's chapter (Chapter 11), which springs from her own role as a senior probation officer and from her research for her University of Cambridge MSt dissertation. She suggests that the increasing numbers of prisoners recalled to prison is not so much an increase in reoffending (interestingly, this is no one's explanation) but a decline in the use of professional discretion. She looks at the US literature, mentioning the 'waste management' model, which suggests that 'dangerous' prisoners are treated as a kind of toxic waste, simply to be contained. Her own research reaches depressing conclusions which need to be heard: for example, those offenders more likely to be recalled are also the most disadvantaged (p. 170). She reinforces the message that recall is both ineffective and costly, and calls for a more 'graduated' response to recalls, and indeed a return to a policy of recall via the courts.

The third chapter focusing explicitly on recall is that of Hamish Arnott, an experienced solicitor in the field, who focuses on the question of disputed facts. In Chapter 12, he asks whether the Board provides a sufficiently adversarial procedure, pointing out the tension between the two tasks of the Board: deciding facts and assessing risks. In relation to both, he challenges the reader to consider whether there is in truth a burden of proof, and he also questions the quality of the evidence upon which the Board is entitled to rely. For the prisoner, he argues, the process is 'unlegal' and bewildering: he questions how a 'status' can be litigated, by looking at decision-making relating to ASBOs, national security and child care orders. He points out that recall only happens because of adverse developments in the community, and he questions the quality of the legal advice and training available to probation staff who initiate recalls. He points out the vital role of the prisoner's legal representative in seeking to improve the quality of the evidence presented to the Board, and urges the Board itself to be clearer in articulating their findings of facts, quite separately from their assessment of risk, since this may have considerable subsequent impact on the prisoner. He concludes with specific recommendations which include a proposed duty on NOMS/the Home Office to take further steps to obtain evidence beyond the Probation Service recommendation prior to revoking a licence.

The session of the conference from which this part of the book developed provoked a particularly lively debate. Clearly some probation or NOMS staff felt that Hamish Arnott's analysis insulted overworked and underpaid probation staff. But solicitors working in this field are clearly also poorly paid and overworked. A certain animosity towards solicitors seemed to reflect both a misunderstanding of their role and the high levels of frustration and pressure under which both probation officers and the Parole Board work in trying to provide a 'good' service. It is not necessarily inconsistent to support both Helen Collins's call for greater trust in probation professionals and Hamish Arnott's call for a more rigorous approach to fact-finding. Perhaps the answer is a more openly adversarial system, with the NOMS witnesses having their own legal representative, and greater clarity about the role of the probation officer and the Secretary of State's representative?

Another intervention from the floor suggested that some recalls resulted from a failure to get other services (particularly psychiatric services) involved early enough. Concerns included the impact of the increased number of licence conditions and the imprecision of the term 'unacceptable failure'. One probation officer reported on a recent trip to the Czech Republic. When she and her colleagues had described the management of offenders in the community in England to Czech colleagues, they were very surprised to be told that it sounded like living under the Russian totalitarian state. They were asked how such practices could be acceptable in the European Union. It was a healthy reminder of the very high price one pays if one loses sight of the individual and of human rights.

While we are frequently reminded of the problem of limited resources, it is helpful to be reminded of the hidden costs of recall: the mental health problems exacerbated in those looking at long periods of recall in prison, or the rupture to drug abstinence courses being successfully followed in the community caused by a period of recall. If release plans are to be realistic, it is urgently necessary for home probation officers to reconnect with 'their' recalled prisoners. There is also an overarching anxiety about rising expectations: is what is expected of probation officers achievable?

Is predicting risk fair?

The fourth part of this book includes three chapters which ask whether predicting risk is fair. Gill Attrill and Glenda Liell, senior Prison Service psychologists, present the results of their research, conducted specifically for this book and the conference, on prisoners' views on risk assessment. They are clearly impressed by the care, eloquence and thoughtfulness with which prisoners present their views. In Chapter 13 the reader will find many echoes of Alison Liebling's theme that fairness really does matter. The prisoners' own words effectively remind the reader of how little control prisoners feel they have over the risk assessment process, while well understanding the importance of the process as well as the impact of the media and of politics. They are perceptive about the limitations of the process. Mistakes happen. These prisoners remind the Board of the need to be accurate and not vague; interestingly, there is a call for the Parole Board to have a more active role in prisons.

This chapter is followed by that of Hazell Kemshall, Professor of Community and Criminal Justice at De Montfort University, who started her professional life as a probation officer before becoming a leading academic authority on risk assessment. Her chapter (Chapter 14) starts with an analysis of recent tragic management failures and of the Home Secretary's attempts to restore public trust. She argues that failures are inevitable, that such failures should be seen as systemic and not as individual failures, and that they can be better managed. According to her, MAPPAs reflect a model of community protection which is 'characterised by the use of restriction, surveillance, monitoring and control, compulsory treatment and the prioritisation of victim/community rights over those of offenders (p. 206). The MAPPA–parole interface creates a number of threats to effective risk management – clashes of culture and the fragmentation of accountability, for example – and it 'may be *as* programmed to produce poor results as it is programmed to produce positive ones' (p. 214). She urges a better understanding of, and more testing of, different risk assessment tools as well as the strategic management of the whole system.

Finally in this part, Jackie Craissati, consultant clinical and forensic psychologist at the Bracton Centre, identifies in Chapter 15 certain paradoxical effects of stringent management, focusing on community failure and sex offenders. Her insights come from her own work, where she says she specialises in 'failure', particularly sex offenders who fail. She looks at the relationship between MAPPAs and offenders and, by looking at individual 'stories', she reveals a number of challenging insights: that the fear of professional/institutional scapegoating may lead to oppressive risk management, which paradoxically raises the sexual reoffending rate, for example, or that some offenders do better simply when left alone. She concludes:

Really thoughtful risk management does not always consist of rights and wrongs, but of dilemmas . . . there is a fine line between control and persecution, one that is difficult to detect at times, and that social exclusion – in the current climate – seems to be an unavoidable consequence of rigorous risk management ... The possibility that stringent risk management approaches embodied within the MAPPA recreates – for some offenders – the disturbing experiences of their early lives seems absolutely clear. That it may paradoxically result in triggering greater levels of offending is an uncomfortable idea, as is the suggestion that in order to reduce risk, sometimes professionals and agencies may need to take risks. (p. 227)

These three chapters again highlight many of the tensions within the release process: most clearly the fairness–effectiveness dichotomy. But again many of the points raised in discussions at the conference were practical: the difficulty or impossibility of identifying the 'critical few', the anodyne nature of some MAPPA reports (from a Parole Board member's perspective) and the recurrent problem of resources.

Pulling the threads together

Finally, two chapters seek to pull the debate of the conference together. In Chapter 16, Christine Glenn, Chief Executive of the Parole Board, focuses on public confidence, which she sees as the real challenge for the Parole Board. She too is hard-hitting in adopting Rutherford's desire to 'get out of the NOMS mud', and her words reveal a real frustration that the Parole Board is still treated (within the Home Office) 'as a rather troublesome child' (p. 232). She does not consider the recall system to be 'fit for purpose' (p. 236). She reminds us of the difficulty for the Parole Board in justifying its decision to a critical press when it is not permitted to publish its reasons. She also raises the problem of training, when a budget is so limited. She highlights the need to improve and enhance the Secretary of State's representation at oral hearings to lead to real equality of arms and for better rules on disclosure. She is concerned that the requirement that the Parole Board consider all recall cases is clogging up the system and causing unnecessary delay (echoes here of Rutherford's 'shallow-end' workload). She also raised the big picture: changes in policy and in sentencing law which need better planning and more resources.

This book closes with Hugh Southey's personal overview, in Chapter 17. As a barrister who represents prisoners before the Parole Board, he is keen to demonstrate that human rights lawyers share common objectives with other participants in the parole process. In the first place, all agree that prisoners who pose an unacceptable level of risk should not be released, and that prisoners who pose an acceptable level of risk should be released as soon as possible. A second common objective is to improve decision-making. Procedural fairness and independence matter not least because they improve decision-making. Thirdly, lack of resources leads to unacceptable consequences. But he also argues that we must accept that the unthinkable may happen, not least because of failures in other parts of the system which may have nothing to do with the work of the Parole Board (his example is that probation budget cuts have resulted in few prisoners enjoying long-term relationships with their probation officers).

Nicola Padfield had the last word at the conference, as she does here, as editor of this book. So – where did this conference take the debate? Will the Home Office note the conference's apparently unanimous agreement on the need for the Parole Board to have greater independence? As we go to press in the autumn of 2006, it seems inconceivable that the government cannot acknowledge that the proper place for the Parole Board is as an independent tribunal within the tribunal service. Improving representation (of both sides to the process) would also lead towards 'equality of arms' and better decision-making. But the reconstitution of the Parole Board within the tribunal service cannot be done on a shoestring. The government's reluctance may be partly affected by a fear of costs: but there are plenty of suggestions in this book that the process is remarkably cheap (it depends on how you count), and that economies at one vital point in the criminal justice process can have huge costs elsewhere. A lack of resources impedes the work, of course, of the probation service and of defence lawyers, as well as of the Parole Board itself. It is depressing to note that chronic underfunding forced the Parole Board to cancel its annual conference in November 2006. If, within NOMS, probation remains the underfunded poor relation of the prison system, so supervision on licence will continue to 'fail' and result in too many expensive recalls.

Thus this book underlines the interconnections between the various players in the resettlement of offenders in the community. Obviously decisions taken at one stage have expected and unexpected consequences elsewhere. The Chief Inspector of Probations Report (HMIP 2006b) on the Rice case is raised by a number of contributors. Clearly the Parole Board felt that confidence in the Board had been damaged (see Sir Duncan Nichol, Chapter 2, this volume, p. 17). Yet a clear message of this book is that a human rights culture can improve decision-making. The European Convention on Human Rights has not put barriers in the way of good decision-making; it provides only minimum protections, and many would argue that it goes not far enough. Article 5 allows for the lawful arrest or detention of a person 'when it is reasonably considered necessary to prevent his committing an offence'. Everyone so detained is 'entitled to take proceedings by which a court shall decide the lawfulness of his detention speedily and his release ordered if the detention is not lawful'. It is difficult to see why this might be controversial.

This book encourages a certain reflection on the complexity of the parole process, but inevitably we skim the surface. We have failed perhaps to discuss the further fragmentation of control and accountability which arises with the increasing privatisation of criminal justice agencies (see Padfield 2005). Who is responsible, for what and when? (A simple example is the prisoner's dossier, for whom no 'body' seems to want to take responsibility.) The need for vigilant 'checks and balances' in this ever more complicated environment is all too apparent.

Other tensions at the heart of the parole process remain unresolved. What is parole and early release for? Most of us would agree that a period on licence is an integral and important part of a (custodial) sentence. The implications of this are of course different for the various players: for Jo Thompson, it means that enforcement is a priority (p. 149), for prisoners, it means they deserve 'due process' and 'fairness' throughout the sentence. But is parole/early release simply for public protection or also for rehabilitation? Stephen Shute argues that the philosophical tensions are no longer so apparent, yet Terry McCarthy argues that there is nothing unfair in a prisoner having the burden of showing himself not to be dangerous before he is set free into the community. This surely assumes that such a prisoner is being allowed a privilege of 'early' release. It is somewhat artificial to see a prison sentence divided into a period designed as punishment followed by a period designed only as public protection. Jo Thompson, a senior NOMS representative, stresses the point that licence conditions are not about punishment but about effective management, and should be both necessary and proportionate. Mark Elliott seems to accept that the punishment and the public protection element of a sentence can be separated. Yet clearly both parts feel like punishments for prisoners, especially when 'unacceptable' breaches result in recall to prison. Do technical breaches indicate risk? What are the implications of accepting that some licence conditions, such as geographical restrictions, have nothing to do with risk?

Perhaps we need to acknowledge that release on licence, for all prisoners, serves a multitude of purposes. Interestingly, several of the calls for more empirical research in this area come from practitioners, not just from academics. There are calls both for more use of discretion and for less (discretion as intuition, as Hamish Arnott puts it). Alison Liebling calls for fairness for criminal justice professionals. Is too much emphasis put on what goes wrong? Sir Duncan Nichol understandably emphasised the Parole Board's own Review Committee which reviews cases of grave and serious reoffending by those released by the Board. The lessons which he says are to be learnt from these reviews (see p. 18) ignore the 'success' stories. Alison Liebling also urges more 'appreciative inquiry' as a research tool. Let us focus also on the Board's successes. Given that those released were invariably supported by probation officers and prison service psychologists, the Parole Board should not try and learn too much from 'its' failures. How good a risk assessment tool is OASys? Should we simply accept that human behaviour is even more difficult to assess than the weather?

Andrew Rutherford's discussion of the 'powerful momentum' towards release suggests that living a sentence looks something like life on a 'snakes and ladders' board: the prisoner is moving along the board, sometimes fast, sometimes slowly, sometimes he goes up a ladder (a move to a different category of prison, enhanced privileges, acceptance on the Sex Offenders Treatment Programme or release), sometimes he gets stuck and sits still, sometimes he slides down the snakes (back to closed conditions, recall). How much should a court or tribunal be involved in all these decisions? The current distinctions between those which affect release and deserve a court-like decision-making body and those which are merely 'administrative' should be re-examined. The law on the administration of sentences deserves a fundamental review. It is interesting to recall some of Halliday's recommendations (see Halliday 2001): particularly, recommendation 20 which called for 'review courts': 'Before the release of a prisoner, the content of the second half of the sentence should be subject to court review, on the basis of proposals prepared jointly by the prison and probation service, in consultation with other potential contributors in the statutory, independent, and voluntary sectors.' Halliday wanted, too, community prisons and a review of the intermediate estate, a joined-up system. The gap between prison and community 'punishment' remains too great. And there is still far too much emphasis in the literature and in practice on 'front-door' sentencing decisions rather than 'back-door' decisions. The rules which govern getting into prison need to be transparent, but so too do those on getting out. This book has sought to shift the spotlight a little.

It remains only for me to thank most warmly all those who took part in the conference from which this book results, and for those key members of both the Parole Board and the Centre for Public Law at the University of Cambridge who worked so hard to support the project. One needs singling out: Felicity Eves, secretary for the Centre of Public Law, who has put in many, many hours ensuring that both the conference and this book smoothly fell into shape. Our thanks to the 'team' at Willan Publishing for their support and professionalism.

Part 1
Setting the scene

Chapter 2

Who should we keep locked up?

Sir Duncan Nichol CBE

I take my title as an invitation to cover the following ground. First, the reasonableness of Parole Board decisions as viewed against a perception that human rights considerations may be undermining our priority to protect the public, against the questioning of our judicial independence and as reviewed through our own internal review process. Second, our track record on release, recall and reconviction, and finally our agenda for promoting safe decisions. I respond at a time when confidence in the Parole Board has been damaged by the Chief Inspector of Probation's inquiries into the cases of Hanson and White (HMIP 2006a) and of Rice (HMIP 2006b).

The reasonableness of Parole Board decisions

The main point I want to make from the Rice inquiry is that judgments about the reasonableness of Parole Board decisions to release or retain in custody cannot be segmented or compartmentalised for the reasons that the Chief Inspector demonstrated in his report on Rice. He pointed to cumulative, collective and in my terms 'whole system' failure, while acknowledging that the Parole Board made a reasonable decision given where the case was in August 2004. I would also emphasise that risk assessments are weighed against risk management plans which should be commensurate to any given risk.

Turning to human rights. The European Convention on Human Rights ensures a fair hearing for life sentenced prisoners by giving them the right to see what is written about them, the right to challenge that, the right to legal representation and the option of an Oral Hearing. Nothing in the Convention or in the Human Rights Act takes away from our prime consideration to protect the public. We advise our members to subordinate any concerns about the possibility of Judicial Review to their concerns about risk. We have been judicially reviewed on 294 cases over five years to the end of 2005, seven of which went against us.

On the question of the Parole Board's independence, our principal function is that of a judicial tribunal at Oral Hearings. However, our status is that of an executive Non-Departmental Public Body (NDPB) sponsored by the Home Office. So the issue does arise as to whether, in perception at least, we are judicially independent given the following points. The Home Secretary is a party to our proceedings and the National Offender Management Service exercises significant sponsorship influence at the same time as managing the offenders we review. Our chair and members are appointed by the Home Secretary, and for shorter three-year periods than the two successive five-year periods deemed appropriate for tribunals. Our close working with our sponsor, including work together on risk assessment, is important but it can be miscon-strued by an independent observer. Our e-mail address . . .@homeoffice . . . , doesn't help if you are looking from the outside. The Home Office has announced that they are to review their NDPBs, and we will take the opportunity in the course of that review to argue the case that we should be sponsored elsewhere. The obvious candidate is the Department for Constitutional Affairs and the most appropriate body for making appointments to the Parole Board could be the Independent Judicial Appointments Commission.

Moving to our own internal review process, our Review Committee is chaired by Neil Butterfield, High Court Judge and Deputy Chair to the Board, who has alongside him a cross-section of members from the Board, and recently the addition of two external members, Peter Neyroud and Stephen Shaw. It reviews cases where there has been grave and serious reoffending. The broad generic lessons learnt are that static risk factors are not always given sufficient weight, that risk issues are not always identified and addressed in reasons and there is drift in following the Directions of the Secretary of State. There are more specific issues. First, around instrumental violence, which makes up a significant number of the cases reviewed, and gives rise to particular difficulties for us, where such offenders present credibly, are compliant in custody and perform well on cognitive courses. Second, the need for all reports to contextualise risk – risk of what, to whom, in what circumstances and with what instrument? Third, the need for all reports to refer to the risk predictor being used and to identify when a professional opinion differs in its conclusions from the predictor. We also suffer from lapses in the transfer of information between different agencies on whom we depend, not just individually, but collectively.

Our track record on release, recall and reconviction

Between 2000/01 and 2005/06 the number of offenders released on Life Licence has trebled almost and the recall rate to prison for alleged reoffending or breach of licence doubled approximately, although it should be noted that the reconviction rate for sex and/or violence reoffending has remained stable at around 3 per cent.

What are the hypotheses or explanations for these trends? What should we attribute to the effect of the *Stafford* decision which relaxed the test for release? Is the Parole Board releasing riskier offenders, either by failing to identify the risk appropriately or by responding positively to optimistic assessment reports? Is a higher proportion of risk management plans breaking down? Has the probation service become more sensitive to potential and actual risky behaviour and therefore become more likely to recall? The uncomfortable truth is that there is a dearth of multi-factorial, system-wide research to answer these interrelated questions.

We looked at similar issues for offenders subject to Discretionary Conditional Release (DCR) in the period between 2001 and 2004, where the numbers had moved from a 10 per cent recall to prison and a 4 per cent alleged reoffending rate to 15 per cent and 7 per cent respectively. Analysis by the Home Office of the Risk of Reconviction (ROR) score for those released did not indicate any significant increase in that score. However, appropriate breach enforcement by the probation service had been a significant contributor to the increase in recalls to prison.

A study by Hood and Shute (2000) showed us considerably more risk averse than probation service report writers in awarding parole in 54 per cent of cases where release was recommended by both home and prison seconded probation officers, as against 79 per cent from a recent internal review. In the Hood and Shute sample the overall paroling rate was 36 per cent and in the current sample it was 52 per cent. For the grave and serious reoffending cases which come to our Review Committee, there is invariably strong support for release from probation officers and prison service psychologists.

I conclude selectively with the Parole Board's agenda for promoting safe decisions. We have a very robust and thorough recruitment process, while subject to some current ambiguity as to how the Home Office is going to introduce victim experience and victim awareness into the attributes of all future members of the Parole Board. In relation to appraisal and accreditation, it is very important that we have embedded a culture of appraisal, albeit a form of appraisal limited by the nature of our organisation to taking snapshots irregularly of the performance of a member at work through the eye of an appraiser on a given day. We are looking to move further to regular accreditation to ensure that the standards which members have developed during training and in practice are being maintained. We believe also that members should be tested against explicit criteria and mock assessments before progressing to more challenging work.

Finally the Board's Lifer Database, developed by Dr Marion Swan and Miss Catherine Appleton, which is potentially so important to us as we accrue the data. Its objective is to identify variables and any combination of variables which are strongly related to failure on licence. We have 311 cases (100 per cent) of released offenders entered for the first year to September 2004 and we continue to input cases for Year 2. The database has the potential of building rapidly into a very rich source for research and evaluation. We envisage two early pieces of analysis, firstly of the static variables, and a second analysis, which will look at all the variables and the recall information for all prisoners who will have had the opportunity to spend at least 12 months on licence. The Lifer Database should be available to external researchers and I welcome such collaboration in the spirit which today's conference will engender.

Chapter 3

Parole and risk assessment

*Stephen Shute**

The parole system in England and Wales is going through difficult times. Scarcely a week seems to pass without some negative report appearing in the press about parolees who have committed serious crimes while on parole licence. One of the more dramatic examples is the *Daily Mirror*'s recent coverage of Her Majesty's Chief Inspector of Probation's report on the Anthony Rice case.[1] The paper published its story under a large front-page headline which made reference to Rice's victim and asked, memorably, 'What about her rights?'[2] Not to be outdone, *The Sun* has also turned its guns on parole, including it in a high-profile 'Charter for Justice' campaign and demanding change.[3]

---

*I am grateful to John Baldwin and Roger Hood for their helpful comments on an earlier version of this essay.

[1] See Her Majesty's Inspectorate of Probation (HMIP) (2006b).

[2] See the *Daily Mirror*, 11 May 2006.

[3] See, for example, an edition of *The Sun* printed on 20 July 2006 which carried the front-page headline 'Blair axes soft sentences'. One of the nine demands made by the newspaper was that 'No criminal should be freed on parole unless the Parole Board agrees unanimously.' This idea has now been taken up by the government. In a speech made in the House of Commons on 20 July 2006, the Home Secretary, Dr John Reid, announced that reform of the Parole Board would include a requirement that, in serious sexual and violent cases, the decision of a Parole Board panel would have to be unanimous before a prisoner could be released on parole. See HC Debs, sixth series, 20 July 2006, vol. 449, col. 472. See also Home Office (2006a: 34, para. 3.45). *The Sun* described this policy change as a 'victory' for its campaign. When implemented, it will mean that any member of a three-person panel will have the power, should he or she deem it appropriate, to prevent a serious sexual or violent offender from being released on parole licence.

With the tabloid press, and even some of the broadsheets,[4] in such a frenzy about parole, it is perhaps not surprising that politicians – including senior members of the Conservative Shadow Cabinet – have been drawn into the fray. The Shadow Home Secretary, Mr David Davis, for example, has claimed that 'more dangerous prisoners' than before are being released into the community.[5] And, in an exchange in the House of Commons at Prime Minister's Questions, the leader of the Conservative Party, Mr David Cameron, challenged the Prime Minister to include early release schemes – which, he said, were causing 'widespread concern' and 'still let far too many prisoners out of prison far too early' – within the review of probation policy that had been commissioned by the Home Secretary.[6]

An improved structure

It is important to remember, however, that parole is currently in a process of radical transformation. Reforms introduced by the Criminal Justice Act 2003 mean that the parole system will no longer be based on considerations of rehabilitation balanced against risk, grafted on to a largely retributive, 'just deserts', sentencing structure, as was the case with the system introduced by the Criminal Justice Act 1991. Instead, in an approach that is plainly in tune with the public protection agenda that has driven criminal justice policy for the last ten to 15 years, the 2003 Act refocuses parole entirely on risk and risk assessment. Under its provisions, the only prisoners sentenced to determinate sentences of imprisonment who will be assessed by the Parole Board as to their suitability for release on parole licence will be those who have been identified as dangerous by the court at the time of their sentence.[7]

The 2003 legislation is complex but, broadly speaking, it operates in the following way.[8] Offenders who receive ordinary determinate senten-

---

[4] For three examples, see 'Parole thief faces life for killing', *The Times*, 15 March 2006, p. 29; 'Record number of lifers freed by parole boards [*sic*] are called back to jail', *The Times*, 7 November 2006, p. 32; and 'Two mothers assaulted by released killer', *The Times*, 12 December 2006, p. 17.

[5] See *The Times*, 7 November 2006, p. 32.

[6] HC Debs, sixth series, 22 March 2006, vol. 444, col. 279.

[7] The court making this assessment must take into account all the information that is available to it about 'the nature and circumstances' of the offence(s) and, where appropriate, 'any information which is before it about any pattern of behaviour of which any of the offences forms a part' and 'any information about the offender which is before it': see s. 229(2) and (3).

[8] The discussion here will be confined to the provisions relating to determinate sentences. It should be noted, however, that the 2003 Act also introduced a new indeterminate sentence of 'imprisonment for the protection of the public' for 'dangerous' offenders

ces of imprisonment of 12 months or longer are to be released automatically at the halfway point of their sentences.[9] Their release will only be able to be delayed beyond that point if they have been awarded 'additional days' for offences against prison discipline committed while in custody.[10] Once released, they will – unless recalled – remain on licence in the community and under the supervision of an offender manager until their full sentence has expired (i.e. until their 'SED' or 'sentence expiry date').[11] However, if an offender is convicted of a 'specified' violent offence or a 'specified' sexual offence for which the maximum sentence is less than ten years, the sentencing judge is required to consider whether there is a significant risk that the offender will cause serious harm to members of the public by committing a further 'specified' offence.[12] If the judge concludes that there is such a risk, the offender *must* be given an 'extended sentence of imprisonment'; the judge has no discretion in the matter.[13] An 'extended sentence of imprisonment' is a determinate sentence which consists of the normal custodial term – that is, the term that would have been imposed upon the offender in any event, irrespective of the risk that he or she is deemed

---

convicted of 'serious' specified offences (i.e. specified offences which are punishable either by life imprisonment or by a determinate period of imprisonment of ten years or more): see ss. 225 (for adult offenders) and 226 (for offenders aged under 18). Those sentenced under these sections are subject to the same release arrangements – contained in the Crime (Sentences) Act 1997, ss. 28–34 – that govern life sentence prisoners. See also s. 230 of, and Sched. 18 to, the Criminal Justice Act 2003. For a discussion of the 2003 Act, see Shute (2006: esp. pp. 75–83). The legislative changes in the 2003 Act meant that extensive revisions had to be made to Prison Service Order 6000 which covers parole release and recall. It was reissued in March 2005.

[9] See s. 244(3)(a) of the Criminal Justice Act 2003. These sentences have been dubbed 'Standard Determinate Sentences'. The provisions relating to 'custody plus' (see ss. 181 and 182), which would have applied to offenders sentenced to less than 12 months, have not been brought into force.

[10] See s. 257 of the Criminal Justice Act 2003. Some of these offenders may be released before their halfway point under the system for 'Home Detention Curfew' (HDC) which was established by ss. 99 and 100 of the Crime and Disorder Act 1998 (amending ss. 34, 37 and 38 of the Criminal Justice Act 1991): see s. 246 of the Criminal Justice Act 2003. The Parole Board plays no role in the release of prisoners under the HDC scheme but it does have responsibility for advising on the recall (i.e. assessing its appropriateness and deciding whether to recommend release) of prisoners serving less than 12 months who were released on HDC and then subsequently recalled after having been charged with an offence committed while on HDC.

[11] See s. 249(1) of the Criminal Justice Act 2003. Adult offenders are supervised by the Probation Service; those under the age of 18 are supervised by the Youth Offending Teams.

[12] See ss. 227 (for adult offenders) and 228 (for offenders aged under 18). An offence is a 'specified offence' if it is a 'specified violent offence' listed in Part 1 of Schedule 15 to the Act or a 'specified sexual offence' listed in Part 2 of Schedule 15 (see s. 224(1) and (3)). More than 150 offences are to be found there.

[13] See ss. 227(2) and 228(2).

to pose – followed by a further 'extension period' during which the offender will be on licence in the community and subject to supervision. The extension period cannot exceed five years in the case of a specified violent offence or eight years in the case of a specified sexual offence,[14] the custodial term cannot be shorter than 12 months[15] and the combination of the custodial term and the extension period cannot be longer than the maximum sentence permitted for the offence.[16]

Unlike prisoners sentenced to ordinary determinate sentences of imprisonment – who, as we have seen, are to be released automatically at the halfway point of their sentences – prisoners sentenced to extended sentences only become *eligible* for release halfway through their designated custodial term.[17] Whether they are in fact released at that stage will depend on whether a Parole Board panel is 'satisfied' that their confinement is 'no longer necessary for the protection of the public'.[18] If the panel is *not* so satisfied, extended sentence prisoners will be required to remain in custody until the end of their designated custodial term. Only at that point will the Home Secretary be under a duty to order their release.[19] Once released, they will remain on licence in the community and under the supervision of an offender manager until the entirety of their sentence – including the full extension period – has expired.

These changes, which apply only to offenders who have been sentenced for offences committed on or after 4 April 2005,[20] finally resolve some of the tensions that have long lain at the heart of the parole system in England and Wales.[21] Sentencing decisions and release decisions for parole-eligible prisoners will, for the first time since the modern system was created in 1967,[22] be subject to the same risk-based criterion. The 2003 Act also abolishes the hard-to-justify distinction between 'long-term prisoners' – those serving determinate custodial sentences of four years or longer who were eligible for parole release at the halfway point of their sentences – and 'short-term prisoners' – those serving determinate sentences of 12 months or longer but less than four

---

[14] See ss. 227(4) and 228(4).

[15] See ss. 227(3)(b) and 228(3)(a). Nor can it be longer than the maximum sentence permitted for the offence: see ss. 227(3) and 228(3)(b).

[16] See ss. 227(5) and 228(5).

[17] See s. 247(2).

[18] See s. 247(3).

[19] See s. 247(4).

[20] See the Criminal Justice Act 2003 (Commencement No. 8 and Transitional and Saving Provisions) Order 2005, SI 2005 No. 950, 24 March 2005.

[21] For a discussion of other tensions, see Shute (2003) and Hood and Shute (2002).

[22] The parole system in England and Wales was established by the enactment of ss. 59 to 62 of the Criminal Justice Act 1967.

years who were released automatically at the halfway point. Introduced by the Criminal Justice Act 1991, this distinction rested upon the questionable assumption that all offenders serving sentences of four years or longer were potentially dangerous and thus needed a risk assessment by the Parole Board.[23] Furthermore, by taking offenders who are not regarded as dangerous at the point of sentence out of the selective system, the 2003 Act enables parole decision-makers to focus their deliberations on those who require it most: that is, on prisoners who were considered by the sentencing judge to pose a substantial risk to the public.[24]

Other improvements

Nor is the structure created by the 2003 Act the only improvement to have been made to the parole system over the years. Parole procedures are also much fairer than they were in 1967. Much of the credit for this lies with the Carlisle Committee, which was established in the late 1980s to review the operation of the parole system in England and Wales.[25] Following the publication of its 1988 report, prisoners were given access to their dossiers, had the opportunity to make representations on their contents and were given reasons for the decisions that were taken.

Finally, the recall process has been improved. Recall cases used to be what might be termed the 'waifs and strays of the system'.[26] They were reviewed at the beginning of an ordinary panel of the Parole Board which had an already full agenda of parole cases to consider. In many

---

[23] See the White Paper, *Crime, Justice and Protecting the Public* (Home Office 1990: ch. 6), and the Carlisle Committee's report, *The Parole System in England and Wales* (Home Office 1988: 62, para. 246). Whatever its original merits, this assumption has become even harder to sustain following the substantial increases in sentence lengths that have occurred since 1991.

[24] Such a system had been considered by the Carlisle Committee but was rejected (Home Office 1988: 65, paras 257 and 258). The Committee set out three drawbacks to its adoption: (a) that 'the power would be generally unwelcome to the judges'; (b) that it could be damaging to 'day-to-day relations in prisons to have inmates serving sentences of identical lengths, some of whom had been marked out in this way by the courts and some of whom had not'; and (c) that it was 'questionable whether the judge, at the time of the trial, is best placed to determine which particular prisoners may pose the greatest risk when released a few years hence'. While observing that not all its members attached 'identical weight' to each of these drawbacks, the Committee said that the third represented 'the most substantial' of its reservations.

[25] See n. 23 above.

[26] See Shute (2003: 430–1).

instances, the decisions were taken quickly on the basis of tabled papers rather than on papers that had been circulated in advance.[27] But, once s. 103 of the Crime and Disorder Act 1998 had been brought into force,[28] that way of dealing with recall cases became unsustainable. The new section, which repealed s. 38 of the Criminal Justice Act 1991, placed the recall of offenders serving sentences of less than four years – like that of prisoners serving sentences of four years or longer – into the hands of the Parole Board rather than magistrates' courts. This increased significantly the number of recall cases coming before the Board, which in turn forced the Board to establish special 'recall panels' to deal with the workload. A further improvement came in 2005 when the decision of the House of Lords in *Smith and West*[29] required the Board to provide recalled prisoners with the possibility of an oral hearing.[30]

Recurrent problems

Yet, despite these improvements, the parole system is still dogged – will continue to be dogged under the new structure – by many of the old concerns: most notably, how can 'good risks' be accurately separated from 'bad risks' and how judicial should the decision-making process be? In the remainder of this chapter, I will discuss some of key issues relating to these questions.

---

[27] The Board would consider recall cases involving offenders serving determinate sentences of four years or longer in three situations: (a) where a recall was proposed but the Board's endorsement was required before that recall could take effect (see s. 39(1) of the Criminal Justice Act 1991); (b) where the Home Secretary considered the risk so great that the prisoner had been recalled to custody before such an endorsement could be obtained (see s. 39(2) and (4)(b) of the Criminal Justice Act 1991); and (c) where the prisoner had been recalled following a recommendation by the Board under s. 39(1) but the prisoner then made written representations against that recall (see s. 39(3) and (4)(a)).

[28] On 1 January 1999: see the Crime and Disorder Act 1998 (Commencement No. 3 and Appointed Day) Order 1998, SI 1998 No. 3263, art. 2(a), 21 December 1998. Breaches of licences by offenders serving sentences of less than four years imposed for offences committed before 1 January 1999 are still handled by the courts.

[29] *R (West)* v. *Parole Board* and *R (Smith)* v. *Parole Board (No. 2)* [2005] UKHL1; [2005] 1 WLR 350.

[30] Another change to the recall procedures occurred with the enactment of s. 254 of the Criminal Justice Act 2003. This placed the initial power to revoke a licence and recall an offender to prison entirely with the Home Secretary, whereas previously (other than in cases where immediate action was required) the Home Secretary could only recall a prisoner if he had been recommended to do so by the Parole Board. This change, which speeds up the recall process, is more palatable now that recalled prisoners are allowed an oral hearing.

'False positives' and 'false negatives'

Risk assessment is of course a notoriously difficult business, particularly as the type of reoffending that is of greatest concern to the Parole Board – very serious violent or sexual reoffending – is that which is least likely to occur.[31] Parole decision-making is thus, of necessity, largely a question of trying to predict a rare event, difficult enough in relation to aspects of the physical world such as long-term weather trends and short-lived meteorological occurrences like tornados, but even more problematic when what is in issue is human behaviour.[32] Furthermore, as the Parole Board has rightly pointed out in its *2004–2005 Annual Report*,[33] any parole system is likely to be judged not by the number of prisoners who are released safely into the community but by the number who fail while on parole licence, in particular by the number who are recalled for committing a further offence, especially a further serious offence.

So how good are parole selectors at distinguishing between those prisoners who are safe to release and those who are not? On one level, the answer is clear. Empirical research has consistently shown that prisoners who are released on parole have lower statistical risks of reconviction than prisoners who are denied it.[34] But this fact alone does not reveal what proportion of those who are denied parole on the grounds that they are a 'high risk' would, had they been released, have confounded that prediction and stayed free from serious offending (so-called 'false positives'). Nor does it tell us what proportion of those who are released on parole licence because they are judged to be 'low risks' in fact end up being convicted for a further serious crime (so-called 'false negatives').

Some light, however, is cast on this issue by the findings of a follow-up study of serious sex offenders that Roger Hood and I published in 2002.[35] Our study grew out of observations that we made of decision-making at Parole Board panels in the early 1990s. The prisoners considered included a sub-sample of 144 male prisoners who had been convicted of a serious sexual offence for which they had received a determinate sentence of imprisonment of at least four years. Using the Offenders' Index, we were later able to track the known reconvictions for this group for four years following their release from prison and to compare these reconvictions with the assessments that Parole Board members had made of the risk that the offenders posed. Bearing in mind that our

---

[31] See O'Leary and Glasser (1972: 194) and Shute (2004: 330).
[32] See Shute (2004: 330) and Monahan (1996).
[33] See Parole Board (2005: 16).
[34] See, for example, Home Office (1979: ch. 8).
[35] See Hood and Shute et al. (2002). See also Shute (2004: 321–5) where the findings are summarised.

findings relate only to reconvictions and not to reoffending, they can be summarised as follows:

- All of the small number of sex offenders (7/144: 4.9 per cent) subsequently convicted for a further sexual crime within the four-year follow-up period had been identified by at least one panel member as a 'high risk'.[36] These prisoners were 'true positives': they were regarded by at least one Board member as a 'high risk' and the subsequent reconviction data revealed that that assessment was correct.

- On the other hand, 91 per cent of the 82 offenders (57 per cent of the sample) who had been identified as a 'high risk' turned out not to have been convicted of a further sexual crime by the end of the four-year follow-up period. In that sense, they were 'false positives'.

- Where no member of the Parole Board had identified the prisoner as a 'high' risk' (62/144: 43 per cent of the sample), that prediction turned out to be correct in all cases. These prisoners were, by this criterion, 'true negatives'. (In other words, there were no 'false negatives' within the four-year follow-up period.)

- The 'false positive' rate was highest (100 per cent) for prisoners who had committed their sexual offence against a child or children within their own family unit.[37]

These findings, therefore, point to an ongoing need to try to reduce the number of 'false positives' identified by parole decision-makers, without of course increasing the number of 'false negatives'. They raise questions about what makes for good risk assessment and good risk assessors and how the process of risk assessment can be supported and refined.

Refining risk assessment

Expertise

From the earliest days of parole it was thought helpful for parole decision-makers to have a good working knowledge of the criminal

---

[36] The degree of risk obviously varied but prisoners were only classified as 'high risk' if a Board member had used a term such as 'he is risky', 'a very high risk', 'a man of violence', 'he scares the living daylights out of me', 'alarming', 'frightening', 'an entrenched sex offender', 'an extremely grave risk to children', 'dangerous', or words of that kind. Where there was no overt mention of 'high risk' or 'danger', it did not mean that the prisoner was regarded as posing no risk at all: as one panel member put it, 'obviously there is a risk, there always is'.

[37] That is, where the prisoner was a relative or step-parent living in the same household as the child, or a grandparent or other close relative with regular access to the child.

justice system and of risk assessment. For this reason, the 1967 legislation stipulated that Parole Board members should be drawn from (but not limited to) four statutory categories: judges, psychiatrists, probation officers (described in the legislation as persons who have 'knowledge and experience of the supervision or after-care of discharged prisoners') and criminologists (described, somewhat quirkily, as persons who 'have made a study of the causes of delinquency or the treatment of offenders').[38] These statutory groups were chosen because it was felt that their expertise would strengthen the parole process. But, over the years, the appointment of many 'independent' members to the Board together with a reduction in panel size – oral recall hearings, for example, are decided by a single 'legally qualified' member – has diluted the influence that these specialists can have on parole decision-making.[39]

The extent of the change in the composition of the membership of the Board and in the size of panels can be seen if we compare the situation in 1967, when the Board was first constituted, with the situation now. In 1967, the Board consisted of a part-time chairman and sixteen other part-time members: four judges, two psychiatrists, two probation members, two criminologists, and six independent members.[40] Forty years on, its membership has grown to 145. Of these, 26 per cent are judges, 10 per cent are psychiatrists, 12 per cent are probation members, 3 per cent are criminologists and as many as 49 per cent are independent members.[41] (It is important to recognise, however, that many independent members also come to the Board with experience of having worked in the criminal justice system. They may, for example, have served as magistrates, have been employed by the police or the prison service, have worked in voluntary agencies or be qualified lawyers.) Over the same period, the size of ordinary panels of the Parole Board has declined from seven or eight members in the first year of its operation to the current level of three.[42]

---

[38] See Sched. 2, para. 1, to the Criminal Justice Act 1967. These categories are now to be found in Sched. 9, para. 2, to the Criminal Justice Act 2003.

[39] See Shute (2003: 421–3).

[40] See *Report of the Parole Board for 1968* (London: HMSO, 1969), 290, p. 5.

[41] These figures are drawn from an analysis of the membership of the Board between 1 April 2005 and 31 March 2006, as given in the *Annual Report and Accounts of the Parole Board for England and Wales 2005–2006* (Parole Board 2006c: 68–76). The Chairman, Professor Sir Duncan Nichol, has been included in the figures. Some of those who have been classified as independent members are psychologists: in 2005–2006 psychologist members accounted for 3 per cent of the Board's membership.

[42] Within a year or so of the Board's creation the workload became such that the panels were reduced to five or six members, and by the mid-1980s the size of ordinary panels had been reduced to four. In 1993 panel size was cut again to three (see Home Office 1993: para. 57). The new recall panels, which were established in 1999 (see text note 28 above), have a membership of two.

The impact of these changes in membership and panel size became even more marked when it was decided that panels that provide oral hearings for life sentence prisoners should include a judicial member (as chair) and, in many cases, a psychiatrist (or psychologist) member.[43] With judicial and psychiatrist members a relatively 'scarce resource' on the Board, this decision meant that members from these specialist categories had to be withdrawn completely from panels which consider applications for parole from prisoners serving determinate sentences of imprisonment.[44] As a consequence, the only members that currently sit on such panels are independent members, probation members and criminologists. The focus of determinate sentence panels will, however, increasingly be on prisoners who are serving extended sentences of imprisonment under the Criminal Justice Act 2003, all of whom will have been deemed to be 'dangerous' by a sentencing judge. It is surely odd, therefore, that the panels that decide whether these 'dangerous' prisoners are safe enough to be released back into the community on parole licence will – unless there is a change of approach – generally not include a judge or a psychiatrist.[45]

Training, appraisal and feedback

Training, appraisal and feedback are also an important way of supporting parole decision-makers. These mechanisms can be prophylactic and curative. They can assist in fostering a common approach to decision-making as well as helping to identify and rectify problems with particular decision-makers should these arise. It is, therefore, encouraging that the Parole Board has taken such matters seriously in recent times

---

[43] The same is true of panels which provide oral hearings for prisoners sentenced under s. 225 of the Criminal Justice Act 2003 to indeterminate sentences of imprisonment for the protection of the public.

[44] See *Member Handbook* (Parole Board for England and Wales, 2006), Section A, Chapter 5, 'Training and Development', para. 4.3. The Board recently announced plans for a further increase in the number of members appointed, particularly judges, psychiatrists, and psychologists: see its *Business Plan 2006–2007*, which was published in April 2006. The expectation on appointment to the Parole Board is that independent members and criminologists will work 115 days per annum for the Board (i.e. two-and-a-half days per week for 46 weeks), probation members 50 days per annum, psychiatrists and psychologists 35 days per annum and judges (serving and retired) 15 days per annum. The Parole Board's Management Board uses these figures to calculate the resource required in terms of numbers of members to be appointed each year: see *Member Handbook*, Section A, Chapter 2, 'Being a Parole Board Member', para. 3.1.

[45] If it is felt that, exceptionally, a determinate sentence case needs input from a psychiatrist or a psychologist, there is a procedure by which that case can be referred, as a one-off, to a three-member panel (on which a psychiatrist is sitting) that has been convened to conduct an oral hearing in a lifer case. The referred case will be considered by that panel 'on the papers' only.

by appointing a dedicated training manager,[46] by establishing a mentoring system[47] and by reinvigorating its appraisal system. The new system of appraisal, which includes peer observation, was introduced by the Board in 2002–2003, and all members of the Board are now appraised by their colleagues 'at regular intervals'.[48] However, somewhat perversely given that what is in issue is the ability to predict risk, the Judges' Council has insisted that the appraisal of judicial members can only be conducted by other judicial members,[49] although some judges have elected to be appraised not by other judicial members but by independent members, on the ground that independent members have a broader understanding of parole decision-making and are in a better position to share their knowledge of best practice.[50] The Board has also recognised the value of hands-on experience. The old notion that all members ought to have the opportunity to chair panels has fallen away and only 'the most experienced' (i.e. the longest-serving) members are now allowed to take on this role.[51] It has also been accepted that chairs need to be trained for the task.[52]

Clear criteria

Well structured and detailed parole criteria provide a further means of underpinning robust decision-making. They go some way towards making risk assessment consistent and ensuring that decision-makers take relevant factors into account and are not affected by considerations, such as ethnicity, that ought to play no part in the parole process.

---

[46] See Parole Board (2005: 18). On their appointment to the Board, all members are required to undertake 'New Member Training'; thereafter, they must participate in the programme of continuing training and development that is organised by the Board.

[47] The Parole Board's mentoring scheme 'aims to provide individual and confidential advice, support and guidance to new members to assist them to understand the workings of the Board and their role within it' (see *Member Handbook*, n. 44 above, Section A, Chapter 5, 'Training and Development').

[48] See Parole Board (2003: 10). The *Member Handbook* (see n. 44 above, Section A, Chapter 5, 'Training and Development') states that members will be appraised according to the following approximate timetable: 'During the last four months of their first year (May–August); during the middle four months of their third year (January–April), prior to re-appointment; and towards the first four months of their fifth year (September–December)'. The *Handbook* adds that '[m]ore frequent appraisals can be an option for those who need development and/or training. In some circumstances where the appraiser has raised significant concerns that need to be addressed, further appraisals will be arranged'.

[49] See Parole Board (2005: 13).

[50] Information about the current appraisal system was kindly provided to the author by Sarah Lightfoot, one of the Board's two full-time members, who has responsibility for the Board's appraisal scheme.

[51] See Parole Board (1998: 19). See also Shute (2003: 428).

[52] Ibid.

Nonetheless, for the first eight years of its existence, from 1967 to 1975, the Parole Board in England and Wales operated without any comprehensive criteria for parole. That gap was partially filled in 1975 when the then Home Secretary, Mr Roy Jenkins, made a 'broad statement of policy' in a written answer in the House of Commons.[53] But it was not until 1992 that detailed parole criteria emerged, and even then they were not prescribed by statute but were brought into being by the Home Secretary (Mr Kenneth Clarke) exercising his power under s. 32(6) of the Criminal Justice Act 1991 to give Directions to the Board on the matters that it must take into account when considering an application for parole.[54]

The latest set of Directions was issued in March 2004,[55] before the 'dangerous' offender provisions in the Criminal Justice Act 2003 came into force. Not surprisingly, therefore, these Directions draw no distinction between the release of parole-eligible prisoners who have been sentenced to determinate terms of imprisonment under the Criminal Justice Act 1991 and the release of parole-eligible prisoners who have been sentenced to determinate terms under the Criminal Justice Act 2003. Yet there is an important difference between the two: for prisoners in the latter category but not the former category will all have been sentenced on the basis that they were regarded as dangerous by the sentencing judge. For this reason, there is a strong argument that new parole criteria are now needed to deal specifically with these cases and to reflect the special considerations that apply to them.

Risk prediction tools

When properly integrated into the process, statistical 'risk of reconviction' scores are also valuable. They can help Board members to ground their risk assessments and the decisions that flow from them on a strong evidential base. Actuarial risk scores began to be included in parole dossiers soon after the modern system of parole was established in 1967. But their influence rapidly waned. Indeed, by the late 1980s, the Carlisle Committee observed that many Parole Board members seemed to pay 'little regard to the score in formulating their views of the case'.[56] Carlisle sought to reverse this trend. It recommended that the Board should be

---

[53] See HC Debs, fifth series, 4 August 1975, Written Answers, vol. 897, cols 25–27. For a discussion of the 'Jenkins initiative', see Shute (2003: 396–400).

[54] See HC Debs, sixth series, 16 July 1992, Written Answers, vol. 211, col. 981.

[55] See the Parliamentary Statement by the Minister of State, Mr Paul Goggins: HC Debs, sixth series, 18 March 2004, Ministerial Written Statements, vol. 419, cols 29–31. The Directions came into force on 1 May 2004. The power to give Directions now derives from s. 239(6) of the Criminal Justice Act 2003.

[56] See Carlisle Committee (1988: 81, para. 330).

'under a duty to take account of all appropriate prediction techniques',[57] and in July 1992 the Home Secretary responded positively to this suggestion by including such a duty in his Directions to the Board.[58] Yet, when Roger Hood and I observed Parole Board panel decision-making in the second half of 1992, we found that risk scores still played almost no part in the assessment of risk.[59]

In the late 1990s, the Home Office discontinued its practice of calculating risk prediction scores for the purposes of parole.[60] This prompted Roger Hood and myself, in a further report on parole that we published in 2000, to argue strongly that actuarial risk of reconviction scores should, once again, be made available to Board members.[61] Eventually, that view was accepted, first by *The Comprehensive Review of Parole and Lifer Processes*, published in October 2001,[62] and later by Home Office ministers. Accordingly, in March 2004, a clause was included in the Home Secretary's Directions to the Parole Board which required the Board to take into account, if available, the indication of predicted risk as determined by a validated actuarial risk predictor.[63]

Nonetheless, despite the introduction into the National Probation Service in 2001 of a new risk assessment tool known as OASys (the Offender Assessment System),[64] risk prediction instruments are, it seems, still not fully integrated into the system. Thus, in his 2006 inquiry into the murder of the financier John Monckton, HM Chief Inspector of Probation recommended that:

> The Probation Service should ensure that a full OASys assessment is completed and that the findings are always available to the parole panel considering an application for early release on licence.[65]

Welcome as it is, this endorsement of the value of using actuarial risk assessment tools to support parole decision-making needs to go hand in

---

[57] Ibid.

[58] See HC Debs, sixth series, 16 July 1992, Written Answers, vol. 211, col. 981.

[59] See Hood and Shute (1994: 72, para. 175).

[60] For a discussion, see Shute (2004: 327–30).

[61] See Hood and Shute (2000: 49 and 78).

[62] See Sentence Management Group (2001: 88, para. 4.3.6).

[63] See n. 55 above.

[64] Assessments are based on 'a systematic assessment of the criminogenic factors relating to each offender': see Her Majesty's Inspectorate of Probation (2005c: 16, para 5.1). OASys scores an offender's 'risk of reconviction' on a scale which runs from 0 to 168.

[65] Practice Recommendation 10.2. See Her Majesty's Inspectorate of Probation (2006a: 38). The Chief Inspector also recommended that 'parole panels and probation staff should be reminded of the importance of static factors in the assessment of risk' (Practice Recommendation 10.4), the implication being that 'clinical' assessments and 'dynamic' risk factors were being given too much weight.

hand with an ongoing programme of work to develop and refine the available risk prediction instruments so as to ensure that they are accurate and up to date. OASys is based both on 'static' and 'dynamic' risk factors: that is, on historical unchanging facts about the offender, such as previous convictions and current age, and factors that are capable of change, such as housing or whether the offender has a current relationship. It has been described by HM Chief Inspector of Probation as 'probably the most advanced tool for [risk assessment] in the world'.[66] Yet, Home Office research has shown that the version of OASys in current use is actually no better at predicting the probability of an offender being reconvicted of a 'Standard List' offence within two years of the commencement of a community penalty or release on licence than is the Offender Group Reconviction Scale (OGRS) which relies entirely on static risk factors.[67] The need for further development is therefore clear and this is being taken forward by the OASys Data, Evaluation and Analysis Team (O-DEAT) in the Home Office. O-DEAT has recently produced a new OASys scoring system which not only outperforms OGRS but includes both a 'general' reconviction predictor and a 'violence' reconviction predictor.[68] It will be piloted for user acceptability in 2007.

Interviews by Parole Board members

What about the vexed question of interviews with prisoners by Parole Board members? The Parole Board's view is that these interviews are conducive to more reliable risk assessments because they provide panels with information about prisoners which would otherwise be unavailable from the dossier. In order to assess the validity of this claim, it is helpful to look at the history of these interviews.

Before 1991, the task of interviewing prisoners who had applied for parole was carried out by a member of the Local Review Committee (LRC). LRCs were prison-based and provided a first tier for parole decision-making.[69] When, on the recommendation of the Carlisle Committee, LRCs were abolished, Carlisle suggested that their interviewing role should be transferred to a 'group of local people who might be termed parole counsellors'.[70] Parole counsellors would study the

---

[66] See ibid., para. 11.12, p. 69. See also HM Government (2006: 11, para. 2.2): 'OASys is considered to be the most advanced system of its kind in the world'.

[67] See Howard (2006: 3). For a discussion of OGRS, see Copas and Marshall (1998).

[68] See Moore et al. (2006).

[69] On the complicated relationship between decision-making by LRCs and decision-making by the Parole Board (and the changes in that relationship that occurred over time), see Shute (2003: 387–91, 394–6 and 402–6).

[70] See Carlisle Committee (1988: paras 338–41).

prisoner's dossier, talk over the main points with the prisoner and help the prisoner to put down in writing his or her own comments. In the event, however, neither Carlisle's suggestion nor a similar suggestion made in the subsequent White Paper that interviewing should be undertaken by 'parole assessors'[71] was adopted. Instead, certain members of the Parole Board – probation members, criminologist members and independent members but not judges or psychiatrists – were designated 'Parole Board Interviewing Members'. PBIMs, as they came to be called, would interview prisoners in prisons and write short reports based on those interviews. These reports would then be considered by a Parole Board panel in London along with all the other documents and reports contained in the prisoner's dossier. The PBIM who had written the report would not sit on the panel that decided the case, nor would he or she be present. PBIM reports were designed to be 'factual' and 'objective'. Interviewing members were firmly told that they should neither express opinions nor make recommendations. Prisoners were provided with copies of the PBIM report and could, if they wished, make written representations to the Board about its contents.

Whether the benefits to be gained from these interviews were sufficient to justify the considerable costs of sending PBIMs to prisons to conduct them was an issue that Roger Hood and I examined in the empirical study of parole decision-making that we published in 2000.[72] By that time, interview work accounted for 'the majority of an average Parole Board member's remuneration'.[73] On the basis of our findings, we were sceptical about whether these interviews added substantial value to the process of risk assessment. One of the primary purposes of the interview, laid out in the instructions given to Board members, was 'to enable the prisoner to clarify or expand upon any matter which the prisoner wished to draw to the attention of the panel'.[74] Yet, according to both the prisoners and PBIMs who were interviewed for our research, 40 per cent of the inmates had been nervous or upset during their interview, and one-third of the prisoners told us that they had not managed to get over to the PBIM all the points that they had wanted to make. Furthermore, transcripts from the 151 PBIM interviews that we observed for the study revealed that, despite the attempts made by PBIMs to ask open-ended questions in the hope of eliciting a full response, prisoners all too often provided only short, single-sentence answers.

Overall, then, there was a strong indication from our research that prisoners found PBIM interviews too taxing to be able to make the best

---

[71] See Home Office (1990: 34, para. 6.27).
[72] See Hood and Shute (2000: ch. 7, esp. p. 75).
[73] See Sentence Management Group (2001: 55, para. 3.5.2).
[74] See Hood and Shute (2000: 69).

of their case for parole.[75] Our research also examined the use that Parole Board panels made of PBIM reports. We found that these reports were referred to in only 10 per cent of the 417 cases that we observed, and even then they appeared to have had only a marginal impact on panel decision-making.[76] There was also a due process problem. Because the interviewing member who wrote the report did not attend the panel meeting, there were cases where panel members made subjective judgments about prisoners on the basis of a reported interview w-1ith no possibility of asking the PBIM or the prisoner whether that interpretation was correct.

We recognised, however, that if it were to be concluded that employing Parole Board members to interview prisoners and write reports was an expense that could not be justified, some of the PBIMs' tasks would have to be carried out by others. The job of ensuring that dossiers were complete, we argued, could be made the responsibility of parole clerks in prisons. But someone else would be needed to ensure that the prisoner was familiar both with parole procedures and with the criteria that the Board was directed to apply, that the prisoner had read and understood the dossier and was in a position to challenge any matter in it and that the prisoner had received all the help that he or she needed to make effective representations to the Board. We thought that these tasks could readily be transferred to voluntary, independent and trained 'parole counsellors', recruited from retired probation officers and others with experience relevant to that role. These counsellors could meet with prisoners at an earlier stage of the process to review and discuss progress and then later assist prisoners with their representations.

The scepticism that we expressed about the value of PBIM interviews was shared by *The Comprehensive Review*, which followed the publication of our research. *The Review* noted that there was 'a potential confusion for prisoners in being interviewed by a Parole Board member', as many regarded it as their Parole Board hearing.[77] Although it concluded that PBIM interviews should continue, *The Review* recommended that, once the Prison Service and Probation Service were satisfied that OASys provided a comprehensive risk assessment tool and was fully operational, the *sole* function of these interviews should be to assist prisoners to make their representations. They should not be used to probe for risk factors.[78]

The Parole Board, however, strongly resisted this move to curtail its interviewing role. In its *2002–2003 Annual Report*, it argued that inter-

---

[75] See ibid., p. 71.
[76] See ibid., p. 73.
[77] See Sentence Management Group (2001: 55, para. 3.5.2).
[78] See ibid., Recommendation 40, pp. 54–5, and the discussion in sections 3.4 and 3.5 (pp. 50–60).

views had 'proved a valuable two-way learning and communication tool between members and prisoners', and claimed that the Board's experience over ten years was that PBIM reports 'constantly inform[ed] panel decisions and often provid[ed] up-to-date information not available elsewhere'. Without these interviews, it said, more cases would have to be deferred because dossiers would be incomplete.[79] But this resistance was in vain and, by 2004, the Board had 'reluctantly accepted that, for financial reasons' (funding had been withdrawn by the Home Office), PBIM interviews would have to 'stop in the vast majority of cases'.[80] The change took effect in April 2004 and, from that point, automatic interviews with prisoners ceased, although the Board could, if it wished, still ask a member to carry out an interview if a panel regarded that as 'essential to inform their decision on risk'.[81]

But the issue did not go away. It was reopened by HM Chief Inspector of Probation in his review of the supervision of Damien Hanson and Elliott White.[82] Hanson, who was serving 12 years for attempted murder and conspiracy to rob, first applied for parole in 2003 when Parole Board members were still carrying out interviews with offenders. A Parole Assessment Report (written by his 'home' probation officer) was optimistic about his prospects, as was the report written by a 'seconded' probation officer in the prison. Yet, according to the Chief Inspector, the report from the PBIM appeared 'to raise important questions' about these assessments. When a Parole Board panel subsequently considered the case, it refused to grant Hanson parole. The Chief Inspector thought that 'there was little doubt' that the PBIM's report had been 'a very significant factor' in that outcome.

A year later, though, a second application for parole was granted, and Hanson was released from a category C prison. He had not been interviewed by a Parole Board member for this second application

---

[79] See Parole Board (2003: 16).

[80] See Parole Board (2004: 16).

[81] Ibid. Chapter 1 ('Discretionary Conditional Release') of Section B of the Parole Board's *Member Handbook* (see n. 44 above) states (para. 11.5, emphasis in the original): 'Where there is important information missing from the dossier that can only be obtained directly from the prisoner; *and* the panel considers that no other report writer is likely to be able to provide that information; *and* the information is critical to the decision, the panel may request that a member of the Board interview the prisoner. The panel should specify clearly what information they want the member to obtain. An interview report should not be used as an alternative to reports that should have been provided by other agencies'. The power to interview is to be found in s. 239(3) of the Criminal Justice Act 2003: 'If in any particular case the Board thinks it necessary to interview the person to whom the case relates before reaching a decision, the Board may authorise one of its members to interview him and must consider the report of the interview made by that member'.

[82] See Her Majesty's Inspectorate of Probation (2006a: 38).

because, by that time, the practice of conducting such interviews had ceased. The Chief Inspector thought that the decision to release Hanson 'was *in principle* a defensible one, despite some contra-indications' (emphasis in the original). But he also argued that, if Hanson's 'long personal statement' had been 'scrutinised closely' by the Board, greater concern might have been raised about both his state of mind and 'the reality of his plans for the future'. For this reason, he recommended that:

> The Parole Board should review its current policy on the question of a member interviewing the offender and reporting independently to parole panels when considering high-risk cases.[83]

A few months after this recommendation was published, the Chairman of the Parole Board, Professor Sir Duncan Nichol, gave further impetus to the idea that PBIM interviews should be reinstated when he told a reporter working for *The Times* that the Board wanted to move away from a position where only about 10 per cent of applicants were seen 'personally' by Board members.[84] Two justifications were given: first, quoting an unnamed psychiatrist member of the Board, Sir Duncan argued that interviews were helpful 'because the person you see on paper is very often not the person you see face to face'; second, he claimed that a 'skilled interview can focus on the risks a specific prisoner presents, digging beneath the surface, challenging bland assumptions'.[85] In November 2006, the Shadow Home Secretary, Mr David Davis, also supported the reintroduction of interviews. He made the strong claim that their abolition had led to 'many more mistakes being made, many more criminals being recalled and many more dangerous prisoners putting the public at risk'. He even went so far as to imply that there was a link between their abolition and cases where 'a number of innocent people [had been] murdered by people who should have been in prison'.[86]

Finally, in its recently published *Annual Report for 2005–2006*, the Parole Board announced that it had committed itself to reintroducing PBIM interviews, from April 2007, for those offenders 'who pose particular concern to the Board, notably those convicted of a sexual or

---

[83] Ibid., Practice Recommendation 10.3, p. 38.

[84] See *The Times*, 25 July 2006, *Public Agenda* section, at p. 5 (interview by Richard Ford).

[85] Sir Duncan was quoted as saying that the Board wanted 30 per cent of those applying for parole who had been given an 'indeterminate sentence' to be interviewed. Over time, he thought the figure should rise to 50 per cent. However, since all prisoners serving indeterminate sentences currently receive a hearing in front of a Parole Board panel, it seems likely that Sir Duncan was referring to 'determinate sentences' and not 'indeterminate sentences'.

[86] See *The Times*, 7 November 2006, p. 32.

violent offence who are recommended for parole by report writers'.[87] The Board added that a renewed funding bid had been submitted to the Home Office but that the outcome of that bid was not yet known.

This revival of interest in interviewing parole applicants is reflected in the fact that, during the 12-month period from 1 April 2005 to 31 March 2006, the Board carried out 16 interviews with prisoners serving determinate sentences, but 51 during the following six months, from 1 April 2006 to 30 September 2006.[88] But whether the re-introduction of PBIM interviews will help to enhance the quality and reliability of risk assessments by the Board must be open to question. So long as interviewing members are not present at panel meetings, the same deficiencies that affected the earlier system are likely to be present in any reincarnation. Moreover, interviews by Board members are not readily compatible with the Board assuming a more judicial function: it would surely be odd for a judge in a court of law to interview and write a report on a person whose case was then considered at a later date 'on the papers' by his or her judicial colleagues.

This does not mean, however, that Parole Board members and prisoners should be kept apart. On the contrary, providing every prisoner who applies for parole with an opportunity to have a full personal hearing before the panel which takes the decision offers the best structure of all. In the short term such a system would be relatively expensive to establish. But in the longer term these costs should fall. This is because, when the provisions of the Criminal Justice Act 2003 Act fully take hold,[89] the number of determinate-sentence prisoners falling into the selective system will reduce substantially. (Under the new structure, it will be recalled, the only determinate sentence prisoners who are to be considered for parole are those who are regarded as dangerous by a judge at the time of their sentence.) With fewer prisoners to consider, fewer resources will be needed to fund personal hearings.[90] But, in any case, the view of this author is that offering personal hearings to prisoners serving 'extended sentences', akin to those that are currently made available to prisoners serving indeterminate sentences, is a far better use of scarce resources than funding the reintroduction of PBIM

---

[87] See Parole Board (2006c: 9).

[88] The author is grateful to Mollie Weatheritt, Director of Quality and Standards at the Parole Board and a full-time member, who kindly made these figures available.

[89] They apply only to offenders who are sentenced for offences committed on or after 4 April 2005: see n. 20 above.

[90] Parole applications will still need to be considered from prisoners who have been sentenced under the Criminal Justice Act 1991 to determinate terms of imprisonment of four years or longer for offences committed prior to 4 April 2004. Over time, the number of such cases will reduce but, until it dwindles to nil, it is surely right that they too should be offered the right to a full personal hearing before the Board.

interviews. It is also a much more just solution. For now that personal hearings are available to prisoners who are sentenced to indeterminate terms because they are considered dangerous at the time of their trial, it is surely indefensible to deny such hearings to 'extended sentence' prisoners who are also given their sentences because they are considered dangerous at the time of their trial.

Recall

I want to conclude by returning, briefly, to the topic of recall. As I indicated earlier, there can be no doubt that the recall system has improved considerably during the last decade. Nonetheless, it still has its weaknesses. One difficulty is the sheer number of released prisoners who are now being recalled – more than 9,000 in 2005–2006.[91] A second is that inconsistencies remain in the mechanisms that are available for recall. If an offender is aged 18 or over and has been released on licence, any recall will be by the Home Secretary via the Release and Recall Section of the Home Office (RRS). The process is quick and easy to use and, if an emergency recall is thought necessary, an arrest warrant can be issued within two hours of the breach papers being received in London.[92] But, if the offender is aged between 18 and 21 and has been released on a notice of supervision under s. 65 of the Criminal Justice Act 1991 rather than on a licence, revocation has to be via the courts.[93]

---

[91] See Parole Board (2006c: 10).

[92] The new 'emergency' (within two hours) recall procedure was introduced in April 2005 to supplement the procedure for an 'immediate' (standard) recall (recall within 24 hours). 'Emergency' recall should normally be used when the offender is subject to oversight by the MAPPA (Multi-Agency Public Protection Arrangements) at Level 3 or where the offender 'is considered to present a high or very high risk of serious harm' or where the offender's behaviour 'has deteriorated to such an extent that re-offending is believed to be imminent'. See *Criminal Justice Act 2003 – Early Release and Recall*, Probation Circular 16/2005, para. 44.

[93] Notices of supervision date back to s. 15 of the Criminal Justice Act 1982 (release from Detention Centre Orders and from Youth Custody). In *Owen Davies (AKA Nicholas Slocombe)* v. *Secretary of State for the Home Department* [2004] EWHC 3113 (Admin) Tuckey LJ held that the fact that notices of supervision could include onerous supervision requirements which extended beyond the prisoner's sentence expiry date did not mean that they violated Article 5 of the European Convention on Human Rights. For offences committed by 18- to 21-year-olds *after 4 April 2005* which lead to a custodial sentence of *12 months or longer*, the provisions of the Criminal Justice Act 2003 apply and recall is via the Home Secretary (unless the offender has been recalled and then re-released on a notice of supervision taking him beyond his SED, in which case recall will still have to be via the courts). The 'custody plus' provisions in ss. 181 and 182 of the Criminal Justice Act 2003, which would have applied to those sentenced to a custodial sentence of *less than 12 months*, however, have not yet been brought into force. If they had been, they

This causes problems because court-ordered revocations are much more cumbersome and laborious to execute than revocations and recalls by the Home Secretary. Moreover, since notices of supervision cannot exceed three months in length, the offender's probation officer may easily find that the notice has expired before the matter is finally resolved.

The thinking behind these notices is that offenders aged between 18 and 21 ought, on their release from custody, to receive at least three months' supervision in the community, irrespective of whether that is possible within the normal sentence expiry date (SED). Notices of supervision, therefore, can allow the supervision period for 18- to 21-year-olds to be extended beyond their SED. They can also allow for three months' supervision for 18- to 21-year-olds where, because the custodial sentence is less than 12 months, there would not normally be any supervision at all.[94] Breach of a notice of supervision is a criminal offence punishable by a fine or a custodial sentence for a period not exceeding 30 days.[95]

The question thus arises: does it make sense to have such a bifurcated system for adult offenders?[96] The answer that this author would give is an emphatic no, especially now that all offenders recalled by the Home Secretary are entitled to an oral hearing by the Parole Board. The revocation procedures for offenders aged between 18 and 21 who have been released on notices of supervision should, therefore, be brought into line with the more streamlined structure that has been created for licence recalls.

Conclusion

This chapter has discussed some of the ways that the parole system has improved over the years and some of the ways that risk assessment might be supported and refined. It has expressed doubts about whether

---

would have done away with the need for notices of supervision for those sentenced to short custodial sentences (less than 12 months) for offences committed after the commencement of the provisions (s. 65 was to have been repealed by Sched. 32, para. 63, to the 2003 Act). But, until 'custody plus' is brought into force, notices of supervision will continue to operate for all 18- to 21-year-olds who are sentenced to custodial sentences of less than 12 months' duration, and any recall must therefore be pursued through the magistrates' courts.

[94] However, in both cases, the supervision ends on the offender's 22nd birthday, if it has not ended before: see s. 65(2) of the Criminal Justice Act 1991.

[95] See s. 65(6).

[96] Young offenders (offenders under the age of 18) released from detention and training orders are also placed on notices of supervision. However, different considerations apply to young offenders, and these may be sufficient to make court-ordered recall desirable for this group.

reintroducing Parole Board member interviews for offenders serving determinate sentences of imprisonment (at least in the form that they took in the late 1990s), while at the same time denying these prisoners a proper parole hearing before the decision-making body, will enhance the reliability of risk assessments made by panels of the Board. It has argued that the better approach would be to offer personal hearings to all prisoners who request them. The chapter has also called for a change in the revocation system for offenders aged 18 to 21 years who have been released from custody on a notice of supervision under s. 65 of the Criminal Justice Act 1991.

Chapter 4

The Parole Board and the changing face of public law

*Mark Elliott**

Introduction

Since it was established in 1968, the Parole Board, like other parts of the criminal justice system, has undergone numerous changes. In three key areas, these reflect the changing face of public law in this country and, in particular, the growing influence of the European Convention on Human Rights.[1] First, there has been a substantial *shift of power* in parole (and associated) matters away from the executive. Secondly, this has been accompanied by the imposition on the taking of parole decisions of more rigorous standards of *due process*. Thirdly, however, the legal constraints which operate in this sphere do not only concern the process by which decisions are made: offenders' *human rights* may, in certain circumstances, substantively condition the range of options open to the Board.

These changes, significant in themselves, also form part of a bigger story in which the foundations of the British constitution itself are shifting. The parole regime which obtained 40 years ago was the product of a system in which politicians had considerable freedom to do – and to fashion a legislative scheme which permitted them to do – very much

*I am grateful to Simon Creighton, Christopher Forsyth, Nicky Padfield and Dirk van Zyl Smit for their helpful comments on drafts of this paper. I am responsible, however, for the opinions expressed and for any remaining errors.
[1] Hereinafter 'ECHR'.

as they pleased. Prisoner release could be characterised as an exercise of administrative benevolence, and prisoners generally had to take the system for the conferral (or non-conferral) of such largesse as they found it. That is a state of affairs which is today almost unrecognisable. Successive decisions of the British courts and the European Court of Human Rights[2] have curtailed the powers of Ministers, reducing their ability to participate in or influence the making of parole decisions, and recasting the parole process as a judicial one (at least in part).

The current debate concerning parole – sparked by high-profile cases[3] which have situated parole decisions firmly in the glare of the media spotlight – illustrates that this is a matter of some frustration to politicians today. There is a growing perception that the judicialisation of the parole process has introduced a bias in favour of 'offenders' rights', undermining the protection of the public. This view fits into a broader discourse, recently joined by the Prime Minister, who argued that it is time to 'rebalance' the criminal justice system 'in favour of the decent, law-abiding majority who play by the rules' (Blair 2006). Against this background, the objective of this paper is to trace how the parole system has changed in recent decades in the three spheres mentioned above; to explain why, properly understood, these changes are to be welcomed; and to demonstrate that the supposed contradiction between due respect for human rights and proper regard for public safety rests upon a false hypothesis.

The erosion of executive power

Political and judicial roles: the emergence of clear dividing lines

Although the executive branch in the United Kingdom is undeniably – some would say problematically (Hewart 1929) – powerful, the evolution of the parole system in recent decades clearly demonstrates the con-straining force of public law vis-à-vis the government.

The courts' powers of judicial review have expanded dramatically in recent years as a counterweight to the might of the executive,[4] enabling the courts to invalidate public bodies' decisions on grounds such as unlawfulness, unfairness and unreasonableness.[5] However, like every-thing in the British legal landscape, judicial review exists in the shadow of legislative supremacy – the long-standing and widely accepted

---

[2] Hereinafter 'ECtHR'.
[3] Most notably that of Anthony Rice, who committed murder while on a life licence (HMIP 2006b).
[4] See Lord Mustill's speech in R v. *Home Secretary, ex parte Fire Brigades Union* [1995] 2 AC 513.
[5] On judicial review, see generally Craig (2003), Wade and Forsyth (2004).

principle that Parliament's law-making power is unbounded, such that no legal rule is immune from alteration or abolition (Dicey 1959).[6] It follows that where Parliament has clearly prescribed some facet of the decision-making process, the judges are powerless to interfere. So, when primary legislation provided that it was for the Home Secretary to decide[7] whether to order the release of mandatory life sentence prisoners on parole, the courts took this as a given. As Lord Mustill said in the *Doody* case, after adverting to the then prevailing view that such sentences were underpinned by a different philosophy than that applying to discretionary life sentences, 'I [do] not argue for one regime rather than another, nor [do I] suggest that each of them is unsatisfactory. This is a question for Parliament and we must take the law as it stands.'[8] Consequently, the question whether it was appropriate for Ministers, as opposed to an independent body, to have the final word on parole decisions was not one which British courts were able to decide. If the sovereign Parliament ordained that such powers should reside with Ministers, then that was that.

Whether this was a good thing depends on one's perspective. Some would argue that, in a democracy, Ministers accountable to Parliament and, ultimately, the electorate should be responsible for making difficult penal decisions. This view, however, reflects a somewhat impoverished vision of the legitimacy of public power. While democratic credentials can clothe with legitimacy the exercise of certain sorts of power, it does not follow that democracy is the only, or an always sufficient, source of legitimacy. Most developed legal systems recognise that different types of power derive legitimacy from different sources. For example, it has been said that the legitimacy of judicial power derives not from any form of democratic accountability – quite the reverse: it consists in, *inter alia*, 'the independence of the judiciary from the political arms of government, guaranteeing an unbiased and objective assessment of the legality of the acts and decisions of the executive' (Feldman 2006: 375). For precisely that reason, it is desirable that certain tasks – including, quite uncontroversially, the sentencing of offenders – be carried out not by Ministers, but by judges whose independence and impartiality enable them objectively and dispassionately to pursue justice under the law. And, as we shall see, it is for substantially similar reasons that decisions concerning the release of prisoners detained solely on the ground of continued dangerousness should also be made independently, not by elected politicians.

---

[6] However, this orthodox view has recently been questioned, *inter alios*, by Lords Steyn and Hope in *R (Jackson)* v. *Attorney-General* [2006] 1 AC 262, [2005] UKHL 56.

[7] Albeit that the Parole Board made recommendations.

[8] *R* v. *Home Secretary, ex parte Doody* [1994] 1 AC 531, p. 556.

However, when the business of judging, thus conceived, yields unpopular results, the temptation is for politicians to interfere. Witness, for example, the Prime Minister's excoriating criticism of a recent decision that four Afghan hijackers could not be deported due to the risk that they would thereafter be tortured.[9] In a similar, but more salient, vein, consider the Home Secretary's instinctive desire[10] to intervene in parole matters in the wake of the Rice case (HMIP 2006b) and in sentencing matters following a public – or at least media – outcry in relation to the case of the paedophile Craig Sweeney.[11] Most legal systems contain immovable dividing lines[12] which prevent political interference in the judicial realm, but this has not traditionally been so in the UK, given the absence of a written constitution (within which such lines might otherwise be found) and the notion that Parliament is sovereign (in effect allowing the governing political party to distribute power as it sees fit). That is why, for instance, it was possible for the Parole Board, when it was first established, only to have the power to *recommend* the release of prisoners – a state of affairs which persisted until quite recently in relation to mandatory life sentence prisoners.

Today, however, things are rather different. Public law now operates in an institutionally constraining sense, by prescribing by whom certain types of decision may and may not be taken. This is so because of Article 5 of the ECHR, the first paragraph of which is, for present purposes, important. Although it generally provides that '[e]veryone has the right to liberty and security of person', deprivation of liberty is permissible where, *inter alia*, it is 'in accordance with a procedure prescribed by law' and involves 'the lawful detention of a person after conviction by a competent court'. Also relevant is Article 5(4), which provides, 'Everyone who is deprived of his liberty by arrest or detention shall be entitled to take proceedings by which the lawfulness of his detention shall be decided speedily by a court and his release ordered if the detention is not lawful.'

Although the Convention now enjoys enhanced status in *domestic* law following the enactment of the Human Rights Act 1998,[13] it is because, as a matter of *international* law, the UK has undertaken[14] to secure to those within its jurisdiction the Convention rights that they enjoy a special status. The UK is bound as a state to ensure that the Convention rights are upheld: unlike the norms of domestic law, the obligations

---

[9] See *The Daily Telegraph*, 11 May 2006, p. 4.
[10] Evidenced in his Parole Board Annual Lecture (Reid 2006).
[11] See *The Guardian*, 14 June 2006, p. 11.
[12] Or at least lines which are difficult to shift (e.g. constitutional amendment may be required).
[13] Hereinafter 'HRA 1998'.
[14] See Article 1 ECHR.

which the UK acquired by becoming a party to the ECHR do not – as a matter of international law – exist in the shadow of parliamentary sovereignty. If, therefore, the Convention were to stipulate that particular types of decisions (certain parole decisions, for example) had to be taken by particular types of bodies (court-like institutions, for instance), the UK would be obliged to make appropriate arrangements. Crucially, the Convention *does* so stipulate. This means that the decisions to which Article 5 is applicable – including, as we shall see shortly, many parole decisions – cannot be taken by government Ministers. By providing precisely the sort of dividing lines – separating the judicial and the political – which the British constitution has traditionally lacked, the Convention has provided a vehicle for challenging the role of the Home Secretary within the penal system, precipitating a fundamental redrawing of the boundaries between his role and that of the Board.[15]

When does Article 5 apply?

Prima facie, it is unclear why Article 5 should be relevant to parole decision-making: the requirements of Article 5(1) appear capable of being met, once and for all, by the sentencing court itself, while it has been held that the entitlement conferred by Article 5(4) can also be realised through the original trial and sentencing process.[16] However, the true position is more complex than this. At the heart of the matter is a distinction between the *punitive* and *security* phases of sentences. In essence, Article 5 applies to parole decisions pertaining to the latter but not the former. The policy underlying this distinction is clear. Deprivation of liberty is a serious matter, and is acceptable only in limited circumstances. If the substance of the right set out in Article 5(1) is to have any value, it must be accompanied by appropriate procedural guarantees, as laid down in Article 5(4). And, although due process before the sentencing court is generally sufficient to meet those requirements, the position is different where that court imposes a sentence which includes a security phase during which the appropriateness of continued detention is dependent upon factors – such as the risk posed by the offender – that are susceptible to change over time.

In some instances, the application of these principles is unproblematic. For example, since long-term sentences under the Criminal Justice Act 1991[17] are regarded as wholly punitive, Article 5(4) has no application to the Board's decisions whether to recommend release within the 'parole

---

[15] The ECHR has yielded similar results in analogous contexts, such as the determination of the minimum period for which lifers must be imprisoned.

[16] See *De Wilde* v. *Belgium* (1979–80) 1 EHRR 373, p. 407.

[17] Hereinafter 'CJA 1991'.

window'.[18] That explains why it is ultimately the Home Secretary who retains the legal power to decide whether such prisoners should be released.[19]

However, life and similar sentences have proven more problematic. A milestone was reached in the ECtHR's decision in *Thynne*, in which it was accepted that discretionary life sentences consist of both punitive and security phases, the former being represented by the 'tariff', or 'minimum detention', period.[20] The court concluded that post-punitive detention raised issues of 'mental instability and dangerousness [which] are susceptible to change over ... time', and that 'new issues of lawfulness may thus arise in the course of detention'. During the security phase of their discretionary life sentences, the applicants were 'entitled under Article 5(4) to take proceedings to have the lawfulness of their continued detention decided by a court at reasonable intervals and to have the lawfulness of any re-detention determined by a court'.[21] This judgment prompted the sweeping changes to the parole system – most notably the creation of discretionary lifer panels (Padfield 2002) – which were introduced by the CJA 1991. Its reasoning was later extended to detention at Her Majesty's pleasure,[22] and ultimately to mandatory life sentences.[23] As a result, the detention of all indeterminate sentence prisoners – including those subject to sentences of imprisonment for public protection[24] – is now a matter for the Board once the minimum detention period has expired.[25]

However, a question mark exists in relation to 'extended sentences' under the CJA 2003. Whereas prisoners serving standard determinate

---

[18] That is, the period between the halfway and two-thirds points of the sentence, during which the prisoner may be released on parole but is not automatically entitled to release.

[19] Albeit that he has delegated that power to the Board in respect of prisoners serving sentences of less than 15 years. See Prison Service Order 6000, para. 5.3.1.

[20] *Thynne* v. *UK* (1991) 13 EHRR 666, p. 693.

[21] Ibid., p. 694.

[22] *Hussain* v. *UK* (1996) 22 EHRR 1.

[23] *Stafford* v. *UK* (2002) 35 EHRR 32; cf *Wynne* v. *UK* (1995) 19 EHRR 333.

[24] Under the Criminal Justice Act 2003 (hereinafter 'CJA 2003'), s. 225.

[25] The minimum detention period is judicially determined under s. 269 CJA 2003 for mandatory life sentences (subject to the principles stated in sch. 21 CJA 2003) and otherwise pursuant to s. 82A of the Powers of Criminal Courts (Sentencing) Act 2000, under which the convention (set out in *R* v. *Szczerba* [2002] EWCA Crim 440, [2002] 2 Cr App R (S) 86) is that the minimum period should be half of the determinate sentence that would otherwise have been imposed (to take account of the fact that determinate sentence prisoners are released – or, in the case of extended sentence prisoners, eligible for release – after serving half of their sentence). The Home Office proposes to end this convention, and is consulting on giving the courts 'discretion to make dangerous offenders serve a higher proportion of their tariff' as well as on the possibility of changing the CJA 2003 regime for standard determinate sentences to allow some offenders to be detained beyond the halfway point of their sentence (Home Office 2006a: 18).

sentences are *entitled* to release having served half of the custodial period, extended sentence prisoners are merely *eligible* for release at that stage. Although the relevant Prison Service Order presupposes that initial release decisions concerning extended sentence prisoners do not attract the operation of Article 5,[26] since such prisoners find themselves in this less advantageous position solely because the court has chosen, *on grounds of dangerousness*, to impose an extended sentence, it may be argued that any detention beyond the halfway point – when they would have been released but for their dangerousness – constitutes preventative detention (Arnott and Creighton 2006: 79–81).

Yet, while the contours of Article 5 may not be entirely clear, the policy behind it is. It reflects the fundamental norm that certain types of decision, including sentencing, may legitimately be made only by independent judicial bodies. It follows that such decisions must either be taken by the court when the offender is sentenced, or, where the sentence passed by that court incorporates a security element during which the appropriateness of release cannot be determined in advance, by an independent body such as the Parole Board.

What does Article 5 require?

This begs an obvious question. Given that Article 5 now applies to many parole decisions, does the Board pass muster? Although the text of Article 5 refers to such decisions being taken by a 'court', the ECtHR has explained that this does not require 'a court of law of the classic kind integrated within the standard judicial machinery of the country'.[27] It does, however, require the body to exhibit certain 'fundamental features', including 'independence of the executive and of the parties to the case'.[28] Although it is generally taken for granted that the Board enjoys the requisite degree of independence,[29] the matter is not beyond doubt (Padfield 2006).

An obvious difficulty is that the Home Secretary is permitted by statute to give directions to the Board 'as to the matters to be taken into account by it in discharging [its] functions'.[30] As Walker J recently noted in the *Girling* case, it is difficult to see 'how directions by the Home Secretary as to matters to be taken into account can be appropriate where the Board is performing a judicial function, especially when that function requires the Board to resolve a dispute between the Home Secretary on

---

[26] Prison Service Order 6000, para. 8.1.5.
[27] *Weeks* v. *UK* (1988) 10 EHRR 293, pp. 315–16.
[28] *De Wilde*, op. cit., p. 408 (see note 16).
[29] See, for example, *Murray* v. *Parole Board* [2003] EWCA Civ 1561, para. 20; *R (Day)* v. *Home Secretary* [2004] EWHC 1742 (Admin), para. 20.
[30] CJA 2003, s. 239(6) (formerly CJA 1991, s. 32(6)).

the one hand and the prisoner on the other'.[31] His Lordship concluded that it was improper for the Home Secretary to possess such a power in cases where the Board has directory powers and is required by Article 5 to act judicially – albeit that there was nothing improper in the Home Secretary issuing directions to the Board vis-à-vis the discharge of its advisory, non-judicial functions, where there is no need for the Board to act as an independent 'court'.

However, this analysis flags up a further issue. As the ECtHR has observed, the text of Article 5(4) makes it clear that 'the body in question must not merely have advisory functions but must have the competence to "decide" the "lawfulness" of the detention and to order release if the detention is unlawful'.[32] The analysis in *Girling* presupposes that in those contexts where the Board still has only advisory power this is unobjectionable: Article 5, it is assumed, does not apply to those functions, and so does not require the Board to have the power of decision; it follows that there can be no impropriety in the exercise of the Home Secretary's direction-issuing power. Yet this begs the question whether the demands of Article 5 are met by the present distinction between the Board's advisory and directory powers, or whether there are any matters in relation to which the Board merely has advisory power but over which it ought (as the relevant 'independent' body) to possess directory power.

In some circumstances, merely advisory power is unobjectionable. For example, it is uncontroversial that Article 5(4) has no application to the initial release of long-term prisoners under the 1991 Act: here, the Board's lack of directory power is acceptable. But can the same be said in relation to the Board's role concerning the progress of offenders through the prison system? While it is possible for the Board to advise the Home Secretary on the transfer of prisoners from closed to open conditions, the Board has no directory powers in this regard: the decision lies with the Home Secretary. Although this has been considered unproblematic at both the domestic and European levels,[33] Rose LJ has observed that 'in reality, transfer to open conditions for a period of testing is generally a necessary preliminary to release'.[34] So, in practice, release of post-tariff lifers from closed conditions is likely only in exceptional circumstances (an approach upheld by the courts),[35] thus allowing the Home Secretary, by refusing to act on the Board's

---

[31] *R (Girling)* v. *Parole Board* [2006] 1 WLR 1917, para. 71.
[32] *Weeks*, op. cit., pp. 315–16 (see note 27).
[33] *Burgess* v. *Home Secretary* (3 November 2000, unreported); *Blackstock* v. *UK* (2006) 42 EHRR 2.
[34] Ibid., para. 14.
[35] *R* v. *Parole Board, ex parte Lodomez* (1994) 26 BMLR 162.

recommendations as to transfer to open conditions,[36] to place the Board in a position where it is in effect unable to direct release because there has been no opportunity to 'test' the prisoner in open conditions. Decisions concerning transfer to open conditions are, in substance if not in form, inextricably linked with the decision-making process concerning the release of post-tariff prisoners. If this is so, it may be argued that the requirement, inherent in Article 5, that *release* decisions be made by an independent body can be given meaningful effect only if that body – namely the Board – also has directory power in relation to *transfers*.

In conclusion, it is noted that the precise location of the dividing line – the drawing of which is required by Article 5 – between the respective roles of the government and the Board remains somewhat uncertain. The crucial point, however, is that Article 5 insists that such a line be drawn. In doing so, it has fundamentally refashioned the parole system by curtailing the role of politicians in what are rightly regarded as judicial matters – a redrawing of institutional boundaries which domestic law, on its own, would have been powerless to secure.

Due process in parole decision-making

The development of the common law principles of fairness

The second way in which the changing face of public law has impacted upon the parole system concerns the way in which decisions are made. Although it is uncontentious that the Board is under a 'duty to act fairly', the nature of this duty has changed substantially in recent decades:

> The procedures involved in parole applications from the creation of the Board until after the coming into force of the [Criminal Justice Act 1991], despite the involvement of judges [as Board members], were far from judicial ... Decisions relating to initial release were all conducted on paper by panels of the Board – there was no disclosure of the material upon which the decisions were made and so no real opportunity to make representations, and no reasons were given (except in recall cases). The standard response given to fixed-term prisoners stated: 'Your case for early release on licence under the parole scheme has been fully and sympathetically considered but the Secretary of State regrets to have to inform you that parole has not been authorised.' (Arnott and Creighton 2006: 3)

---

[36] Something which it is said the Home Secretary 'frequently' does (Padfield 2002: 136). For examples, see *R* v. *Parole Board, ex parte Hirst* (21 October 1997, unreported); *Blackstock*, op. cit. (see note 23).

It would unquestionably be unlawful for the Board to act thus today. The duty to act fairly is more rigorous than it was 40 years ago: the reasons underlying its evolution are complex, and form part of a more general renaissance in administrative law in recent decades. That reflects (and is, in turn, constitutive of) a fundamental shift in the relationship between the individual and the state. As the Home Secretary recently remarked in a speech to the Board, such bodies 'are more accountable to the public than ever before . . . Forty years ago, decisions were taken . . . that had serious ramifications but very often hardly anyone knew about the nature of the decision, the evidence base behind it or the potential outcome' (Reid 2006). The position today is quite different. Established conventions of deference to, respect for and trust in public bodies have all but evaporated (O'Neill 2002). Greater public awareness of the business – and shortcomings – of the public sector, together with the increasingly evident impotence of Parliament to exercise meaningful control over government departments and public bodies and a more general drift towards litigiousness, have combined to produce a growing number of legal challenges to public bodies' decisions and a general sense in the courts that it is their responsibility to ensure that power is exercised fairly and lawfully.[37]

As a result, the Board, being a public body charged with making decisions that affect the fundamental interests and rights of individuals, now finds itself under a rigorous duty to act fairly. So, for example, it is abundantly clear that it would now be unlawful for the Board to make a decision on the release of a prisoner without first disclosing to him the information available to it and affording him an opportunity to make representations in response.[38] Equally, the Board would today act unlawfully if it were to make a decision without giving adequate reasons – an obligation which requires the Board to furnish the prisoner with 'an intelligible summary of [its] reasoning, enough to show him that his application has been fairly considered and explain to him why the decision has gone against him',[39] and which may require the Board to address specific points in the prisoner's favour and to explain why they were regarded as insufficient to outweigh factors pointing away from release.[40]

That these safeguards now exist is to be welcomed. Adherence to the standards described above is central to the existence of a decision-making system which adequately recognises the dignity of the individ-

---

[37] See, for example, the case cited above at note 4.

[38] *R* v. *Parole Board, ex parte Harris* (15 September 1997, unreported). However, the duty of disclosure may be qualified in exceptional circumstances: see, for example, *R (Roberts)* v. *Parole Board* [2005] UKHL 45, [2005] 2 AC 738.

[39] *R* v. *Parole Board, ex parte Oyston* (1 March 2000, unreported), *per* Lord Bingham CJ.

[40] *R (Tinney)* v. *Parole Board* [2005] EWHC 863 (Admin).

ual, given what is at stake for him; which is equipped to assess risk as accurately as possible, thus improving outcomes; and which is encouraged to make decisions in a rigorous manner through the discipline which flows from a duty to give adequate reasons.[41]

The impact of the ECHR

However, while domestic law's role in this context has been important, the ECHR – which can now be enforced against the Board in national courts via the HRA 1998[42] – has been pivotal.

For instance, English courts long refused to accede to the argument that the Board should give reasons to 'lifers', explaining why they had not been released and thereby equipping them to make more meaningful representations as part of their next review.[43] The turning point was the *Wilson* case in 1992, in which the Court of Appeal held that the claimant was entitled to know why his last review had not recommended release.[44] The court was (exceptionally) persuaded to depart from its own previous case law, partly because a case decided two years earlier by the ECtHR[45] (and brought, *inter alios*, by the present claimant) had held that 'the Parole Board procedure [in discretionary lifer cases] which did not afford the normal incidents of a court hearing, including disclosure, was a violation of Article 5(4) of the Convention'.[46] That decision did not automatically change English law or, at that time, establish rights enforceable by prisoners in domestic courts,[47] yet, as *Wilson* illustrates, it caused English judges to rethink the position at common law, thus imposing new obligations – here, of disclosure – on the Board as a matter of domestic law.

However, the ECHR's role in driving up due process standards is most obvious in relation to oral hearings. This becomes apparent when we compare situations in which judges have simply applied common law standards of fairness with those in which the law has been changed – either legislatively or judicially – because Article 5 has been held applicable. In the former category, prisoners have traditionally been able to insist on an oral hearing only in specific, often exceptional, circumstances, if at all. The line that there is no general entitlement at common

---

[41] On these different aspects of the desirability of procedural fairness, see, *inter alios*, Galligan (1996), Allan (1998) and Fordham (1998).

[42] Section 6 obliges public authorities, of which the Board is one, to act compatibly with the ECHR.

[43] *Payne* v. *Lord Harris of Greenwich* [1981] 1 WLR 754; *Gunnell* v. *Parole Board* (*The Times*, 7 November 1984); *R* v. *Parole Board, ex parte Bradley* [1991] 1 WLR 134.

[44] *R* v. *Parole Board, ex parte Wilson* [1992] QB 740.

[45] *Thynne*, op. cit. (see note 20).

[46] Ibid., p. 751.

[47] The decision preceded the HRA 1998.

law to an oral hearing has been maintained throughout a wide range of circumstances, including decisions on the categorisation of prisoners within the prison system;[48] the early release both of prisoners serving 'longer than normal' sentences under section 2(2)(b) of the CJA 1991[49] and of long-term determinate sentence prisoners under the CJA 1991 within the 'parole window';[50] and (prior to the ECtHR's decision in *Stafford*) the release of post-tariff mandatory lifers.[51] Indeed, even after the ECtHR had ruled[52] that Article 5 applied to persons detained at Her Majesty's pleasure, the English courts refused (pending legislative implementation of the Strasbourg judgment) to hold that an oral hearing had to precede release decisions in such cases.[53] All of this is of a piece with the standard common law approach which, as noted earlier, is highly context-sensitive, and which therefore tended to insist on an oral hearing only where there was some specific, compelling reason for such an approach.

The position is very different in relation to decisions where Article 5 is operative: here, it is taken as read that an oral hearing will be required if the Board's procedure is to pass muster.[54] The context-sensitivity of the common law contrasts with the category-based approach of Article 5: provided the case falls within one of the classes to which Article 5 applies, an oral hearing is automatically supplied. That is why the landmark judgments extending Article 5 to release decisions concerning discretionary lifers,[55] HMP prisoners[56] and then mandatory lifers[57] prompted such stark changes in Parole Board practice, precipitating a shift from the common law-informed position of affording hearings where necessary (which was generally taken to mean only exception-ally), to a situation in which such hearings are now the norm.

The most recent of those landmark cases is *Smith* v. *Parole Board*,[58] in which the House of Lords held that the Board had acted unlawfully by not giving oral hearings to two recalled determinate sentence prisoners.

---

[48] *R (Williams)* v. *Home Secretary* [2002] EWCA Civ 498, [2002] 1 WLR 2264.

[49] *R* v. *Parole Board, ex parte Mansell* (*The Times*, 21 March 1996).

[50] *R* v. *Parole Board, ex parte Harris* (unreported, 15 September 1997).

[51] *R* v. *Parole Board, ex parte Davies* (unreported, 27 November 1996).

[52] In *Hussain*, op. cit. (see note 22).

[53] *R* v. *Parole Board, ex parte Downing* (unreported, 24 October 1996). The position would have been different had the HRA 1998 been in force.

[54] See, for example, *Hussain*, op. cit., p. 26 (see note 23); and, in *Mansell*, op. cit. (see note 50), it was noted in relation to discretionary lifers that, following *Thynne*, the 'Secretary of State ha[d] recognised' that oral hearings were necessary 'in order to bring the United Kingdom in line with their Treaty obligations arising out of art. 5(4) of the [ECHR]'.

[55] *Thynne*, op. cit. (see note 20).

[56] *Hussain*, op. cit. (see note 22).

[57] *Stafford*, op. cit. (see note 23).

[58] [2005] UKHL 1, [2005] 1 WLR 350.

Although the Law Lords were at pains to stress that their decision was based in common law, it is clear that the infringement of common law principles of fairness found in *Smith* was fundamentally influenced by the ECHR itself. This is most readily apparent from Lord Hope's speech. He concluded that the Board, by not providing an oral hearing, had failed to supply the level of 'procedural fairness that the common law requires of a court', stressing that '[p]rocedural fairness is a requirement of the common law'.[59] That may be so. However, as Lord Hope acknowledged, the common law required this level of fairness in the first place because Article 5(4) was applicable and 'require[d] that the continuing detention must be judicially supervised' such that the Board had to act 'as a court would act'. It is therefore somewhat inaccurate to suggest that *Smith* is simply a product of common law reasoning: the ECHR played a fundamental part, since it determined, in the first place, the appropriate level of fairness by requiring that the Board behave like a court by (*inter alia*) supplying an oral hearing – a requirement which, as noted above, the common law on its own has been notably reluctant to impose.

All of this points to two conclusions. First, the ECHR has played a pivotal role in driving up the procedural standards applicable to parole decisions. It is highly unlikely, for instance, that in the absence of Article 5 the right to an oral hearing before the Board would be as widespread as it is today. Secondly, and just as importantly, Article 5 – by identifying categories of cases in which the right to an oral hearing is the norm – has brought a welcome degree of clarity to the law in this area. This is to be contrasted with the approach at common law which, as one commentator has noted, raises difficulties 'in terms of certainty and predictability' (Loughlin 1978: 237) – two characteristics which are always desirable in the law, but particularly so where something as fundamental as the liberty of the individual is at stake.

Prisoners' rights and the protection of the public

None of the developments traced above impede the making of decisions which properly safeguard the public. The fact that such decisions must now be made by the Board rather than by the Home Secretary does not make it any less likely that prisoners eligible for parole will be detained to the extent necessary for public protection. Nor is the fact that parole decisions must now be taken pursuant to exacting standards of procedural fairness incompatible with protecting the public: indeed, one of the principal virtues of procedurally proper decision-making is that it is liable to yield more accurate outcomes – risk assessments, in the present

---

[59] Ibid., para. 75.

context – by ensuring that decision-makers are in receipt of, and equipped fully to test, all relevant information.

Nevertheless, there is a view abroad that public law – in particular, human rights law – is getting in the way of adequately safeguarding the public. This discourse has acquired prominence in the parole context following the Anthony Rice case, recently singled out as a 'conspicuous and sobering example of the operational problems which have arisen for key agencies' due to 'misconceptions' about the impact of the HRA (DCA 2006: 5). The focus of this discourse is not primarily the procedural constraints (considered above) under which the Board and other decision-makers find themselves, but the notion that human rights law substantively restricts discretionary powers, requiring the interests of the public to be subjugated to those of the offender. Although, as we explain below, these perceptions are misguided, they are still highly damaging: they risk distorting priorities in the decision-making process, something of which the Parole Board stands accused in the Rice case (DCA 2006: 25; Reid 2006), in turn undermining public confidence in the Act and in the whole notion of human rights (Home Office 2006a: 16).

It is perhaps unsurprising that misconceptions have grown up in this area: if the Board is now required by the HRA[60] to act compatibly with prisoners' entitlements to (*inter alia*) respect for private and family life,[61] freedom of assembly and association,[62] and freedom of expression,[63] surely offenders must be granted parole at the first opportunity? How can continued detention be lawful, given that it will (at best) limit or (at worst) preclude the enjoyment of these rights? The answer is that, although offenders do not, simply because they are offenders, lose their human rights,[64] many of the rights contained in the ECHR[65] exist in qualified form only. In certain circumstances it is therefore perfectly lawful to limit a person's rights.

For example, it stands to reason that imprisonment – whether as a direct consequence of a sentence imposed by the trial court or due to a later decision of the Parole Board – will affect an individual's private and family life, the right to respect for which is enshrined in Article 8. However, this right – which appeared to be a factor in the Board's decision in the Rice case (HMIP 2006b: 36) – can lawfully be limited in the interests of (*inter alia*) 'public safety', provided that any such limitations are 'in accordance with the law' and 'necessary in a democratic society'. What, then, does this mean for the Board?

---

[60] Section 6.
[61] Article 8 ECHR.
[62] Article 11 ECHR.
[63] Article 10 ECHR.
[64] See, for example, *Raymond* v. *Honey* [1983] 1 AC 1; *Hirst* v. *UK (No. 2)* (2006) 42 EHRR 41.
[65] Including those cited above at notes 61–3.

In attempting to answer this question, we begin with the proposition that there is 'no question that a prisoner forfeits his Convention rights merely because of his status as a person detained following conviction'. It follows that 'any restrictions on [prisoners' qualified rights] require to be justified, although such justification may well be found in the considerations of security . . . which inevitably flow from the circumstances of imprisonment'.[66] This means, in the first place, that a decision ordering further detention, and so interfering with the prisoner's rights, must be suitable to achieve the competing policy objective of upholding public safety. The measures designed to meet the objective must therefore be 'rationally connected to it',[67] a requirement that will straightforwardly be met in parole cases, since imprisonment is an obviously effective way of protecting the public by disabling offenders from committing acts which may harm others.

This is a necessary but not sufficient condition of lawful decision-making. The limitations placed upon a right in the pursuit of a competing policy objective must also be proportionate: that is, the steps taken must be necessary for the protection of the public, the crunch question being whether the public safety objective could satisfactorily be secured by something entailing a smaller impact on the individual's rights than that entailed by detention:[68] for instance, release subject to particular licence conditions, perhaps including very close supervision. Of course, such considerations are hardly alien to the Board. For example, it may not direct the release of lifers unless it is 'satisfied that it is no longer necessary for the protection of the public that the prisoner should be confined' (Home Office 2004b). However, the Convention makes the obverse proposition true as well: further detention should *not* be ordered unless this *is* necessary. This does not fundamentally change what the Board must do – the central question remains whether further detention is necessary – but it does introduce a new dimension by requiring the appropriateness of detention to be judged by reference not only to its potentially beneficial impact on the public but also its inevitably detrimental impact on the prisoner's rights. In this sense, the Board, in seeking to make a lawful decision, now has a narrower target to aim for: it is still obliged (by the CJA) to detain if this is *necessary* on public safety grounds, but is *also* obliged (by the HRA) to release where further detention is *unnecessary*.

Although this may suggest that the Board's decisions are now highly vulnerable to legal challenge, the courts have traditionally been reluctant

---

[66] *Hirst*, op. cit., paras 69–70 (see note 64).
[67] *De Freitas* v. *Permanent Secretary of Ministry of Agriculture, Fisheries, Lands and Housing* [1999] 1 AC 69, p. 80.
[68] See, for example, *A* v. *Home Secretary* [2004] UKHL 56, [2005] 2 AC 68, paras 35 and 155.

to second-guess the Board's risk assessments. The case law highlights very particular reasons for deferring to the Board – reasons which survive the introduction of the HRA. For example, in the *Martin* case the court acknowledged that its role was not to 'attempt some sort of second guessing exercise in relation to the [Board]'s decision'.[69] As the court recognised in *Bradley*, the Board has 'a grave responsibility fraught with anxiety especially in the field of those serving life sentences for grave crimes': the courts, on judicial review, had to 'bear in mind that the panel considering [lifers'] cases[70] will be presided over by a High Court judge, and includes others having relevant knowledge and experience in judging risk'.[71] This recognition of the special position of the Board is reflected in other judgments: in *Hart*, for instance, Turner J noted that the Board is 'uniquely qualified',[72] while Jackson J observed in *Blake* that the Board has 'both experience and expertise . . . which judges lack'.[73]

Although courts are now generally more willing to interfere in the substance of decisions where human rights are at stake, judges continue to recognise the need for 'deference' to decision-makers' conclusions where there is a good reason for this – and it is widely acknowledged such a reason is supplied by the expertise of the decision-maker. For instance, in the *International Transport* case, in the course of setting out general principles concerning the intensity of judicial scrutiny of governmental decisions, Laws LJ argued that judges should be more willing to defer to decision-makers where 'the assessment of [the] matters [in question] . . . is . . . far more within the competence of government than the courts'.[74] In a context different from – but, it is submitted, relevant to – that which is presently under consideration, these principles were recently applied by the House of Lords in the *Belmarsh* case. On the question whether there was a 'public emergency' justifying counter-terrorism measures that were prima facie at odds with the ECHR, Lord Bingham accepted that 'great weight should be given to the judgment of the Home Secretary, his colleagues and Parliament'. This was because it 'involved making a factual prediction of what various people around the world might or might not do, and when (if at all) they

[69] *R* v. *Parole Board, ex parte Martin* (unreported, 20 November 1995).

[70] Such cases were singled out because it was the decision of a DLP that was under consideration in this case.

[71] *R* v. *Parole Board, ex parte Bradley* [1991] 1 WLR 134, p. 147 (but note that Panels are now routinely chaired by circuit judges and sometimes by legally qualified non-judicial members).

[72] *R* v. *Parole Board, ex parte Hart* (unreported, 24 May 2000).

[73] *R* v. *Parole Board, ex parte Blake* (unreported, 23 February 2000).

[74] *International Transport Roth GmbH* v. *Home Secretary* [2002] EWCA Civ 158, [2003] QB 728, para. 87.

might do it, and what the consequences might be if they did. Any prediction,' his Lordship noted, 'about the future behaviour of human beings . . . is necessarily problematical.'[75] Although that case arose in a different context, the general principles underlying the court's deference to the government's risk assessment is pertinent to the question presently under consideration. The parole context also calls for the making of difficult and careful assessments of risk on which reasonable minds might differ – a task to which the Board is peculiarly well-suited, in view of its expertise and its ability to take (and judge the veracity of) first-hand evidence from relevant parties.

Against this background, it is worth considering the *Buxton* case,[76] in which the claimant complained that the Board had inappropriately focused upon and prioritised public safety at the expense of his Article 8 rights. Rejecting this view, Forbes J agreed with counsel for the Board that it is 'not required to balance the protection of the public against the interests of the individual prisoner in determining whether or not to recommend release on licence';[77] rather, its only task is to 'determine whether or not release on licence presents an unacceptable risk of reoffending', and the offender's personal circumstances are relevant only as far as they bear upon that assessment of risk. None of this, said the judge, involved an unlawful limitation of the claimant's rights, since the 'extent to which private and family life can in practice be respected is constrained by the fact that the Claimant is a serving prisoner'.[78] The Board's decision would therefore be 'unassailable' provided that 'there [was] no flaw in [its] assessment of risk'.[79]

This, it is respectfully submitted, is not entirely correct. Even if the reviewing court refuses to interfere with the Board's view of the dangerousness of the offender, it does not follow that a decision to order further detention is 'unassailable'. The concept of proportionality, which, as explained above, is central to the HRA, requires that further detention must be *necessary* – a condition that will only be met if the acknowledged risk posed by the offender cannot satisfactorily be managed in the community. The Board will therefore have to be prepared to defend its

---

[75] Op. cit., para. 29 (see note 68).

[76] *R (Buxton)* v. *Parole Board* [2004] EWHC 1930 (Admin).

[77] Ibid., para. 41.

[78] Ibid., para. 49. Since this case was decided, the Home Secretary has issued new directions on the recall of determinate sentence prisoners. Although the new directions have a 'different emphasis' (Arnott and Creighton 2006: 32), the Board's decision as to when the prisoner should be re-released still turns on public safety considerations, the key questions being whether the prisoner presents an acceptable risk to public safety and whether adequate risk management arrangements are in place.

[79] Op. cit., para. 51 (see note 76).

view that release coupled with supervision would not be an adequate means by which to manage the risk posed by the offender.[80]

Like the assessment of risk in the first place, the Board's decision as to whether the risk can adequately be dealt with in the community or only by detention involves the use of expertise and the making of value-judgments, and so, in line with the principles described above, is likely to be accorded a good deal of respect by the courts. Yet judicial deference to such judgments is not limitless. For example, in the *Belmarsh* case, while the court did not displace the government's assessment of the nature and gravity of the risk posed by terrorism, it refused to accept that it was *necessary* to detain suspects: the government, noted Lord Scott, had failed to 'show that monitoring or movement restrictions less severe than incarceration in prison would not suffice'.[81] Similarly, in *Ploski v. Poland*, the applicant prisoner, who had been denied leave to attend his parents' funerals, succeeded in his Article 8 challenge, because the authorities had failed to show that public safety could be upheld only by ongoing detention rather than by, for example, temporary but *escorted* leave.[82] In both cases, the defendant governments had, perhaps surprisingly, failed to address modes of risk-containment falling short of detention, making it relatively straightforward for the courts to hold that detention had not been shown to be necessary. For that reason, these cases should not be taken to indicate that the courts will readily interfere with a reasoned determination by the Board that it is necessary to detain an offender in order acceptably to manage the risk he poses. *Belmarsh* and *Ploski* do, however, demonstrate that the Board will need to show, and be prepared to defend, exactly why it considers further detention – rather than release subject to supervision – necessary.

Of course, none of this prevents the Board from ordering the detention of those who present an unacceptable risk. It does, however, point to two important conclusions. First, if the Board's decisions – unlike those in *Belmarsh* and *Ploski* – are to withstand scrutiny, it will need to justify them carefully. In this way, the possibility of judicial review on *substantive* grounds acts as a further incentive to adhere to high *procedural* standards, in particular in the recording and provision of reasons for decisions; in this way the *necessity* of detention can be demonstrated. Secondly, provided the Board acts in this way, the courts are, for the reasons noted above, unlikely to second-guess its risk assessments or decisions as to how risk can satisfactorily be managed. However, this does not make successful judicial review, on substantive

---

[80] Of course, the Board already takes account of the resettlement plan for the offender (Home Office 2004a; Home Office 2004b).
[81] Op. cit., para. 155 (see note 68).
[82] 12 November 2002, application no. 26761/95.

human rights grounds, inconceivable. The deference which courts are likely to pay to the Board's decisions on these matters means that it retains a measure of discretion, but that discretion is not a boundless one, and it is clear that the advent of the HRA precludes the adoption of the sort of *unnecessarily* cautious approach to release decisions which the tabloid press would no doubt applaud.

Conclusions

In the parole context, as elsewhere, it has become fashionable (in some circles) to decry the interference, as it is presented, of the law – particularly human rights law. This paper has attempted to show that while the changing face of public law in the UK has had a major impact on the way in which parole decisions are made, its influence has been positive, and has left intact the Board's capacity to safeguard the public. This is apparent in each of the three spheres in which the role of public law has been considered.

First, it is clear that Article 5 ECHR has effected a major erosion of executive power over parole matters. This is an entirely positive development. All developed legal systems recognise that it is fundamentally inappropriate for certain functions to be discharged by certain types of decision-maker, a proposition nowhere more obviously correct than in relation to the sentencing of offenders – a task which encompasses the release of those subject to sentences incorporating preventative elements during which the appropriateness of detention is liable to change. The need for objectivity and independence makes this a task for judicial, not political, decision-makers. The suggestion that depriving elected politicians of the power to make such decisions is undemocratic is spurious; as argued above, it rests on an incomplete conception of democracy. Nor does this shift of power reduce the capacity of the system to protect the public: it simply ensures that decisions are made impartially and dispassionately, free from the pressures and populist instincts to which political decision-makers may be prone.

Secondly, we have seen that the development of public law – both domestically and under the influence of the ECHR – has led to radical changes in the way in which the Board operates in procedural terms. Disclosure of dossiers, rights of participation and (in many instances) oral hearings are now the norm in parole proceedings. Again, this is to be welcomed. One of the consequences (indeed, purposes) of due process is to promote the reliability of decision-making by ensuring that the evidence in play is adequately tested and the ultimate determination based on as accurate an appreciation of the relevant factors as possible. None of this is inconsistent with the making of decisions which pay proper regard to public safety: the latter interest is in no way advanced by decisions which needlessly elongate detention because, for example, evidence adverse to the prisoner was untested due to non-disclosure or inadequate opportunities for challenge.

Thirdly, and perhaps most controversially, public law undoubtedly places some substantive limits on the discretion of the Board. This has always been so: it has long been possible for courts to intervene in the event of (for example) a manifestly unreasonable risk assessment. There is, however, a perception that the Board's capacity to make decisions upholding public safety is unduly compromised by the HRA. It has been argued in this paper that such perceptions are essentially false, and that the Board remains able to order detention where this is *necessary* for public protection – notwithstanding that the HRA now prevents further detention where this is *unnecessary*.

The view that public and human rights law distorts decision-making in the parole context may have captured the public and political imagination, but it is one that does not withstand analysis. To the extent that the parole system has been impacted by the changing face of public law in the UK, the resulting changes have been for the better. The political and media debate has generally been founded upon the false premise that respect for individual rights and the protection of the public are mutually incompatible. The reality is different. The procedural changes which public law has precipitated in the parole system ensure that individual prisoners' cases are more fully and transparently considered, something which should only improve the quality of decision-making. And, although prisoners do possess substantive human rights which may seem to cut down the powers of the Board, this misses the fundamental point that the ECHR – the source of those rights – is premised on the notion that the interests of the individual must yield where this is necessary in the interests of public safety.[83] Properly understood, there is no inconsistency between due respect for human rights and a parole system which adequately protects the public.

---

[83] Making further legislation such as has been proposed (DCA 2006: 39) unnecessary.

Chapter 5

Why fairness matters in criminal justice

Alison Liebling

Fairness is getting off with quite a lot but not too much. An incident happened the other week when I talked back and was abusive to an officer on the wing. He banged me up and told me that I had to move wing. Later that day he got me on my own and explained why I needed to move wing. He explained that the new prisoners on the wing had to learn that you can't talk to an officer in that way. After the incident he treated me fairly by explaining that I had to be moved to prove to the other prisoners that you can't talk that way. It was fair 'cause he explained it to me. (Prisoner, Doncaster, cited in Liebling assisted by Arnold 2004: 270)

'Fairness' and 'order' are conceptually two of the most important ideas in political theory (Bottoms 1999). They have been the subject of close theoretical and empirical scrutiny in the prison context over a number of years. In this chapter, I draw on the results from some of this work to suggest that fairness matters in criminal justice for several reasons, including its relationship to various outcomes. This chapter provides both a summary of arguments laid out in further detail elsewhere (e.g. Liebling assisted by Arnold 2004; Liebling et al. 2005) and an extension of some of these arguments.

A word on fairness

Rawls's theory of justice as fairness is derived from an imaginary 'original position',[1] in which rational actors are behind a 'veil of ignorance'. In this state, they choose the principles of justice. According to Rawls, fairness should *generate trust* (Rawls 1980: 497–8). Others have argued that fairness 'involves an ability to consider consistently and without contradiction the interests and intentions of others' (Siegal 1982: 1). It requires impartiality (Barry 1989). On the other hand, it expresses the 'value of persons' (Raphael 2001: 248). Fairness, in relation to the individual, depends on *how* decisions are taken, the *frame of mind* in which they are taken, and the results (Lucas 1980: 4). In other words, fairness is intrinsically bound up with the *quality of the behaviour* of individuals, especially those in power (Tyler 1990). Judgments of fairness depend to a significant extent on the *manner* of one's treatment as well as (sometimes, more than) outcomes (Paternoster et al. 1997; Tyler and Blader 2000).[2] Fairness is related to, but is more than, equality. It often requires the resolution of competing claims and interests. Raphael argues that, while utility is not irrelevant to fairness, 'some of the most perplexing conflicts are conflicts between the principle of utility and an aspect of justice' (Raphael 2001: 201).[3] One of the problems facing criminal justice in an era of managerialism and the modernisation of public services is precisely the principle of utility.

My focus below is on what fairness is, rather than what it is not (the former is more difficult to articulate), but for completeness, let me report that prisoners include in their examples of unfair treatment: being disbelieved, treated with scepticism, treated as an aggregate, singled out as undeserving, and staff not following through on promises (see further Liebling assisted by Arnold 2004: 270–2 and *passim*).

---

[1] The 'original position' is a hypothetical (artificially contrived) situation in which free and rational actors find themselves in a situation of equality; it corresponds to the state of nature in traditional social contract theories (Rawls 1980: 11–12).

[2] Judgments about fairness often involve perceptions of the treatment of others. In this sense it is not an exclusively self-regarding value. 'Young children are quick to complain that action which discriminates in favour of one child or one group is unfair, and they do not confine this complaint to thought of their own advantage but are ready to speak up for the claims of others' (Raphael 2001: 208).

[3] We sometimes distinguish between 'what is right in the circumstances' and 'what is just' (Raphael 2001: 212).

A word on what fairness is not

Fairness should be distinguished from *laxity* and from *care* – two slippery concepts whose mistaken identities caused considerable trouble in two maximum security prisons during the mid-1990s. In a story told elsewhere (covered in some detail in *Prisons and Their Moral Performance*), Lord Justice Woolf's careful concept of fairness as justice was misunderstood as laxity, care or smooth relationships, in some important places, with some disastrous consequences. Prisoners at the Special Security Unit in Whitemoor prison were found with 84 boxes of property, some Semtex and a bicycle, following the high-profile escapes from that unit in 1994. This was the consequence of a systematic wearing away of the normal rules and procedures of prison life in the interests of good relationships, as a means of avoiding disorder, and in a context in which it is actually impossible for prison staff to enforce all the rules at their disposal if they are to make it through the day. The important point for the purposes of this chapter is simply that we should be precise when we use important words like fairness, and we should think through their application 'on the ground' before we fool ourselves into a false sense of security as to their meaning. One of the reasons that fairness has become unfashionable and politically unappealing is that it is so frequently mistaken for laxity.

The relevance of fairness to prison life

Prisoners are sophisticated commentators on the meaning and role of fairness in prison. The quotation above from the prisoner at Doncaster was one of many used to generate a working definition of fairness via a route I explain further below. This definition went more or less as follows:

> Free from dishonesty or discrimination. To be treated clearly, consistently (but also flexibly, where appropriate), impartially (but also with mercy), in conformity with rules or standards, with access to redress, competently, and courteously.

In order to proceed with this argument, I shall explain my term 'moral performance', show how it incorporates fairness and recount briefly how it emerged out of organised and 'appreciative' deliberations with staff and prisoners about how prison quality should be measured. But first, I shall outline some further context. Research on the role of fairness in prison has developed rapidly since the link was explicitly made between a major series of disorders in English prisons and the perceptions of prisoners that they were not being treated *fairly*. Fairness, according to the Woolf Report, included due process or procedural justice (for example, being informed about reasons for decisions made) but also decent facilities, programmes, means of redress and the manner of prisoners' treatment by staff (Home Office 1991a, 1991b).

An unpublished doctoral study arising out of discussions held at the time of the Woolf Inquiry (see Sparks et al. 1996: appendix B) constitutes the first comprehensive empirical analysis of fairness in prison. Ahmad set out to explore 'the perceived fairness of day-to-day life in prison' (Ahmad 1996: 64) by conducting detailed structured interviews with 230 prisoners in three prisons of different types: a local prison, a Category C prison and a maximum security prison. He argued that fairness in prison had three main components: the fairness of staff; the fairness of the regime; and the fairness of procedures (for example, disciplinary and grievance procedures). Ahmad argued that there is 'a direct relationship between the nature of rule enforcement and the quality of life that inmates experience inside the prison' (Ahmad 1996: 26). He found that prisoners emphasised interpersonal aspects of fairness (which he suggests included being 'treated with respect and humanity', Ahmad 1996: 84). Prisoners wanted 'understanding and concern', and 'equality' (ibid.).[4] Rules, procedures and relationships together provided fairness. If the staff were perceived as fair, then the regime was also likely to be perceived as fair (and vice versa). Relational aspects of staff behaviour, such as personal contact, helpfulness and positive attitudes, were strongly related to judgments about staff fairness. Ahmad hypothesised that prisoners saw staff as having more control over these variables than over specific details of the regime, which they could blame on the governor (Ahmad 1996: 144).

Secondary multivariate analysis of Ahmad's data conducted by Bottoms and Rose showed that 'when prisoners assess overall staff–prisoner relationships in a prison, their perceptions of the fairness of the uniformed staff are of central importance to their judgment of the overall quality of staff–prisoner relationships' (Bottoms and Rose 1998: 223).

Perceived staff fairness was seen as the 'main determinant of perceived overall regime fairness' (ibid.; and see Figure 6.1 in Liebling assisted by Arnold 2004: 265). Prisoners' perceptions of staff–prisoner relationships and prisoners' perceptions of staff fairness were very highly related. Perceptions of fairness in prison were 'substantially more dependent' on perceptions of staff fairness and staff–prisoner relationships than they were on 'the objective quality of various specific regime features' (that is material provision), or prisoners' evaluations of the fairness of these

---

[4] These might be in tension, of course.

regime features: 'In a very real sense, therefore, it would seem that staff actually embody, in prisoners' eyes, the regime of a prison, and its fairness' (Bottoms and Rose 1998: 227).

This is a crucial insight, and it has significant implications for our understanding of prisons, for the way in which they are evaluated by prisoners and for our thinking about the work of prison officers. It also has implications for other areas of criminal justice work, as ongoing research on policing, probation and immigration detention is beginning to show (see, for example, Tyler and Huo 2002; Mair 2004; Prison and Probation Ombudsman 2004).

Returning to my own recent research, I was converted to the use of 'appreciative inquiry' [AI] during an exploration of the work of prison officers. Instead of focusing on 'problems', we were asking questions like, 'when do you perform at your best, in here?', 'tell me about your best moment in the job', 'what was going on at the time, to make this day so special?' and so on. We found this technique creative and energising, and it helped us to discover new ways of looking at the work of prison officers. Their peacekeeping role, the constructive uses of discretion, the way they made refined judgments about complex situations and the way they underused their formal authority more often than they overused it, all emerged out of a deliberately appreciative look at their work (see Liebling et al. 1999; Liebling and Price 2001). Likewise, it seemed better to attempt to measure a prison's quality positively than to rely solely on measures of failure, like a suicide or an escape. Prison staff in difficult prisons seem to be more prepared to talk about poor performance and to discuss possible explanations for it if investigators show that they have measured the good bits as well as the bad bits. As John Braithwaite has argued, people and organisations experience negative, defensive reactions when they are simply stigmatised or criticised (Braithwaite 2002). The legitimacy-compliance framework applies to the workforce as well as to offenders. A 'low respect' or 'low fairness' prison often has a wing, or a shift, or several 'micro-climates' where respect and/or fairness can be found.

Our research was an exploratory project in which we aimed at positive measurement for understanding rather than negative measurement for control. The most important feature of the study is the fact that we worked in detail, from staff and prisoners 'upwards', to identify what should be measured. Staff and prisoners assisted in the identification of statements or items felt to reflect each dimension and in the wording of the questionnaire. We used exercises with workgroups in each prison, over a number of days, asking staff to reflect on where the strengths lay in their establishment, and a discussion of what values underlay all their best hopes for the prison. We used scenarios to explore what was meant by each of these values, and we conducted some training in AI for staff and prisoners and some practice interviews, which we discussed together.[5] We referred to our methodology as a form of 'strong evaluation': that is, prisoners and staff engaged with us in complex moral reasoning about their condition. We were trying to bring a deep sense of what was important to them to definition, getting past distortions and shallow evaluations, and encouraging the expression of what they valued most highly.

There are two ways in which we were measuring the prison positively: the questions were based on positive values, arising out of a vision of where those living and working in the prison wanted to be (and because of the nature of the exercises, this vision was grounded in real experiences). Second, the survey captured some of everything – in a low-trust prison, we still found some trust. We knew what it looked like and where it was experienced. We conducted 'appreciative interviews' with most of the respondents in the study, as well as asking them to complete the survey questionnaire, so we were able to invite continual elaboration on what it felt like to be treated with respect, fairness and so on.

There was a surprising degree of consensus both between prisons and between prisoners and staff about what the most important aspects of prison life were. They explained that these were the areas of prison life that varied most, and that it was these variations that gave individual prisons their distinctive tone. The dimensions identified were: Respect, Humanity, Staff–Prisoner Relationships, Trust, Support, Fairness, Order, Safety, Well-being, Personal Development, Family Contact, Decency, Power and Relationships among prisoners. These are empirical and theoretical constructs in the sense that they emerged out of our deliberations, and were refined in the analyses that followed. We were trying to do justice to the complexity of the prison experience, while also striving for meaningful quantification. The survey represented how prisoners felt morally treated by the prison. We found a pattern to prisoner evaluations of a prison's moral performance, so that levels of order were much higher than levels of respect, humanity, trust or personal development, for example. Levels of all of the things that mattered were quite low, but importantly they varied between prisons of the same type. If we take fairness on its own, we found in the original survey that only two out of five prisons were regarded as at all fair by prisoners, and that prisons failed on quite distinct aspects of fairness, for example privilege distribution, clarity, consistency or relational aspects of fairness (Liebling assisted by Arnold 2004: 276).

One of the important steps we were able to take using this survey was to investigate how the dimensions were related to each other and to

---

[5] Charles Elliott, the author of an authoritative book on Appreciative Inquiry, led these exercises at our request (see Elliott 1999; also Elliott et al. 2001; Liebling et al. 2001).

outcomes. For example, Fairness was significantly positively correlated with all other dimensions. It was most highly correlated with: humanity (.774), trust (.739), relationships and respect (.730) and order (.707).[6] It was possible to find three sub-dimensions using all the fairness items together. They fell into three factors or groups: staff fairness, clarity and formal or procedural justice. This framework was supported when we combined the fairness with the relationships items, suggesting that these distinct dimensions of fairness are reasonably robust (see further Liebling with Arnold 2004: 277–81).

The relationship between fairness, moral performance and outcomes

The following section briefly outlines some of the links between aspects of moral performance and two outcomes: order and disorder, and distress and suicide.

Order

Further analysis of the associations between the dimensions revealed clear statistical links between the concepts of respect and relationships, fairness, perceptions of safety and order in establishments, as hypothesised in the literature. Interestingly, we found a statistical relationship between levels of respect and fairness and levels of well-being among prisoners. I shall return to this later.

One of the first prisons we studied in the development of the questionnaire (Holme House) went on to have a major disturbance six months after we had surveyed it in detail. As we had also gathered considerable qualitative data at this site, we knew the prison well. Our diagnosis of its moral performance had been that this was a modern, well-equipped prison with reasonable levels of activity but slightly overbearing staff. Prisoners said, 'they treat you fair, but it's not respect'. At the time of our survey, the prison had been under its normal population figure, resulting in unusually good access to facilities. As the population began to climb, access to activities became restricted. Prisoners united in a protest on one wing in particular, almost destroying it. A second disturbance followed two months later. This was the first empirical illustration we had of the Sparks et al. thesis (in *Prisons and the Problem of Order* (1996)) that cooperation depended on perceptions of legitimate treatment, including respect. It looked, at Holme House, as if prisoners had been complying with the regime for

---

[6] Correlation coefficients using Pearson's r.

instrumental rather than normative reasons. As soon as their material quality of life declined, they withdrew this consent. We know that in other prisons, staff can 'sell' an impoverished regime by treating prisoners in a civil and friendly manner. This illustrates something that is increasingly recognised about fairness: that its full meaning incorporates relational as well as material treatment.

Suicide and distress

Turning to suicide and distress, we showed in a recent study that there is a direct statistical relationship (at least in high-turnover, local prisons) between mean or average levels of distress among prisoners in individual establishments and three-year moving average suicide rates in those prisons (Liebling et al. 2005). In other words, if one is interested in how at risk of suicide a particular prison's population are, one can acquire some indication of this by measuring mean or average levels of current distress in that prison. We did this using our own 16-item measure of distress, devised for use in prison, and the GHQ-12, a short screening instrument used in community samples to indicate anxiety and depression. We found that prisons of the same type differed significantly in levels of distress among prisoners, and that only a small proportion of the variance in levels of distress could be accounted for by prisoner characteristics or what we have called elsewhere 'imported vulnerability'. A considerable and significant amount of the variation in levels of distress was explained by prisoners' feelings of safety, their perceptions of fairness and their evaluations of their relationships with staff. These findings were related, so that how safe prisoners felt was linked to the responsiveness and fairness of staff or prisoners' 'trust in the environment'. Prisons differed in this respect, and it has been a significant development of our understanding of suicides in prison that lack of fairness, safety and respect can increase levels of distress among already vulnerable prisoners, for reasons that make sense. I am now intrigued to investigate whether these in-prison effects have longer-term influence on well-being, including desistance from offending, following release from custody. There are reasons to believe that a prison experience that is perceived as reasonably fair and respectful will be less painful and damaging than one that is unfair and hostile (see further Liebling et al. 2005).

Implications for criminal justice

What are the implications of this analysis for criminal justice more generally? There are at least two. First, fairness matters, for both normative reasons (we are considering a criminal justice system, after all) and also for instrumental reasons. Being treated unfairly leads to negative consequences – non-compliance and, importantly, distress. We need just institutions of criminal justice if we are to avoid hypocrisy, disaffection and further damage. But second, we need to be clear about what fairness is and what it is not. This means we need to talk about it more, investigate it further and reflect regularly on how far real criminal justice practices approximate, deliver or depart from clearly articulated principles of fairness. Finally, and this is opening up another topic entirely, we should bear in mind that criminal justice professionals need to be treated fairly too.

Chapter 6

The New Zealand Parole Board, its independence and some domestic and international legal challenges

Tony Ellis

Introduction

This paper will address three topics:

- independence of the New Zealand Parole Board;
- heavier penalties provisions (see Article 7 of the European Court of Human Rights (ECHR) and Article 15 of the International Covenant on Civil and Political Rights (ICCPR);
- the legality of interim recall hearings and associated rights.

Background – New Zealand Parole Board

The Parole Act 2002, divided from the Sentencing and Parole Reform Bill at the third Reading, created the New Zealand Parole Board ('NZPB').[1] Prior to that major conceptual change to the approach to sentencing and parole, a Parole Board existed which had jurisdiction to deal with

---

[1] 1 May 2002.

prisoners serving seven years or more,[2] while a number of District Prison Boards dealt with those serving less than seven-year sentences.[3] A High Court or District Court Judge, or a retired member of those benches now chairs the NZPB.[4] The first Chairperson A. A. T. Ellis QC[5] was a retired High Court Judge, unlike the previous Parole Board, which had a serving High Court Judge, Heron J. The current Chairperson Judge D. J. Carruthers is the retired Chief District Court Judge. A considerable number of current District Court Judges sit as Conveners[6] of the Board at various locations around the country, together with two of the 17 lay members. The Extended Board sits with five members and customarily deals with difficult cases. The Chairperson or a Convenor has the power to issue an interim recall order; otherwise a quorum is three members.

Members of the NZPB are appointed for a three-year term.[7] Such a short term, coinciding with New Zealand's triennial general election cycle, is the subject of concern. Until recently, following a still ongoing Judicial Review,[8] the NZPB shared an office floor with the Department of Corrections legal section.

The greatest change brought about by the Parole Act 2002 was possible release at one-third of the sentence rather than the mandatory release at two-thirds. This change has clearly benefited post-2002 offenders by providing for their earlier possible release. The argument as to whether this lighter penalty should have been made retrospective is subject to challenge before the UN Human Rights Committee ('HRC').[9]

During the preparation of this paper the NZ Law Commission produced a final paper *Sentencing Guidelines and Reform*[10] that advocates 'truth in sentencing', a reversal of the one-third sentencing

---

[2] See s. 97, Criminal Justice Act 1985.

[3] Ibid., s. 100.

[4] Section 112, Parole Act 2002.

[5] No relation to the writer.

[6] Twenty-two were last noted on the Board's website as at August 2006 (see: http://www.paroleboard.govt.nz/nzpb/aboutus/whoswho.html).

[7] Section 111(1), Parole Board Act 2000: appointed by the Governor-General on the recommendation of the Attorney-General; s. 120 provides for a three-year term.

[8] *Miller & Carroll* v. *New Zealand Parole Board and Attorney-General* Civ. No. 2004-485-1460.

[9] In *Van Der Plaat* v. *New Zealand*, Comm. No. 1492/2006. New Zealand has ratified both the International Covenant on Civil and Political Rights and the Optional Protocol allowing individual complaints. Since ratification the only successful case has been *Rameka, Harris, and Tarawa* v. *New Zealand*, Comm. No. 1090/2002, CCPR/C/79/D/1090/2002, Views of 15 December 2003 (Human Rights Committee), 7 HNRZ 663, a preventive detention case (IPP prisoner in UK terms). The writer of this paper was counsel for the 'authors' in that case, as the complainants are described in UN terminology. See discussion below at pp. 75–6, 86.

[10] NZLC R94 (see: http://www.lawcom.govt.nz).

regime, longer prison sentences and the establishment of a Sentencing Council. The place of executive power and influence in the sentencing framework raises serious policy issues and the doctrine of the separation of powers. This latest review of sentencing and parole only four years after the last major review in my opinion shows that insufficient consideration has been given to the New Zealand political scene, the independence of the NZPB and the constitutionality and independence of the proposed Sentencing Council. Trendy political amendments are no substitute for a principled approach. Proper discussion of that topic would need a chapter of its own. The real questions and underlying themes are first in my view the prison population (which in the western world is second only to the US), and secondly, the perception of increased crime (see Table 6.1).

Independence of the New Zealand Parole Board

A judicial review still awaiting hearing in the New Zealand High Court raises the interesting question of whether the NZPB and its predecessor are independent. The challenge had its genesis in the comment made by

Table 6.1 Comparative study of prison population for New Zealand, England and Wales, Scotland, Australia and Canada

Country	Prison population total (no. in penal institutions incl. pre-trial detainees)	Date	Estimated national population (millions)	Prison population rate (per 100,000 of national population)	Source of prison population total
New Zealand	6,802	Mid-2004	4.06	168	NPA, Asia-Pacific annual conference
England and Wales	75,320	25/02/05	53.02	142	NPA
Scotland	6,742	25/02/05	5.11	132	NPA
Australia	23,362	Mid-2004	19.9	117	NPA
Canada	36,389*	2002–2003	31.44	116	Statistics Canada

*Average daily population, including young offenders, 1/4/2002–31/3/2003.
Source: Walmsley (2005).

the majority on the HRC in *Rameka* v. *NZ*.[11] Addressing the issue of arbitrary detention in the context of a detainee's right to have his detention regularly reviewed by an independent body with judicial character, the HRC commented:

> 7.3 . . . The Committee is of the view that the remaining authors have failed to show that the compulsory annual reviews of detention by the Parole Board, the decisions of which are subject to judicial review in the High Court and Court of Appeal, are insufficient to meet this standard . . .
>
> 7.4 Furthermore, in terms of the ability of the Parole Board to act in judicial fashion as a 'court' and determine the lawfulness of continued detention under article 9, paragraph 4, of the Covenant, the Committee notes that the remaining authors have not advanced any reasons why the Board, as constituted by the State party's law, should be regarded as insufficiently independent, impartial or deficient in procedure for these purposes. The Committee notes, moreover, that the Parole Board's decision is subject to judicial review in the High Court and Court of Appeal . . .

The majority of the HRC decided that New Zealand's system of 'preventive detention' (the equivalent of Imprisonment for Public Protection (IPP) in England) by which convicted offenders who are considered to pose a serious risk to the safety of the community can be given an indeterminate (open-ended) sentence of imprisonment, violated Article 9(4) of the Covenant.[12] They also decided the challenge to the absence of rehabilitation courses was inadmissible for want of substantiation, because the authors had given insufficient particulars.[13]

Geiringer[14] comments on *Rameka* that three features of the case are worth emphasis. Firstly, of the 16 members nine dissented. Of those nine, six were in favour of more breaches and three in favour of none. She states that 'the second feature worth comment is the circumscribed nature of the violation the Committee found to have been established. Rameka will go down in the annals of legal history as the first occasion on which a human rights treaty body held New Zealand in breach of one of the human rights treaties. The case is, though, just as significant for

---

[11] *Rameka* v. *New Zealand* No.1090/2002 UNHRC 7 HRNZ 663.

[12] Article 9(4) (which is similar to Article 5(4) of the ECHR) provides: 'Anyone who is deprived of his liberty by arrest or detention shall be entitled to take proceedings before a court, in order that that court may decide without delay on the lawfulness of his detention and order his release if the detention is not lawful.'

[13] Para. 6.4.

[14] Geiringer (2005: 193).

the breaches that were held not to be established.'[15] Geiringer is of course correct that it is significant what was not established. However, frankly I had not considered the Parole Board independence point, and did not have the information on rehabilitative courses to effectively challenge them. The judicial review in *Miller* was brought about in an attempt partly to progress *Rameka* particularly on these Parole Board and rehabilitative points. The judicial review (was initially) primarily based on the absence of rehabilitation, and Article 10(3) of the Covenant (a unique provision not reflected in the European Convention) which states that 'the penitentiary system shall comprise treatment of prisoners the essential aim of which shall be their reformation and social rehabilitation'.

The judicial review had migrated from an initial appeal from a postponement order whereby the consideration of Miller's parole was postponed for three years. That was not, in my opinion, a regular review for purposes of Article 9(4) of the Covenant (cf. Article 5(4) ECHR).[16] That High Court appeal was won, but the accompanying habeas corpus based on the rehabilitative courses was lost.

On appeal to the Court of Appeal, it became apparent that a 'member' of the Parole Board, Dr Chaplow,[17] was not what he seemed. In an affidavit, Dr Chaplow quite frankly admitted he had attended meetings of the NZPB as if he were a member (he had been a member of the pre-2002 Board but had retired) and contributed to the Board's private deliberations and 'decision making'. On receipt of that affidavit, the habeas corpus appeal was withdrawn and a judicial review filed. As for Dr Chaplow, the Parole Board website states:[18] 'The Solicitor-General's opinion is that the participation of Dr Chaplow in the decision-making process of the Board was not authorised by the Parole Act 2002 and that offenders should be offered a rehearing if they felt aggrieved by Dr Chaplow's participation.'

It was somewhat disturbing that the Chairman, a retired High Court judge, could invite Dr Chaplow to stay on as a member, and numerous other judges who sat with the Chairman on extended Boards did not demur. The judicial review pleadings allege that both the Parole Board (pre-30 June 2002) and the NZPB were neither an independent nor an impartial tribunal – as they breached the doctrine of the separation of powers, exhibited a lack of independence and impartiality, had the

---

[15] Ibid., p. 194.

[16] *Blackstock* v. *UK*, ECHR Application No. 59512/00, 21 June 2005. *Spence* v. *UK* Application No. 1190/04, 30 November 2004.

[17] The government's Chief Psychiatric Adviser and Director of Mental Health in the Ministry of Health.

[18] See: http://www.paroleboard.govt.nz/nzpb/media/media/. Media release was 21 July 2004.

appearance of bias and failed to comply with fair hearing rights. There are a large number of alleged reasons, such as:[19]

- lay members' appointments are political and their term of office was too short (PB and NZPB);

- there were insufficient guarantees against outside pressures on the lay members (PB and NZPB);

- the structural interweaving of the Department and Board destroyed any appearance of independence, if not independence itself (PB and NZPB);

- the Psychological Service of the Department provides on the request of the Board psychological reports to the Board (PB and NZPB];

- the Psychological Service of the Department provides intensive training to members of the Board (PB and NZPB).

The best example of political appointments is that of David Major. He was appointed to the old Parole Board by the then ruling National Government.[20] The Secretary of Justice responding to the Minister of Justice advised he had sought nominations from the Government Caucus, and approximately 20 members were nominated. The list was not compiled in alphabetical or any date received order. The first listed nomination was recorded as David Major nominated by 'the Office of Prime Minister' but not by the Prime Minister, i.e. a corporate rather than an individual nomination, and a clear example of executive sponsorship and gerrymandering of the list. David Major was described as Chief Executive of the National Party, a Salvation Army Officer of 21 years' standing and the founding Chairperson of the Auckland Central Victims Support Programme. Subsequent approval, or at least no dissent, was

---

[19] Another interesting reason is the Parole Board policy discouraging legal representation set out at p. 70 of the Parole Board Guide under the heading Legal Representation: 'Experience has shown that unless there is some special need for counsel, her/his involvement does not operate to the advantage of the offender. It commonly puts the Board at one remove from the offender, reduces the Board's ability to achieve a close and frank relationship with offenders, and makes them less inclined to exercise their own initiative or work out what may best be done to meet their particular needs based upon their knowledge.' This requirement for leave to appear is a breach of the concept of inequality of arms as the Department has no such restriction. It does not bode well for the proposition that the Board is a court. What court requires counsel to seek leave to appear before it?

[20] Strictly speaking the majority party in a coalition, NZ not having had a single party with sufficient MPs to form a majority government since the MMP (mixed member proportional) system was introduced in 1996 (half constituency MPs and half list MPs with each voter having two votes).

obtained from parties supporting the government. The opposition was not consulted.

No consideration was given as to whether David Major had a conflict of interest at common law, or as described in the State Services Commission Guidelines on Board Appointments and Induction Guidelines referred to in the Cabinet Manual at para. 6.3.[21] In my opinion, as National Party Chief Executive, David Major had a conflict of interest. He also had a conflict of interest being a founder Chairman of the Auckland Central Victims Support Programme, or if that conflict was no longer current had the appearance of a conflict.

On 24 June 1999 the Minister of Justice sent the recommendation for appointment of David Major to the Governor-General. No reference whatsoever was made in the supporting papers sent to the Governor-General that the candidate David Major was Chief Executive of the National Party. David Major was described as a Salvation Army Officer of 21 years' standing, the founding Chairman of the Auckland Central Victims Support Programme, an experienced teacher and a Rotarian. The failure of the Minister of Justice to provide the full details of David Major's status, namely that he was Chief Executive of the National Party, was not full and frank, and was not in accordance with the Minister's duties to keep the Governor-General fully informed as prescribed by the Letters Patent Constituting the Office of Governor-General of New Zealand,[22] and the Cabinet Office Manual para. 1.11. The failure of the Minister to supply the requisite information destroyed the independence of the process, and/or the appearance of independence of the process, and the appointment. The Governor-General appointed David Major *Minister of Religion* to be a member of the Parole Board on 24 June 1999. During his term in office David Major appeared in the Parole Board Annual Report as David Major, *Chief Executive of the National Party*.

The term of the appointments of Parole Board members was,[23] and NZPB still are, three-year terms (or less),[24] regrettably short and unfortunately conveniently pandering to the three-year electoral cycle in NZ, making political appointment or their appearance as such inevitable. In *Campbell and Fell* v. *UK*[25] in relation to Prison Boards of Visitors, the European Court of Human Rights observed that while the three-year terms were short, the members were unpaid and this made it difficult to find members. However the NZPB members are paid.

---

[21] See: http://www.dpmc.govt.nz/cabinet/.
[22] Clause XVI, 1983 SR 1983/225.
[23] Section 130, Criminal Justice Act 1985.
[24] Section 120, Parole Act 2002.
[25] ECHR Application No. 7819/77; 7878/77 28 June 1984.

The important differences are here that Parole Boards, as will be seen, are subject to public pressure. National Party nominees – at least such high-ranking ones as David Major – will not be re-nominated by the Labour Party. Why does a political party in government want its Chief Executive on the Parole Board? The two most obvious reasons are either as jobs for the boys or to exert the party line. Neither is acceptable, and even if not true, an independent observer would not be convinced. Other nuances here are that the Department of Corrections itself nominated six members, fortunately not successfully, but joined with the Chairperson to seek re-appointment of a member who is still currently a member of the New Zealand Parole Board. How government departments and entities such as the *Office of Prime Minister* can nominate for such positions is startling in itself. In *Thaler* v. *Austria*:[26] '. . . whether a tribunal can be considered as "independent", regard must be had, *inter alia*, to the manner of appointment of its members and their term of office, the existence of guarantees against outside pressures and the question whether the body presents an appearance of independence . . .'

What independence or impartiality is there with this type of appointment? Matters get worse when one considers the formal training run for members of the Board is organised by and provided by the Department of Corrections, particularly the Psychological Service. Senior psychological staff provide significant training. The reality for a prisoner (lifer, or preventive detainee, or violent sexual offender) is that a positive psychological report is needed for release, or to prevent a s. 107 order.[27] That training by the Department officers,[28] and particularly the psychologists, in my view irretrievably taints all Board members, especially as expert witnesses from the Psychological Service then give evidence before Parole Boards. Additionally, sharing premises with the Department (until recently) does not give the appearance of independence, nor does sharing staff or computer facilities, or having an e-mail address such as *[Firstname.lastname]@corrections.govt.nz*. For instance, Leggatt (2001), at para. 2.20,[29] comments that it cannot be said that tribunal decisions are independent and that the evidence is to the contrary: departments pay for tribunals' administrative support and IT support, and there may be an appearance of common enterprise. More allegations

---

[26] ECHR, Application No. 58141/00 3 May 2005.

[27] An order that the prisoner not be released while a 'risk' which is reviewed every six months, but for most finite sentenced prisoners it means they will have to serve the final one-third of their sentence.

[28] For example, a General Manager in the Department will be the applicant for recall orders, or s. 107 orders.

[29] See: http://www.tribunals-review.org.uk/leggatthtm/leg-00.htm; see also Creighton and Thornton (Chapters 7 and 8 respectively) in this volume.

when the *Miller* judicial review discovery process is completed are likely.[30]

Heavier penalties – Article 7 ECHR and Article 15 ICCPR

Article 15 of the ICCPR provides that a heavier penalty than the one that was applicable at the time when the criminal offence was committed cannot be imposed. Padfield (2006: 18) refers to the potential impact of *R (on the application of Uttley)* v. *Secretary of State for the Home Department* [2004] 1 WLR 2278; [2005] 1 Cr. App. R. 15, where Articles 5, 6 and particularly Article 7 of the ECHR were in issue. This brings into sharp focus the nature of parole. The issue is whether the change to release entitlements can constitute a penalty, thereby engaging Articles 7 and 15.

The Supreme Court of New Zealand, now the final appellate Court,[31] considered this issue in *Morgan* v. *The Superintendent, Rimutaka Prison* [2005] NZSC 26 SC 13/2005 and *Mist* v. *The Queen* SC12/2005 [2005] NZSC 77. It was held in *Morgan* that parole and early release are matters of administration or management of a sentence rather than the penalty itself. The 'effective maximum approach' was also endorsed which is based on the theory that 'penalty' refers to the maximum, as opposed to the actual, penalty to which an offender was liable at the time of committing the offence.

The author believes that following these Supreme Court decisions, the New Zealand position in regard to Articles 15 and 7 is antithetical to the spirit and true meaning of the Covenant and Convention. This will be shown through the critique of relevant jurisprudence from the United Kingdom, together with the analysis of an insightful dissent from the New Zealand Supreme Court in *Morgan*.

The majority judgment in *Morgan* relied on the two decisions, one of the Privy Council, *Flynn* v. *Her Majesty's Advocate*[32] (UKPC) and the other of the House of Lords in *Uttley*. Both cases concerned the issue in point, whether changes to the way in which early release obtained can constitute a penalty within the meaning of article 7(1) of the European Convention. Elias CJ, dissenting in *Morgan*, indicates that a range of views appears in the judgments,[33] an observation which is not made in the majority judgment.

Uttley had committed rape before 1983, when the maximum sentence for rape was life imprisonment, but he was not convicted and sentenced

---

[30] See also Creighton and Thornton (Chapters 7 and 8 respectively) in this volume.
[31] Replacing the Judicial Committee of the Privy Council on 1 January 2004.
[32] [2004] SCCR 281.
[33] *Morgan* v. *The Superintendent, Rimutaka Prison* [2005] NZSC 26 para. 18.

for the offence until 1995. He was sentenced after a legislative change and received 12 years' imprisonment. The issue was whether more onerous conditions of release constituted an increase in penalty, contrary to Article 7(1) of the European Convention.[34] Their Lordships considered that Article 7(1) would only be infringed if a sentence was imposed on a defendant which constituted a heavier penalty than that which *could* have been imposed on the defendant under the law in force at the time that his offence was committed.[35] Baroness Hale endorsed the principle adopted in *Coeme* v. *Belgium*[36] stating that 'The court must therefore verify that at the time when an accused person performed the act which led to his being prosecuted and convicted there was in force a legal provision which made that punishable, and that the punishment imposed did not exceed the limits fixed by that provision.'[37] Baroness Hale also considered that the issue concerned a sentence of imprisonment, which could have been of any duration up to life imprisonment.[38]

In the Privy Council in the Scottish decision of *Flynn* v. *Her Majesty's Advocate* Lords Rodger and Carswell first formulated the effective maximum approach and then repeated their reasoning in *Uttley*: 'The penalty "applicable" was that which a sentencer could have imposed at that time.' However, criticism of these two cases is found in the dissenting judgment of Chief Justice Elias in *Morgan*, where the Chief Justice points to the fallacies in *Flynn* by looking at the observations made by Lord Bingham, Lord Hope and Baroness Hale. The Chief Justice first considers the issue of the 'administration of sentence'/'penalty' distinction. Lord Bingham considered that the changes to the mechanism

---

[34] As indicated by Lord Philips, if Mr Uttley had been sentenced to 12 years' imprisonment under the old regime he would, subject to good behaviour, have been released on remission after serving two-thirds of his sentence, which would then have expired. Under the new regime he was released at the same time, but he was subject to a number of restrictions on his freedom.

[35] Lord Carswell stated at para. 65: 'The maximum sentence for rape, the most serious of the offences committed by the respondent, was imprisonment for life both before and after 1983 and so remains. A court sentencing the respondent before 1983 could if it thought fit have imposed imprisonment for life or for a term very much longer than 12 years. It is in my opinion impossible to regard a sentence of 12 years, even with the new element of a licence, as a heavier penalty than that which could have been imposed at the time when the offence was committed.' This view was supported by their Lordships. Lord Rodger observed that for the purposes of Article 7(1), the proper comparison was between the penalties which the court imposed for the offences in 1995 and the penalties which the legislature prescribed for those offences when they were committed around 1983. Therefore the cumulative penalty of 12 years which the court imposed was not heavier than the maximum sentence which the law would have permitted it to pass for the same offences at the time they were committed.

[36] Reports of Judgments and Decisions 2000-VII.

[37] Page 75 at para. 14.5.

[38] *Flynn*, para. 109.

by which prisoners sentenced to mandatory life imprisonment were considered for parole offended the spirit of Article 7.[39] The Elias CJ also noted that Lord Hope had stressed the need to look to the substance of the burden imposed in stating that '. . . the introduction into the system of a new component that had the effect of requiring the adult mandatory life prisoner to serve a longer period in custody than he would be likely to have served under the pre-existing system would constitute a heavier penalty[40] and would, for this reason, be incompatible with the Convention right.'[41]

Elias CJ also clearly rejects the effective maximum approach. She quotes para. 99 in *Flynn*:[42]

> It is as 'completely unrealistic' to regard the penalty that could lawfully have been imposed in this case as seven years imprisonment as Lord Hope and Baroness Hale thought it was to regard the penalty imposed in Flynn as imprisonment for the rest of the prisoner's life. A sentence of seven years imprisonment could not lawfully have been imposed on Mr Morgan. It would not have been competent because such a sentence would have been overturned on appeal.[43]

Elias CJ's view of *Flynn* points to a clear indication that both decisions represent an interpretation of Article 7 (and so of Article 15 of the Covenant), which is wholly inconsistent with the ICCPR. Principally, the reasoning adopted betrays a serious error with regard to the interpretation of the purpose of Article 7(1). The spirit of the article(s) is to clearly ensure that the offender is to be punished in the same way, as he would have been at the time of the offence, if this would result in a lesser penalty.[44] If this were not the case, the full protection guarded under Article 15 for individuals who have fallen victim to the mere accident of legislative changes would not be guaranteed. Throughout the text of the Covenant and other international treaty documents it is patently clear that emphasis is placed on the date of the commission of the offence as

---

[39] At paras 18 and 19.
[40] His 'grave doubts' were only overcome by his view that the High Court would be entitled to take into account the prisoner's expectations under the old system in fixing the punishment tariff before which eligibility for parole could not be considered.
[41] At para. 46.
[42] 2004 SCCR 281, UKPC, at para. 99.
[43] At para. 25.
[44] Lord Rodger in Uttley considered that the purpose was not to ensure that the offender was punished in exactly the same way as he would have been at the time of the offence but to ensure that he was not punished more heavily than the relevant law passed by the legislature would have permitted at that time.

the determinative temporal factor. The long recognised criminal law principle of *nullum poena sine lege* proscribes the imposition of a heavier penalty than that which 'was applicable at the time when the criminal offence was committed'. In the leading Canadian case of *R* v. *Lyons*,[45] Wilson J dissenting stated that 'It is a principle of fundamental justice under section 7 of the Charter that the accused know the full extent of his jeopardy before he pleads guilty to a criminal offence for which a term of imprisonment may be imposed.'

The primary rationale of this principle is fairness. In the words of Keith J in *Mist* v. *The Queen*: '. . . the state, through its institutions, should make determinations of criminal guilt and impose serious penalties only by reference to the law in force and applicable to the accused at the time of the crime.'[46] To apply the maximum sentence prescribed under the law at the date of the offence as the lesser penalty is to undermine the very principles of fairness, accessibility and foreseeability which lie behind the article itself. It is to perpetuate, not alleviate, the injustice that is being produced by the legislative change. The issue is not what the law could have imposed at the time, but what would have been lawfully imposed at the time of the offence. This assessment would be undertaken with regard to the factors normally taken into account when a sentence is imposed, i.e. seriousness of offending, culpability, aggravating and mitigating factors etc. Indeed, if every attempt is not lent to applying the same penalty that would have been fixed under the regime at the date of the offending, the convicted person is not afforded his full rights under Article 15 of the Covenant. An outcome, which is inconsistent with the above, would be a superficial approach to what conceivably is one of the foundation blocks of legality. Although it could be said that life imprisonment was 'always available' (in the words of Baroness Hale) in the sense that it was on the statute book at the time of the offending, the sentence was clearly not applicable to *Uttley* as the sentencing judge considered that 12 years was sufficient for the crime committed.[47] A proper construction of the test for the court therefore would be to adopt the opposite of Baroness Hale's proposition as suggested in para. 71, to formulate the following test: 'The court must make a comparison between the sentence the offender would have received if sentenced

---

[45] [1987] 2 SCR 309.

[46] At para. 29

[47] '67. Turning to the words of Lord Carswell, the missing step in his argument is that the court which did sentence Mr Uttley could also have been minded to impose a sentence of life imprisonment, but did not. It is clearly admitted by his Lordship that the maximum sentence for rape was imprisonment for life before, after 1983, and at the time of the sentencing. It is conceded by Your Author that as pointed out by his Lordship, the court sentencing Mr Uttley shortly after the commission of the offence could have imposed imprisonment for life or for a term longer than 12 years.'

shortly after he committed the offence and the sentence the court was now minded to impose.'

Once this test is undertaken, the issue as to whether there is a heavier penalty or not will be easily resolved. It is suggested that authority relied on for the effective maximum approach including *Coeme* v. *Belgium* is not persuasive. As Elias CJ states in *Morgan*, to endorse this approach 'is to apply the type of reasoning deprecated in *R* v. *Home Secretary ex parte Pierson* and rejected by the European Court of Human Rights in *Stafford* v. *United Kingdom* and Weeks v. *United Kingdom*.'[48] The observations as to substance and form made by Lord Steyn in *R* v. *Secretary of State for the Home Department ex parte Pierson*,[49] and in *Stafford* paras 77–9 are relied upon.[50] Indeed, the decision of *Uttley* itself gives an indication that a flexible approach should be adopted vis-à-vis the scope of Article 7 with regard to the definition of the 'heavier penalty'.[51] Baroness Hale states that Article 7 is not limited to sentences prescribed by the law which created the offence. It could also apply to 'additional penalties applied to that offence by other legislation'.[52] Her Ladyship also reports that the maximum duration of the sentence of imprisonment might not be the only factor: 'There might be changes in the essential quality or character of the sentence which made it unquestionably more severe.'[53]

Changes made to parole eligibility dates through legislation strikes at the very core of the 'essential quality or character of the sentence'. This would accord with the observations made by Lord Philips. This would also be consistent with His Lordship's comments regarding a Practice Note, which was issued by the Lord Chief Justice when release on licence

---

[48] At para. 25.

[49] [1998] AC 539, at para. 585.

[50] 'In public law the emphasis should be on substance rather than form. The case should not be decided on a semantic quibble about whether the Home Secretary's function is strictly "a sentencing exercise". The undeniable fact is that in fixing a tariff in the individual case the Home Secretary is making a decision about the punishment of the convicted man . . .'

[51] '77. . . . then in the case of *Anderson and Taylor*, which concerned a challenge under Article 6(1) to the role of the Secretary of State in fixing tariffs for two mandatory life prisoners, the Court of Appeal was unanimous in finding that this was a sentencing exercise which should attract the guarantees of that Article, following on from clear statements made by the House of Lords in the cases of *ex parte T and V* and *ex parte Pierson*. [. . .] 79. The Court considers that it may now be regarded as established in domestic law that there is no distinction between mandatory life prisoners, discretionary life prisoners and juvenile murderers as regards the nature of tariff-fixing. It is a sentencing exercise.'

[52] At para. 46.

[53] Her Ladyship gives as examples a sentence of hard labour, the automatic conversion of a sentence of imprisonment into a sentence of transportation and the replacement for juvenile offenders of committal to the care of a local authority with determinate prison detention.

was first introduced in 1991.[54] This Note had advised sentencing judges that if the changes introduced could lead to prisoners 'actually serving longer in custody than hitherto, it would be necessary for the sentencing judge to adjust the sentence to have regard to the actual period likely to be served.'[55] This clear acknowledgment made by the Lord Chief Justice is evidence that legislative changes regarding release entitlements *can* result in a protracted period spent in detention. This accordingly must signal that parole eligibility must be construed as a penalty. Likewise, clear admission was made by the Chief Justice in para. 21 of *Morgan* that, in New Zealand, the imposition of sentences is made without 'consideration of remission or parole'. Such a view is not conducive to a broad interpretation of Covenant terms, which is capable of ensuring that rights are 'practical and effective'.

A new case to the UN: Van Der Plaat

Somewhat inspired by the Chief Justice's dissent in *Morgan*, this analysis led to the further complaint to the HRC on behalf of Van Der Plaat.[56] Morgan (who represented himself) is now released. Van Der Plaat, relying on *Morgan*, claims that the New Zealand sentencing regime breaches Articles 15 and 26 (discrimination), and to the extent necessary he says that if this is correct, his detention is arbitrary and in breach of Articles 9(1) and (4). The author,[57] a 70-year-old man who is almost blind, has served six years of a 14-year sentence for sexual offences against his daughter. He still maintains his innocence. His sentence appeal was based on grounds that his sentence was 'manifestly excessive and crushing' with regard to his age. The Court of Appeal dismissed his appeal, which effectively exhausted his domestic remedies.[58] His conviction appeal was withdrawn on the advice of counsel. He complains that since sentence, new domestic legislation had reduced sentences for persons in his position but he has not been given that benefit. It will obviously be several years[59] before the views of the Committee become known. The writer awaits with

---

[54] At para. 57: 'If statutory changes were made to the release regime of those serving mandatory life sentences those changes might affect the severity of the sentence that the law required. The remission regime is an integral feature of the sentence of imprisonment. When considering how heavy a penalty has been imposed by the sentence it is necessary to consider the overall effect of the sentence.'

[55] At para. 15.

[56] *Van Der Plaat* v. *New Zealand*, Comm. No. 1492/2006.

[57] Author is the term used by the UNHRC for the person bringing the communication. Cf. plaintiff or appellant.

[58] As at that time the Privy Council was the Final Appellate Court. Less than 15 criminal appeals in 150 years had been granted Special Leave to Appeal.

[59] The HRC typically take two to three years from lodgment to decision.

Table 6.2 Offenders recalled to resume indeterminate sentence

Life imprisonment	16
Preventive detention	2
Total	18

Table 6.3 Recalls

	2002/03	2003/04	2004/05
Parole (total)	284	293	237
Approved	231 (81.3%)	222 (75.7%)	195 (82.2%)
Home detention (total)	80	96	97
Approved	71 (88.7%)	76 (79.1%)	78 (80.4%)

interest those views and new developments in the New Zealand statutory scheme in the interim.

Given Geiringer's comments above and the wafer thin majority 7–6 in *Rameka* for not finding more breaches, it will be of no surprise that *Harris* (one of the original three *Rameka* authors) is lodging a second communication which addresses the main arguments again in light of *Mist*, is asking the HRC to reconsider its views on preventive detention and is also raising the independence of the Parole Board issue above.

The legality of interim recall hearings and associated rights

Obviously recalls are much smaller in number in NZ than England in relative numerical terms, but the underlying philosophy of the recall is important and raises issues of fundamental human rights law. The statistics available from the 2005 annual report of the NZPB[60] are shown in Tables 6.2 and 6.3.

Under sections 59–61 of the Parole Act 2002, the Chief Executive of the Department of Corrections or a probation officer may apply to the Board to have an offender recalled to continue serving a sentence in prison. Grounds for recall are that the offender poses an undue risk to the safety of the community, has breached release conditions or detention conditions, or has committed an offence punishable by imprisonment. In the case of an offender on home detention, grounds for recall include the

---

[60] See: http://www.nzpb/pdf/nzpb-annual-report-2005.pdf.

offender jeopardising the safety of any person at their residence or a suitable residence no longer being available. In the case of an offender required to attend a residential programme, grounds for recall include the offender jeopardising the safety of any person at the residence, the offender failing to remain at the residence for the duration of the programme, the programme ceasing to operate, or the offender's participation being terminated. One particular example will be focused on. The relevant statutory provision is section 62, Parole Act 2002:

> 62 Making interim recall order
>
> (1) On receiving a recall application, the chairperson or any panel convenor must make an interim recall order if he or she is satisfied on reasonable grounds that –
>
>   (a) the offender poses an undue risk to the safety of the community or to any person or class of persons; or
>
>   (b) the offender is likely to abscond before the determination of the application for recall; or
>
>   (c) in the case of an offender on home detention, a suitable residence in the area where a home detention scheme is operating is no longer available.

In *Manuel* v. *Superintendent Hawkes Bay Prison*[61] the appellant was a recalled murderer. He had been sentenced to four months for fresh relatively minor offences, and served two months, in accordance with the statutory scheme, and was then released. He was re-detained the next day, primarily on the basis that he was an immediate threat to the public (somewhat odd having just been released). The interim recall order was never produced as it could not be found. So a question of jurisdiction to detain was in issue. The NZ Court of Appeal, on a habeas corpus application, rejected the approach adopted by the European Court in *Stafford* v. *UK*.[62] The Court of Appeal[63] held that once the relevant tariff period had passed, continued detention could only be justified on considerations of risk and dangerousness associated with the possibility of violent offending. The court recognised the applicability of *Stafford* to New Zealand conditions[64] and the NZBORA but determined they were inapplicable to habeas proceedings and must be advanced on judicial review. The Court of Appeal observed:[65]

---

[61] 2005 1 NZLR 161.

[62] 35 EHRR 1121.

[63] Ibid., para. 74.

[64] Ibid., para. 75.

[65] Ibid., paras 16/17.

[16] The case for the lawfulness of the appellant's detention is relatively simple:

(1) The appellant was convicted of murder on 20 July 1984 and sentenced to life imprisonment.

(2) He was released on parole on 18 January 1993.

(3) On 29 January 1996 the chief executive of the Department of Corrections applied for his recall to prison. The chief executive of the Department of Corrections had power to do so, see s. 107I(1).

(4) The Parole Board had jurisdiction to direct his recall if satisfied that any of the grounds relied on by the chief executive had been established, see s. 107L(2).

(5) The Parole Board, being satisfied that all grounds relied on by the chief executive had been made out, ordered the appellant's recall.

[17] The broad complaints of the appellant as to the lawfulness of his detention involve the following heads of argument:

(1) The interim order should not have been applied for ex parte.

(2) No interim recall order was made by the chairperson of the Parole Board.

(3) Section 23 of the New Zealand Bill of Rights Act 1990[66] was not complied with when the appellant was taken into custody on the warrant issued by the chairperson.

(4) The hearing date stipulated in the original application for the appellant's recall was incorrect (given the statutory framework) and, after a fresh and conforming hearing date was arranged, the appellant's 'consent' to an adjournment (see para [8] above) was not legitimate.

(5) The decision to recall the appellant to prison was inappropriate given international human rights jurisprudence, the New Zealand Bill of Rights Act 1990 and the true interpretation of the relevant provisions of the Criminal Justice Act 1985.

(6) The chairperson of the Parole Board (who presided over the hearing on 19 March 1996) was biased given his role in the interim recall decision.

The Court of Appeal considered that, on the facts, there was a difference with *Stafford*: 'In *Stafford* it was agreed that there was no ongoing risk of violence. Yet on the papers which we have seen, it appears to us that it was the risk of violence which the appellant was perceived as presenting

---

[66] Footnote added for present purposes the right to a lawyer, and the right to apply for habeas corpus.

which led to his recall.'[67] But it was not a serious[68] risk of violence and he had already served his sentence of four months on the offences, except for an assault charge which was pending which meets the statutory test of serious violence, but on which he was subsequently not convicted. *Manuel* v. *NZ*[69] has been taken to the HRC. As Manuel's counsel I have raised a raft of issues of concern to human rights lawyers. It is not simply just a challenge to the recall jurisdiction, but also on the adequacy of habeas as a remedy in NZ, and many other points. The views of the Committee are hopefully expected before the end of 2006.

A prisoner has a right of hearing and counsel for a final recall order; however, no such right exists in respect of an interim order made on the papers by a Convener, or the Chairman of the Board. The proposition that a prisoner can be subject to an interim *ex parte* recall by the Board but denied a hearing on that for at least 14 days[70] engages rights against arbitrary detention.[71]

Nicola Padfield's article[72] refers to the decision to recall in England being taken by an executive casework manager level, and that the recall team issues a revocation order. This is even more alarming than what occurs in New Zealand. If this is not plainly executive recall then what is? In the words of Bingham LCJ (as he then was) referring to the substantive imprisonment (not just the initial stage of recall) in *Stafford*[73] in the Court of Appeal: 'The imposition of what is in effect a substantial term of imprisonment by the exercise of executive discretion, without trial, lies uneasily with ordinary concepts of the rule of law. I hope that the Secretary of State may, even now, think it right to give further consideration to the case.'

The Communication to the UN Human Rights Committee in *Manuel* includes the following:[74]

2. [An interim] order is so fundamentally wrong that it is completely alien to the concept of the rule of law. It is an arbitrary detention caused by arrest and imprisonment by an administrative tribunal *on the papers*, or possibly *ex parte*.

---

[67] 2005 1 NZLR 161, para. 77.
[68] Section 2, Criminal Justice Act 1985 (where a period of imprisonment of two years or more applies).
[69] Comm. No. 1385/2005.
[70] Parole Act 2002, s. 65: '... the final recall order is determined ... at least 14 days after, but not more than 1 month after, the date of the interim order'.
[71] Section 22, New Zealand Bill of Rights Act 1990 ('NZBORA'), Article 9(4) ICCPR; cf. Article 5(4), European Convention.
[72] 'The Parole Board in transition' [2006] *Crim. LR*, 3: 8–9.
[73] Cited by the European Court at para. 24 of *Stafford* v. *UK* [2002] 35 EHRR 32.
[74] Renumbered paragraphs and footnotes are used for ease of presentation.

3. The interim order causes a detention without notification of your right to a lawyer, or to apply for habeas corpus. The detention is for a minimum of 14 days, and a maximum of one month or eight days longer without consent, and unlimited time with consent.

4. Additionally, there is an effective denial of the right to be brought before a court to challenge one's imprisonment. No Board[75] hearing can be heard before 14 days. Even an alleged murderer receives an immediate bail hearing before a court.

5. Fortunately no other administrative tribunal (but see *Wade*)[76] has such a draconian power to imprison without trial and deny rights.

6. Counsel is reminded of the very causes of the English civil law and the Dispute between the executive and Parliament in the time of Charles I. It is somewhat strange that the very arbitrary rights the English Parliament went to war to protect are now encompassed in legislation.

7. Replacing Parole Board for Minister the words of Lord Aitkin are adopted:[77] 'I protest, even if I do it alone, against a strained construction put upon words, with the effect of giving an uncontrolled power of imprisonment to the Minister.'

One could perhaps add that the types of detention currently allowable under terrorist legislation without immediate right to be brought before a court have no place in Parole Board legislation or jurisprudence. Manuel is subject to recall for life, and any such recall must be lawful. Immediate challenge to that must be possible, by habeas or judicial review.[78] Habeas is unavailable[79] according to both *Manuel* v. *Superintendent Hawkes Bay Prison*,[80] and *Bennett* v. *Superintendent, Rimutaka Prison*,[81] at least in domestic law terms. It remains to be seen whether an international habeas right is available.

---

[75] The NZBORA and the ICCPR are relevant. For Covenant purposes the Board is arguably not a court. See Article 9(3) of the ICCPR which states: 'Anyone arrested or detained on a criminal charge shall be brought promptly before a judge or other officer authorized by law to exercise judicial power and shall be entitled to trial within a reasonable time or to release.' In *Dean* v. *New Zealand* 1512/2006, whether the Parole Board is a court is under attack.

[76] Wade, W. and Forsyth, C. F. (2000) *Administrative Law*, 8th edn. Oxford: Oxford University Press, at p. 529.

[77] *Liversidge* v. *Anderson* (1941) 3 All ER 338, 361.

[78] Sections 22, 23(1)(c), NZBORA; s. 14, Habeas Corpus Act 2001 (and the common law); Article 9(4), ICCPR; Article 5(4), European Convention; Article XXV of the American Declaration; Article 70 of the American Convention; Article 7(1)(a), African Charter.

[79] For an alternative view see Ellis (2005).

[80] 2005 1 NZLR 161.

[81] [2002] 1 NZLR 616 (CA) (five judges sat).

Conclusion

The short-term appointments for NZPB members and the Board's wider role need serious reconsideration. Public pressures, alas, have intruded too far into the judicial process. If the Parole Board, as the Law Commission espoused, is essentially a judicial body and certainly each panel is convened by a judge, then it should be free from political appointments and pressures and executive influence and actually be independent and impartial. Members cannot be 'trained' by the Department of Corrections despite a legislative permit to provide administration and training services.[82] We have thankfully not yet reached the position where the police train judges.

It remains to be seen what the HRC makes of recall applications and the applicability of penalty provisions as canvassed in the *Uttley* and *Morgan* arguments. Equally whether our Parole Board actually is independent or impartial remains to be confirmed or otherwise by the NZ courts. In *State* v. *Mamalbolo*,[83] 11 judges of the Constitutional Court of South Africa said:

> Under the doctrine of separation of powers it [the judiciary] stands on an equal footing with the executive and the legislative pillars of state; but in terms of political, financial or military power it cannot hope to compete. It is in these terms by far the weakest of the three pillars; yet its manifest independence and authority are essential. Having no constituency, no purse and no sword, the judiciary must rely on moral authority.

What hope then for the Parole Board?

---

[82] Parole Act 2002, s. 110: *'Department of Corrections to provide administrative and training support to Board*: (1) The chief executive must ensure that the Board and the chairperson are provided with the administrative and training support necessary to enable them to perform their functions efficiently and effectively.'

[83] CCT 44/00, 11 April 2001.

Part II
Dealing with indeterminacy

Chapter 7

Dealing with indeterminacy: life sentences and IPP – the view from within

Terry McCarthy

Introduction

'The Parole Board is the independent body that protects the public by making risk assessments about prisoners to decide who may safely be released into the community and who must remain in or be returned to custody.' This is the Board's published statement of purpose. It highlights the Board's primary duty which is to protect the public. This is reinforced by the statutory provisions relating to the release of life sentence prisoners and those sentenced to IPP (both collectively referred to henceforth as 'lifers'). Section 28(6) of the Crime (Sentences) Act 1997 states that:

> The Parole Board shall not give a direction under subsection (5) above [for release] with respect to a life prisoner to whom this section applies unless:
> (a) the Secretary of State has referred the prisoner's case to the Board; and
> (b) the Board is satisfied that it is no longer necessary for the protection of the public that the prisoner should be confined.

Those sentenced to IPP come within this framework by virtue of s. 225(4) of the Criminal Justice Act 2003.

Clearly the Board's prime function is to protect the public. However, there are various parties affected by Board decisions and the reviews that lead to decisions being made. Each has certain rights in law relating to fairness, some of which compete with one another. This paper looks at these in turn.

Fairness to the prisoner

As recently as 1990, a Parole Board decision was not required to be accompanied by reasons; there was no such thing as an oral hearing; the prisoner was not entitled to disclosure of the written material in the review dossier; and the final decision on release fell to the Secretary of State. There have been a series of decisions in Europe and the domestic courts that have brought us where we are today.

September 1989	A decision of the European Commission of Human Rights in *Thynne, Wilson and Gunnell*[1] found that discretionary lifers who had served the punitive part of the life sentence (the tariff) were entitled to have the lawfulness of their continued detention decided by a court. As part of the required judicial process, they were entitled to full disclosure of the material considered by the decision-making body.
Criminal Justice Act 1991	Gave statutory effect to the report of the ECHR and transferred the decision-making power for discretionary lifers to the Parole Board.
February 1996	A decision of the European Court of Human Rights in *Singh and Hussain*[2] in respect of those who committed murder under the age of 18 and who were subsequently sentenced to detention during Her Majesty's Pleasure (HMP) extended to them the right to have the lawfulness of their detention decided by a court. Moreover, in order to satisfy the requirements of Article 5(4), there must be an adversarial procedure and an oral hearing.
Crime (Sentences) Act 1997 Part 2	Gave statutory effect to the decision of the ECtHR for those sentenced to HMP; the Act

[1] 13 EHRR 666, (1990) *Times* 10 December, ECHR.
[2] 22 EHRR 1, 1 BHRC 119, (1996) *Times* 26 February, ECHR.

	introduced the so-called 'automatic' life sentence for those convicted of a second serious offence. In respect of both these and the HMP sentences, the decision-making power was transferred to the Parole Board.
May 2002	A decision of the ECtHR in *Stafford*[3] extended to adult mandatory lifers the right to have the lawfulness of their detention post-tariff decided by a court.
Criminal Justice Act 2003	Gave statutory effect to the decision of the ECtHR in respect of mandatory lifers; the Act introduced the new sentences of indeterminate imprisonment for public protection and brought both them and mandatory lifers within the scope of Part 2 of the Crime (Sentences) Act 1997.

It has been held that the Parole Board fulfils the role of a court for the purposes of Article 5(4) (ECtHR, in *Weeks*, 2 March 1987,[4] and ECtHR, in *Hirst*, 21 March 2000[5]).

The Board therefore sits as a court when it considers the release of lifers in England and Wales. However, it is not a court for the purposes of Article 6 – i.e. a formal criminal or civil court and its procedures are governed by the Parole Board Rules (the latest version being that of 2004) laid down by the Secretary of State in pursuance of his power under s. 32(5) of the Criminal Justice Act 1991 and s. 239(5) of the Criminal Justice Act 2003. Because rules of evidence and procedure in the traditional sense do not apply to Parole Board proceedings (Rule 19 refers), the Board enjoys flexibility and a wide discretion in how its hearings are conducted. This gives significant scope for applications for judicial review by prisoners who believe that one or more of the procedures used in a given case have resulted in unfairness.

In general terms, and in keeping with the principles of fairness within an adversarial procedure, each prisoner is entitled to:

- full disclosure of the material considered by the Board;

- legal representation and legal aid;

- appear at an oral hearing with the legal representative;

---

[3] 35 EHRR 32, 13 BHRC 260, (2002) *Times* 31 May ECHR.
[4] 10 EHRR 293, (1987) *Times* 5 March, ECHR.
[5] Crim LR 919, (2001) *Times* 3 August, ECHR.

- call and question witnesses;
- full reasons for the decision.

This might suggest some element at least of proceedings akin to those in a criminal or civil court where such rights are necessary to meet the standards of fairness. However, the Board is afforded wide discretion on how its proceedings are run and there have been a number of areas where the courts have adjudged a procedural decision to be within the standards of fairness where the decision of the Parole Board is concerned, despite the fact that it would not be so in the arena of a criminal or civil court, or both.

Withholding information from the prisoner

Parole Board Rule 6(2) states:

> Any part of the information or reports referred to in paragraph (1) which, in the opinion of the Secretary of State, should be withheld from the prisoner on the grounds that its disclosure would adversely affect national security, the prevention of disorder or crime or the health or welfare of the prisoner or others (such withholding being a necessary and proportionate measure in all the circumstances of the case) shall be recorded in a separate document and served only on the Board together with the reasons for believing that its disclosure would have that effect.

Rule 8(2)(d) states that the Board may make directions:

> as regards any documents which have been received by the Board but which have been withheld from the prisoner in accordance with rule 6(2), whether withholding such documents is a necessary and proportionate measure in all the circumstances of the case.

The Rules further state that where a direction is given to this effect, the document shall be served on the prisoner's legal representative on the understanding that it shall not be disclosed, directly or indirectly, to the prisoner (6(3)).

It is envisaged, therefore, that information arising out of the criteria in 6(2) may be an exception to the normal presumption of full disclosure. In practice such information will commonly take the form of statements from victims who are in fear of the offender; information from informants whose safety would be in jeopardy should their identity be revealed; and information from the police relating to an ongoing investigation that may affect the assessment of risk but which would be put at risk should the prisoner be tipped off about it.

While the assumption is that withheld material will be disclosed, the Board has gone further in one case and directed that material relevant to the case be withheld from both prisoner and his legal team, and that a Specially Appointed Advocate (SAA), akin to the procedure which is statutory in other areas of the law, be instructed to represent the prisoner's interests (*Roberts* v. *Parole Board*, House of Lords, 20 and 21 April 2005).[6] Interestingly, in *Roberts*, the grounds for appeal were concerned with whether withholding information from the lawyer was compatible with Article 5 of the Convention (rather than the more general point of whether it could be withheld from the prisoner himself) and whether the Board had the power to adopt the SAA procedures.

By 3:2, the Lords decided that the appeal failed and it boiled down to what constitutes the minimum standards of fairness, and a balancing act between the competing points of a 'triangulation of interests', in this case the prisoner, the source of the withheld material and the public. These were summarised by Lord Woolf thus:

(i) An administrative body is required to act fairly when reaching a decision which could adversely affect those who are the subject of the decision.

(ii) This requirement of fairness is not fixed and its content depends upon all the circumstances and, in particular, the nature of the decision which the body is required to make.

(iii) The obligation of fairness to which I refer can be confined by legislation and, in particular, by rules of procedure, provided that the language used makes its effect clear and, in the case of secondary legislation, it does not contravene the provisions of the Convention (in the context of the present appeal this means article 5(4) as it is accepted article 6 has no application).

It is established, therefore, that while the Parole Board has a duty of fairness to the prisoner, a duty that the Board has always accepted that it works under, there are others too that are affected by its decisions and to whom the Board also owes a duty. But the Board's overriding duty is to the public, and this holds true even where these interests compete with those of the prisoner, although the Board accepts the judgment of Lord Woolf where he said that the possibility of full or partial disclosure to the prisoner must be kept under regular review during the process of

---

[6] UKHL 45, (2005) *Times* 8 July, HL.

the review of detention, and that there will be 'minimum requirements of fairness' that must be observed in order to comply with Article 5(4).

In *Roberts*, there were strong dissenting arguments from Lords Bingham and Steyn. While the latter could be criticised, correctly in my view, on the basis that his judgment at best gave lip service and at worse ignored the triangulation of interests and focused almost solely on the rights of the prisoner, there was in Lord Steyn's judgment an acknowledgment that 'the Parole Board is bound to give preponderant weight to the need to protect innocent members of the public against any significant risk of serious injury.'

Lord Bingham referred to the Court of Appeal in *R v. Parole Board ex p. Watson* 1996[7] where the duty of the Board to protect the public was described as 'paramount'.

This power to withhold information may, in certain circumstances, require a prisoner to be absent from a hearing or part of a hearing where such evidence is aired; its powers further extend to ordering a prisoner out of the oral hearing while evidence is being given, even though the prisoner may know the nature of that evidence as a result of documents that have been disclosed to him.

In the case of *Gardner* (Administrative Court 21 December 2005),[8] the chair of an oral hearing directed that the prisoner should be removed from the room while his ex-wife gave evidence about alleged incidents that had led to his recall to prison and the revocation of his life licence. The prisoner was aware of her allegations and the contents of her written statements but because the witness was scared to speak in front of the prisoner, indeed refused to do so, the chair ordered her evidence to be given in the prisoner's absence. At the ensuing judicial review, the Board relied on Rule 19(2) and (3) which afford the Board the power to (a) 'conduct the hearing in such manner as it considers most suitable to the clarification of the issues before it' and (b) 'The parties shall be entitled to appear and be heard at the hearing and take such part in the proceedings as the panel thinks fit.'

Giving judgment, Mr Justice Mumby referred to *Roberts* and the triangulation of interests. He pointed out that a decision to remove the prisoner must be proportionate and justified. He said: 'In this balancing exercise one has to have regard not merely to the interests of the prisoner but also to the public interest and the interests of those who give evidence.'

Again, in the Board's view, the court here indicated the overriding nature of the Board's statutory duty to the public when balanced against the duty to give the prisoner a fair hearing. In *Gardner* the Board would

---

[7] [1996] 2 All ER 641.

[8] At the time of writing, the case is pending before the Court of Appeal.

have been denied the evidence of the crucial witness had it ruled otherwise in relation to the prisoner's attendance. By implication, it may have been prevented from receiving evidence that went to the heart of its statutory job – to assess the level of risk to the public. The Board cannot countenance a situation whereby the public may be put at risk because the principle of fairness to the prisoner comes before that of fairness to the public.

Hearsay evidence

Rules of evidence that apply in criminal trials do not apply in Parole Board proceedings. Parole Board Rule 19(5) states: 'The panel may adduce or receive in evidence any document or information notwithstanding that such document or evidence would be inadmissible in a court of law, but no person shall be compelled to give any evidence or produce any document which he could not be compelled to give or produce on the trial of an action.'

In the case of *Brooks*,[9] the prisoner had been recalled to prison in similar circumstances to those in the case of *Gardner* above. In this case, the allegation was made from his ex-partner to a probation officer to the effect that the licensee had been abusive and violent, and had raped her. The Board made directions for the ex-partner and probation officer to attend the oral hearing to give evidence before the panel. The ex-partner refused to attend and, at the hearing, the prisoner argued that the Board could not receive hearsay evidence in lieu of the primary evidence that was now not available. The Board rejected that submission and proceeded to hear from the probation officer, saying that it was for the Board to consider the weight to be attached to each piece of evidence.

At the judicial review, the issue of hearsay evidence was considered by Mr Justice Elias (among other issues that do not apply here). He upheld the Board's decision to accept hearsay evidence and the case proceeded to the Court of Appeal (10 February 2004). The relevant ground of appeal was as follows:

The learned judge erred in not finding that there are some cases, and the appellant's was one such, where the potential harm to the prisoner of a finding based on an allegation contained in hearsay evidence is so great that it should not be considered by the Board without the prisoner having an opportunity to cross-examine its maker.

In his grounds of appeal the appellant argued that it could equate such a course of action with the duty to act fairly towards the prisoner.

---

[9] EWCA Civ 80, (2004) 148 SJLB 333, CA.

By 2:1, the Court dismissed the appeal. In the view of Lord Justice Kennedy:

> The duty of the panel was to decide whether it was satisfied that it was no longer necessary for the protection of the public that the claimant should be confined. In making that assessment it was entitled, and indeed bound, to have regard to all relevant information placed before it, including hearsay (see *Sims*) [*sic*] provided that the claimant was given a proper opportunity to respond, and that opportunity was in fact given.

Lord Justice Wall gave a judgment the following extract from which mirrors the Board's view exactly:

> The issue of fairness cannot be divorced from the function which the Board has to perform. Although the issue was whether the claimant had raped [the alleged victim] the Board was not conducting a criminal trial. As Sir Thomas Bingham MR (as he then was) said in *R v. Parole Board ex parte Watson* [1996] 1 WLR 906 at 916H, in the passage cited by Kennedy LJ in paragraph 28 of his judgement, the Board had to balance the hardship and injustice of continuing to imprison a man who is unlikely to cause serious injury to the public against the need to protect the public against a man who is not unlikely to cause such injury. In the final balance, however, as he said, the Board is bound to give preponderant weight to the need to protect innocent members of the public against any risk of significant injury.

This issue, more than anything else, illustrates the underlying reason behind which the normal standards of fairness enjoyed by a defendant in a criminal trial are lowered when he comes before the Board seeking release on life licence. In a criminal trial the question is guilt, which must be proven beyond reasonable doubt. The Board however, is assessing the *risk* of that offender committing serious offences in the community. The two issues are quite separate and are justified by the Board's statutory duty towards the public.

The court also had cause to consider what powers the Board might have to enforce the attendance at a hearing of such a reluctant witness. Hearsay must have its limits and there will be occasions where (a) the evidence received is so remote from the primary source as to be unreliable; or (b) fairness dictates that only by considering the credibility of the primary evidence can the requirements of fairness be secured.

The court made it clear that either party can apply for a direction from the Board for the witness to be compelled to attend. The mechanism would be by way of a direction to the Secretary of State to obtain a witness summons by virtue of CPR 34.4. However, the Board should be 'slow' to do so unless a party had applied for such a course, and should take account of practical considerations such as the likelihood of the witness refusing to speak once in the hearing.

The case of *Pearson* (20 June 2003),[10] where the primary witnesses were four juveniles whose evidence was central and hotly disputed, offered some further clarification. The Board accepted hearsay evidence from individuals to whom they had made allegations against the prisoner and a written statement from one of the children but rejected an application for the children to attend for cross-examination. Aside from pointing out the difficulties inherent in bringing reluctant children into a hearing within a prison environment where hearings are normally held (Parole Board Rule 18(1)), the Hon. Mr Justice Wilson emphasised that the Board was entitled to proceed and make a finding:

> The exercise upon which the Board was engaged was the proper implementation of the court's sentence in the light of all that had by then occurred relevant to the risk of further such offences . . .
>
> . . . I am in no doubt that the claimant's right to a fair hearing demanded that in these circumstances the Board should look not only very carefully but also very critically at the material which suggested that he had taken the children to the bonfire. But I find it impossible to say that, having made the reasonable decision on 20 August to proceed to hear the available oral evidence and then to consider whether it was possible to reach a fair decision without calling for further oral evidence, it was improper for the Board on 5 September to rely at all on what the boys had said.

'Burden of proof'

This phrase has evolved to cover the principle that, in applying the statutory test in s. 28 of the 1997 Act, the Board acts under the presumption that a lifer will remain in custody unless the Board is satisfied that the public no longer requires protection. Prisoners have argued that this places upon them an unfair burden to prove their case, and that it should be upon the state to demonstrate that the prisoner is still a risk.

The use of the word 'proof' is misleading because the Board does not operate under criminal standards of proof. Nor, in some cases, is there any burden on the prisoner at all. It is true that in a case where the bulk or all of the evidence is against the prisoner, there may be an evidential

---

[10] [2003] EWHC 1391 (Admin).

burden upon him to rebut the rest of the material, but in other instances, where the reports of the Secretary of State are unanimously in favour of release, the prisoner may not have to say anything at all.

In a criminal trial, of course, there is a burden on the prosecution and that burden requires proof beyond reasonable doubt. Moreover, the 'burden' is reversed in the case of a prisoner serving an extended sentence following recall (*William Sim*, Court of Appeal, 19 December 2003)[11] and in relation to ss. 72 and 73 of the Mental Health Act 1983 (the case of *H*[12]). However, the Parole Board has steadfastly maintained that no authority yet exists to persuade it that the 'burden', if such a term applies at all, is reversed in the case of a convicted lifer.

In 1994, in the case of *R v. The Parole Board ex parte Victor Lodomez*,[13] the Divisional Court grappled with these concepts. Lord Justice Leggatt put it like this: "The Board must be satisfied that it is not necessary that he should be kept in prison, and not that there would be a substantial risk if he were released. In other words it has to be shown that the risk is low enough to release him, not that it is high enough to keep him in prison.'

This principle raised its head once more in 1996, when the Court of Appeal in *R v. Parole Board ex parte Watson* ruled that the same application of the statutory test must apply where a lifer who has been released on life licence is recalled to custody following the revocation of the licence. The Court upheld *Lodomez* and saw no reason why the same should not apply to recalled lifers. As Lord Justice Roch put it:

> The test is justified if the protection of innocent people is to be placed above the personal liberty of one who has been guilty of grave offending and who may still represent a danger to others. In my opinion, it is incontrovertible that Parliament in the 1991 Act has manifested an intention to put the protection of the public as the overriding consideration.

Of course it will be pointed out that the cases of *Sim* and *H* have since thrown doubt on the judgments in *Lodomez* and *Watson*. The issue came once more before the Court of Appeal in 2002 in *Hirst v. Parole Board and another*.[14] However, since at that point the Board had not made a decision on the prisoner's suitability for release, the court dismissed his appeal on the basis that there had as yet been no act of the Board and that therefore Mr Hirst could not claim to have been a victim of that act.

---

[11] EWCA Civ 1845, [2004] QB 1288, [2004] 2 WLR 1170 CA.
[12] [2001] EWCA Civ 415, [2002] 3 WLR 512, CA.
[13] [1994] 26 BMLR 162, [1994] COD 525, (1994) *Times* 3 August, QBD.
[14] [2002] EWCA Civ 1329.

Nevertheless, the comments of the court suggest that this issue has yet to be finally determined and made it clear that the Board may have to decide for itself in any given case where the burden lies. Lord Justice Laws said that, in relation to the then forthcoming hearing of the case, that:

I would expect that the DLP [Discretionary Lifer Panel of the Parole Board] would grapple with the issue of the construction of Section 28(6)(b) and the question of the burden of proof in the light of the Human Rights Act unless it was quite satisfied as to the merits of the case wherever any burden lay.

Lord Justice Keene agreed and added that the Board, faced with submissions by the prisoner about which way the burden lay, would need to exercise its own mind about it and could not remain silent about how it had approached the question.

There may yet be some mileage in this issue, although the Board submits that a common-sense approach must legislate that the decisions in *Lodomez* and *Watson* are correct. The Board is dealing not with a patient suffering from a mental disorder but a person convicted of a grave offence of a violent or sexual nature. The burden of proof was correctly imposed on the prosecution at trial and was met when the jury returned a finding of guilt. In the knowledge therefore that it is faced with an individual who has been proved capable of the most serious of offences, there is nothing unfair whatsoever in asking that the prisoner accept the burden of showing himself not to be dangerous before he is set free into the community. If it were otherwise, the situation would be that (a) the guilty party has no burden to prove himself at any stage of the criminal justice process, and (b) the real danger would exist that the Board would have to direct the release of prisoners when they remained at risk of causing serious harm to others.

Fairness to the victim

In legal terms, the victim or family of the victim of the prisoner is not a party to the proceedings. Unless a victim has knowledge of material that would affect the current assessment of risk (for example, where the prisoner had made recent threats against them) victims rarely play a part in the decision to release. Nevertheless, they are affected by the Board's decision to a great extent and the Board has a duty of fairness towards them. This is reflected in *The Code of Practice for Victims of Crime*, published by the Office for Criminal Justice Reform and agreed by the Home Office, Crown Prosecution Service and Department for

Constitutional Affairs.[15] It states that the Parole Board has the following obligations:

> The Parole Board must consider any representations that victims have offered to the Probation Service on the conditions to be included in the release licences of prisoners serving sentences subject to consideration by the Parole Board and reflect these considerations in the parole decisions. Conditions relating to the victim should be disclosed to the victim through the Probation Service, and where a licence condition has not been included, the Parole Board should provide an explanation for the non-inclusion.
>
> The Parole Board must consider any information regarding the victim that relates directly to the current risk presented by a prisoner in deciding whether or not to grant or recommend release and reflect this in the parole decision.

These provisions have been echoed in the Home Secretary's Directions to the Board.

In most cases where the victim's view impacts on the Parole Board, it involves one or more conditions to be placed on the parole or life licence. The Board frequently imposes a condition to prevent the licensee attempting to contact or approach a victim and/or the imposition of a geographical area into which the licensee may not go. Usually these cause no problem; however, where the victim lives in an area where the prisoner has family of his own or intends to work, then the proportionality test that is evoked by Article 8 of the Convention must be applied. This can in some cases cause difficulties and the case of *Stephen Craven* v. *SSHD and the Parole Board*, 5 October 2001[16] demonstrates these vividly.

In that case the prisoner's life licence contained a condition preventing him from entering the area of Newcastle/Tyneside. This was designed to protect the murder victim's family from any accidental contact with the offender. However, Mr Craven's parents and his close friends also lived in Newcastle, and he had to enter the city as part of his employment. In order to resolve the conflicting rights of the victim's family and Mr Craven's rights under Article 8, very specific areas of Newcastle had to be identified and defined by particular streets in order to balance those rights.

The case is noteworthy for its confirmation that fairness to the victim may apply even where issues of risk to the public do not arise. There was no suggestion that the family of the victim were at risk of physical harm from Mr Craven, and he was entitled to have his Article 8 rights taken into account. But, as the Hon. Mr Justice Stanley Burton said:

---

[15] Office for Criminal Justice Reform, February 2006. Ref. 253347.
[16] [2001] EWHC Admin 850, QBD.

A democratic society should be sensitive to the emotional harm caused to victims of crime, particularly of the most serious of crimes, to their anxieties and concerns, and to the risks of emotional or psychological harm in the event of an encounter between convicted murderer and the family of his victim ... the concerns of the victim of the murder committed by Mr Craven were matters that the Parole Board and the Home Secretary were entitled, indeed bound, to take into account when deciding what conditions were to be included in the licence for Mr Craven's release.

Fairness to witnesses

We have discussed above that the courts have recognised that the Parole Board owes a duty to those giving evidence to the panel. The 'triangulation' of interests includes the source or sources of information who may have good reason for not wanting the prisoner to know who they are or what they are saying in evidence.

In a criminal trial, witnesses are identified and heard in open court unless there are public interest immunity grounds. We have seen that the Parole Board Rules allow for not only the identity of the witness, but the nature of certain types of evidence to be withheld from a prisoner in much wider sets of circumstances. It was in the case of *Roberts* that this was taken to its extreme and led to material being withheld not only from the prisoner, but also from his legal representative. The concept of fairness to others besides the public and the prisoner was not the end of it and as Lord Woolf put it:

> In addition in a situation where the Board has to consider whether to withhold evidence from a prisoner, for example to protect an individual whose life could be threatened if his identity were revealed, the Board is under a duty to protect this individual's interests. Not to do so could involve the breach of Article 2 or 3 of the ECHR.

Lord Rodger pointed out the practical difficulties if this approach was deemed unlawful. Either the 'informant' would be identified and his life perhaps put under threat, or the evidence would be lost to the Board which might then take a decision to release a prisoner who remained a danger to the public. He said about that latter option:

> In other words the Board should close its eyes to evidence, even though it would be relevant to the decision which Parliament has charged them to take for the protection of the public. That solution

too would be – again, to say the least – unattractive and, moreover, hard to reconcile with the Board's statutory duty not to direct a prisoner's release on licence unless they are satisfied that it is no longer in the interests of the public that he should be confined.

Summary – fairness to the public

We have mentioned that the prisoner's rights to a fair hearing may be measured against rights enjoyed by victims and witnesses. We have also looked at the 'triangulation of interests' that involves the right of the public to be protected against decisions to direct the release of dangerous offenders. This 'triangulation' then is perhaps better described as a 'quadrangle' of competing interests. When considering whose rights win out, the courts have said time and time again that the Parliamentary duty to protect the public is 'paramount' or 'preponderant'.

Since this is a paper about "perceptions of fairness" it is only right to record that many prisoners do not perceive that the process is always fair. When taking account, for example, of the fact that information may be withheld from them or that primary sources of evidence may not be available for cross-examination, that is understandable. On the other hand, there have been moves in the media recently to suggest that the prisoner enjoys too many rights in respect of Parole Board hearings, that the Convention affords them rights that interfere with the public's right to be protected. These are misplaced, however. Those cases decided in the prisoner's favour, both in Europe and the UK, have served only to enshrine the right to a fair hearing and by far the majority of those where the prisoner's rights compete with others have gone against the prisoner.

An underlying explanation is called for to explain why prisoners' rights to a fair deal may be restricted in favour of those whose rights would not be as relevant in a criminal trial. Lord Woolf in *Roberts* put it as eloquently as anyone:

> ... although the decision of the Board is of the greatest importance to a prisoner, the prisoner has inevitably already been found or pleaded guilty, and in the case of a prisoner sentenced to life imprisonment, the offence would have been a grave crime. Furthermore, any decision to find an offender guilty is a once and for all decision, but in the case of a decision of the Board, the decision can always be changed with the passage of time. Finally, the task of the court is to determine the guilt or innocence of a defendant, while the task of the Board is to determine whether it is safe for the prisoner to be released.

Chapter 8

The Parole Board as a court

Simon Creighton

Introduction

Assessing the status of the Parole Board[1] as a court within the domestic legal system is more than an academic exercise. It carries profound implications for the work of the Board, from its constitution through to its working practices and, arguably, to the extent of its powers. The difficulty in carrying out this assessment lies in the manner in which the Board's role has evolved over the years. This evolution has been marked by sudden episodes of profound change leaving the Board having to fulfil a hybrid role as both court and advisory body and it is necessary to examine how those changes have come about in order to understand the consequences for the Board.

At first glance, the Parole Board's primary function of assessing risk and protecting the public has remained unchanged since its inception. It is now 40 years since the Parole Board was first established and the 1965 White Paper, *The Adult Offender*, which presaged the creation of the Parole Board[2] had envisaged a system where: 'prisoners who do not of necessity have to be detained for the protection of the public are in some cases more likely to be made into decent citizens if, before completing the whole of their sentence, they are released under supervision with a liability to recall if they do not behave.'[3]

---

[1] Referred to as the Board hereafter.
[2] Which occurred with the Criminal Justice Act 1967, the Board commencing operations in 1968.
[3] Quoted in Livingstone et al. (2003: 394).

Although these aims have remained consistent the Board's powers and its procedures have been revolutionised in the intervening period.

When the Board was created, it was very clear that there was no need – or intention – for it to be anything other than a further administrative arm of the Home Office. It was established as a corporate body wholly sponsored by the Home Office and retains that constitution to this day.[4] Its members are appointed by the Secretary of State and originally, its staff were nearly all drawn as seconded placements from the Home Office's prisons department. The statutory conception of release on parole as being no more than an executive act of mercy and the Board's purely advisory role (although its decisions were binding in recall cases) in that process were reflected in the concerns expressed in the Board's Annual Reports. In 1977 their report agonised over the extent to which the Board's advice should be influenced by public opinion on notorious criminals and in 1986 the Board felt it necessary to spell out that public perceptions were part of the risk assessment process with the Board taking into account 'the degree of abhorrence with which society regards that offence and the likely public reaction to the offender's early release from custody'. This can be contrasted with the long-standing principle that public reaction is not relevant to judicial sentencing and release decisions. In the highly emotive James Bulger case, for example, public outrage was roundly dismissed as having no relevance in the sentencing and release decisions for his killers.[5]

The changes made to the parole system have tended to be attributed to the impact of the European Convention on Human Rights ('ECHR') on domestic law. This was first apparent in the case of *Weeks* v. *UK*,[6] a decision of the European Court of Human Rights in 1987 ('ECtHR'). In *Weeks*, the ECtHR held that the recall and release arrangements for a young offender sentenced to a discretionary life sentence[7] for robbery violated his Article 5(4) rights. Having decided that the decisions to recall and re-release Mr Weeks raised new issues concerning the lawfulness of his detention, the ECtHR found that the parole process for juvenile discretionary lifers required

---

[4] Criminal Justice Act 2003, s. 239.

[5] See *R* v. *Home Secretary ex parte Thompson and Venables* [1998] AC 407 and *Bulger* v. *Home Secretary & Lord Chief Justice* [2001] EWHC Admin 119.

[6] (1988) 10 EHRR 293.

[7] For a description of the different types of life sentence available to the sentencing courts see Arnott and Creighton (2006: 85–93).

a court-like body to make the relevant decisions. Domestic law was in breach of Article 5(4) as the proceedings were not sufficiently judicial due to the lack of disclosure of relevant material to Mr Weeks[8] and because the Board only had an advisory role in the process.

It is wrong to see this judgment as an unexpected attack on the English system of life imprisonment. The domestic courts had been grappling for some years with the inherent unfairness of a system of sentencing and release that fell wholly within the discretion of the executive and had been seeking to ameliorate the unfairness by imposing more rigorous standards of procedural fairness.[9] While some progress was being made in relation to disclosure of relevant material, there was little that could be achieved in the domestic courts in relation to the legality of the decision being taken by the executive as opposed to the judiciary, this being a statutory provision. A close reading of decisions in *Weeks* and the subsequent *Thynne, Wilson and Gunnell* v. *UK*[10] illustrate that it was the progression made in the analysis of domestic law by the English courts – even in judgments that went against the prisoners – which made it possible for Article 5(4) to be applied to indeterminate sentences. As JUSTICE noted in their exploration of the reforms needed to the life sentence system:

> During the 1980s there was a growing body of opinion that there was an unacceptable lack of openness and accountability in the lifer system and that the rules for making decisions on the minimum length of custody and the release of all life sentence prisoners were both haphazard and unfair.[11]

In the *Weeks* decision, however, the ECtHR decided to go beyond a simple determination of whether Article 5 had been breached and, faced with some criticism of the Board's constitution, examined whether it was, in theory, capable of fulfilling the role of a court required by Article 5. Their conclusion has been hugely influential in shaping the subsequent development of the Board:

> The 'court' referred to in Article 5(4) does not necessarily have to be a court of law of the classic kind integrated within the

---

[8] Weeks (op. cit. note 6), para. 66.
[9] In the context of tariff setting, for example, see cases such as *Handscomb* [1988] 86 CAR 59 relating to discretionary life sentences and *Doody* [1994] 1 AC 531.
[10] [1991] 13 EHRR 666.
[11] JUSTICE (1996: 20–1).

standard judicial machinery of the country ... The term 'court' serves to denote 'bodies which exhibit not only common fundamental features, of which the most important is independence of the executive and of the parties to the case ..., but also the guarantees' – 'appropriate to the kind of deprivation of liberty in question' – 'of a judicial procedure', the forms of which may vary from one domain to another ... In addition, as the text of Article 5(4) makes clear, the body in question must not have merely advisory functions but must have the competence to 'decide' the 'lawfulness' of the detention and to order release if the detention is unlawful. *There is thus nothing to preclude a specialised body such as the Parole Board being considered as a 'court' within the meaning of Article 5(4) provided it fulfils the foregoing conditions.*[12] (Emphasis added)

The problem created by the reliance upon an international court as the mechanism for change is twofold. First, as a matter of public perception, change forced upon the government by the ECtHR can be seen as unduly lenient and as creating a culture of rights for the undeserving which take primacy over the rights of the public at large. This is a problem which will be examined in more detail below. Second, the role of the ECtHR is to assess the compatibility of domestic law with the Convention and has a subsidiary role to domestic authorities. It is unable to determine the nature of the refinements needed to the domestic system once a violation has been found and is restricted to commenting upon the facts before them.[13] In the context of the parole system, the ECtHR identified the areas where the Board was deficient and noted those areas where it might be considered to meet the requirements of a court-like body. As noted above, the Board was not considered to meet the requirements of Article 5(4) in relation to disclosure of material or the extent of its powers, but having found that the Board could theoretically take on that role, the ECtHR did not consider that there were any concerns arising in relation to the question of the Board's independence from the executive:

The applicant maintained that the Parole Board is not independent of the Home Secretary, primarily because he appoints the

---

[12] Note 10 para. 61.
[13] For example: *Sunday Times* v. *UK* (1980) 2 EHRR 245; see also *Chahal* v. *UK* (1997) 23 EHRR 413 where a comment of the court as to Canadian procedures for dealing with sensitive evidence led to the adoption of the Special Advocate system in SIAC (Special Immigration Appeals Commission) cases, subsequently transplanted into the parole process (see below).

members of the Board, provides its staff and makes the rules under which it conducts its procedures. The Parole Board sits in small panels, each of which in the case of life prisoners includes a High Court judge and a psychiatrist ... The manner of appointment of the Board's members does not, in the Court's opinion, establish a lack of independence on the part of the members ... Furthermore, the Court is satisfied that the judge member and the other members of the Board remain wholly independent of the executive and impartial in the performance of their duties. There remains the question whether the Board presents an appearance of independence, notably to persons whose liberty it considers ... On this point, as the Government stated, the functions of the Board do not bring it into contact with officials of the prisons or of the Home Office in such a way as to identify it with the administration of the prison or of the Home Office. The Court therefore sees no reason to conclude that the Parole Board and its members are not independent and impartial.[14]

The nature of the changes

The *Weeks* judgment was followed by that in *Thynne, Wilson and Gunnell* v. *UK*[15] and this in turn prompted the legislative changes of the Criminal Justice Act 1991 which judicialised the tariff setting and release procedures for all discretionary lifers. As the ECtHR did not have any fundamental objection to the Board taking on the role of a court-like body, providing it had the necessary powers, the Board was charged with the task of creating discretionary lifer panels[16] to undertake the review process for this one group of prisoners. There was no accompanying legislative change to the Board's constitution, with the CJA 1991 simply reaffirming the arrangements contained in the CJA 1967. Although the new Act allowed the Secretary of State to introduce the Parole Board Rules to provide a procedural framework for the review process,[17] the Rules had no legislative force as they were not – and are still not – laid by statutory instrument.[18] The functional model that provided a framework for the DLP process was that of the Mental Health Review

---

[14] Footnote 10 para. 62.
[15] (1992) 13 EHRR 666.
[16] Usually abbreviated to DLPs.
[17] CJA 1991, s. 32(5).
[18] The current version of these rules, the Parole Board Rules 2004, are still not laid by statutory instrument although this is planned for the next version.

Tribunals.[19] The MHRTs made a good starting model as there has always been considerable overlap between hospital orders and discretionary life sentences[20] and both bodies were charged with assessing the change in the level of danger posed by people who were susceptible to change with the passage of time.

The real difficulty with these changes is not the model they followed, but the decision to simply graft them onto a Parole Board which had no experience of acting as a court and which was still predominantly concerned with advising the Secretary of State on matters that were outside the protection of Article 5. One study of the DLP process noted:

> [The] remedial actions have been necessarily piecemeal and they have not, by and large, altered the general character and context of UK law and policy . . . Hence the post-*Thynne* DLP legislation was, on the ground and in practice, implemented by persons and institutions that might have only a partial understanding of the conceptual underpinnings of the jurisprudence of the ECHR.[21]

The extent to which the new duties imposed upon the Board were very much an adjunct to its more normal business can be illustrated by the number and type of cases that it was required to process. The Board's Annual Report for 1992[22] provides an excellent insight into the impact the new DLP system had on its workload as it provided figures for the new DLPs it had been required to conduct but had not yet had to start work on the new determinate parole cases introduced by the same legislation. The number of determinate parole cases remained at 25,000 for the year – a figure that had changed very little in the previous ten years. The Board also dealt with the cases of 552 mandatory lifers which were still processed on the papers alone and without the safeguards of

---

[19] The Parole Board Rules 2004 still mirror the MHRT Rules in many key respects such as the provisions on representation and disclosure.

[20] See, for example: *AT* v. *UK* [1995] 20 EHRR CD 59 which contains the following comments made by the trial judge in relation to a prisoner convicted of matricidal manslaughter: 'I am still of the opinion that the proper disposal in your case would be by means of a hospital order, but because of the lack of facilities – the lack of a bed – I am unable to make that order. The only possible alternative order I can make is to sentence you to an indeterminate period of life imprisonment. Now that, in your case, I am confident, does not mean life, it will mean somewhat less. How long you stay in prison depends upon your improvement and how you behave there, but in order that your medical condition shall be fully appreciated by staff at hospital . . . I shall invite the prison authorities to consider whether, in the light of [. . . medical opinions . . .] it would be possible to transfer you to a hospital where you could receive proper treatment for your illness.'

[21] Padfield and Liebling, with Arnold (2000: 135).

[22] Parole Board (1993).

Article 5(4) applying. In addition, a total of 44 DLPs were held. The next major expansion of the lifer system came with the Crime (Sentences) Act 1997 which extended the oral hearings system to prisoners who had been detained at Her Majesty's pleasure as juveniles and to the new group of automatic lifers.[23] The Board's Annual report for 1998/1999[24] shows that the number of determinate cases considered was just over 6,000, the number of lifer cases other than DLPs was 462 and the number of DLPs was now 291. In the space of five years since the Board had been required to act as a 'court-like body', the percentage of cases where this duty arose had increased from 0.1 per cent to 4.5 per cent. By 2004/2005, the last year for which figures have been published, nearly 20 per cent of cases were oral hearings. The requirement to hold oral hearings for recalled determinate sentenced prisoners came into force in early 2005[25] and the number of prisoners serving indeterminate and extended sentences is increasing every year. In the Board's most recent Business Plan it has estimated that for 2006/7 the split between paper decisions and oral hearings will be roughly 50:50.

The rapidity of the change in these primary functions and duties helps explain the problematic situation that faces the Board as it seeks to fulfil its two roles. On the one hand it is required to advise the Secretary of State on issues of risk and is free to do so without any formal judicial constraints. On the other hand, it is required to discharge a judicial function, in full compliance with the jurisprudence of the ECtHR, in deciding upon the fundamental right of liberty. It is difficult to envisage how an institution which is now so central to the workings of the criminal justice system and which falls under such close public scrutiny can be expected to discharge such different legal roles without the danger of cross contamination between them. Balancing the deference that must be shown to the executive on advice cases with the robust independence that is required on Article 5 cases is no easy task.[26]

As the *Weeks* case illustrates, the Board has consistently been considered to meet the Convention guarantees of independence. The reasoning in *Weeks* was followed relatively recently by the Commission in rejecting a further attempt to impugn the independence of the Board.[27] Although these decisions are fairly clear-cut, the law in relation to independence and impartiality of tribunals has not remained stagnant over the last 20

---

[23] Crime (Sentences) Act 1997, s. 28.
[24] Parole Board (1999).
[25] *R (Smith)* v. *Parole Board* [2005] UKHL 1.
[26] Bingham LJ (as he was) in *R* v. *Watson ex parte Parole Board* [1996] 1 WLR 906 held that the Board's advisory role did not compromise its independence when acting judicially (915 E) but this was at a time when oral hearings were the exception.
[27] *Hirst* v. *UK* (1 December 1998) App No. 40787/98. This was a Commission decision which declared a complaint on delay admissible but rejected a complaint that the Board was not independent.

years and many aspects of these decisions may no longer stand up to closer scrutiny given the far more stringent attention that is now paid to institutional independence. In keeping with its duty to adjudicate upon the compatibility of domestic law with the Convention, the ECtHR is required to demonstrate deference to the different historical and legal traditions of its member states. In the context of the complex system for delivering administrative law in this country, it is unsurprising that Strasbourg would not look beyond the identity of the decision-makers as a basis for ascertaining independence. The simple fact that the Article 5 tribunal is chaired by a judge was always likely to be sufficient to meet the necessary Convention standards.[28]

Domestic law and the Convention paradox

Although there has not yet been a direct challenge to test the Board's credentials as a court, the issue has begun to flare up in domestic law as the High Court has grappled with the dual role imposed upon the Board. Table 8.1 is a summary of the Board's powers.

There are a number of anomalies arising from these arrangements which illustrate the uncertainty in the current settlement:

- The release of determinate prisoners does not require a court-like body to be involved but their recall does. However, once recalled, the safeguards of Article 5 no longer apply to any further release decisions.

- The initial release of prisoners serving extended sentences does not require a court-like body but their recall does and so do any subsequent release decisions.[29]

- The release of prisoners serving longer than commensurate sentences is not within the ambit of Article 5, despite the fact that the sentence is longer than would normally be imposed as the characteristics of the offender suggest that there is a need for public protection.[30]

- Pre-tariff parole reviews for all lifers are all simply advice cases as the only issue to be determined is the suitability for a move to open conditions.

---

[28] In the familiar context of prisons, it should be recalled that the European Court considered that Boards of Visitors were sufficiently independent of the prison system to conduct prison disciplinary hearings which fell within the protection of Article 6: *Campbell & Fell* v. *UK* (1985) 7 EHRR 16.

[29] *R (Sim)* v. *Parole Board and Home Secretary* [2003] EWCA Civ 1845.

[30] *R (Giles)* v. *Parole Board* [2003] UKHL 42.

Table 8.1 Summary of the powers of the Parole Board

Type of sentence	Decision	Article 5 applies?
Determinate sentence[a]	First release	No
Determinate sentence	Recall	Yes
Determinate sentence	Further release after recall	No
Extended sentence[b]	Release	No
Extended sentence	Recall	Yes
Extended sentence	Further release after recall	Yes
Life/indeterminate sentence	Pre-tariff parole review	No
Life/indeterminate sentence	Release	Yes
Life/indeterminate sentence	Recall	Yes
Life/indeterminate sentence	Further release after recall	Yes
Life/indeterminate sentence	Move to open conditions	No
Life/indeterminate sentence	Period until next review	No

[a] The position is even more complicated by the fact that the Secretary of State has authorised the Parole Board to direct the release of prisoners serving under 15 years but only permits the Board to advise him on prisoners serving sentences of 15 years or more: Parole Board (Transfer of Functions) Order 1998 SI No. 3128.
[b] It should be noted that there is a conceptual difference between the first release of extended sentence prisoners sentenced under the CJA 2003 and the CJA 1991 but this is not important for the purposes of this table.

- All post-tariff, periodic reviews of lifers and decisions on their recall must be Article 5 compliant but this right is exhausted if release is not directed. If the Board goes on to consider the suitability of open conditions or the timing of the next review, Article 5 does not apply.

In analysing these conflicting duties, Padfield has asked whether 'the judicial function of the Board can be separated from its other functions? Should there be any such distinction?'[31] In answer to those questions, there are hard-edged, practical consequences flowing from these conflicting duties. At lifers' parole hearings, for example, the ambit of what the Board is permitted to consider is set by the Secretary of State.[32] In cases where both release and suitability for open conditions is being considered, the Secretary of State may give directions to the Board in relation to

---

[31] Padfield (2006: 16).
[32] CJA 2003, s. 239(2) sets out the current statutory basis for the referral and in *R (Mills)* v. *Home Secretary* [2005] EWHC 2508 the High Court confirmed that the Board could not consider a lifer's suitability for open conditions at a recall hearing unless directed to do so by the Secretary of State but instead was restricted to simply examining whether the lifer was suitable for immediate re-release or not.

the appropriate factors to consider when assessing suitability for open conditions but similar directions issued in respect of release decisions have been held to compromise the Board's independence.[33] Although the High Court ultimately decided that the contents of the directions were, as a matter of substance rather than form, unobjectionable and did not compromise the independence of the Board, the underlying principle identified has not been satisfactorily resolved given the importance now accorded to the perception of fairness in the administration of justice. As a matter of substance over form, it is also very difficult to separate out the real legal difference between those directions issued by the Secretary of State and the Parole Board Rules which are issued by him without any form of Parliamentary approval.

The fact that the duty to act as a court arose from the jurisprudence of the ECtHR whereas the nature of that duty has largely been a matter for interpretation domestically can lead towards a conflict between the requirements of common law fairness and the limits imposed by the Convention case law. This can be seen in two judgments which have had to confront these two strands. In *R (Day)* v. *Home Secretary*,[34] the High Court was required to assess whether it was a breach of Article 5 for the Secretary of State to set the timing between a lifer's parole reviews and to decide on his suitability for open conditions rather than the Board. Gibbs J observed that:

> 44 ... I can see the merit in the argument that, because the Parole Board is the body with the statutory duty of determining release, it should also be able, if it recommends against release, to determine when the next review should take place. The period of two years laid down by statute is a maximum period and the Parole Board may well be in a good position to say whether a review before that date would meet the justice of the case.

> 45. But the issue here is not whether there would be arguable merit in such a scheme: the fact is that the existing statutory scheme does not provide for the Parole Board to make such a determination. A precondition under the statute for the Parole Board's review powers is the reference of the case to it by the Secretary of State. The question therefore is whether the existing scheme falls foul of Article 5, not whether some other scheme might arguably have more merit. It seems to me that Mr Fitzgerald's broad argument, that 'judicialisation' of the decision-making on release must logically render it legally necessary to confer on the Parole Board the decision-making power on the timing of reviews, cannot be sustained. The case law

---

[33] *R (Girling)* v. *Parole Board* [2005] EWHC 546.
[34] [2004] EWHC 1742.

indicates that there are aspects of the release procedures which remain and properly remain administrative procedures under the control of the Secretary of State, for example the category of prison conditions under which a prisoner is held (see *Ashingdane* v. *United Kingdom* at 14/1983/70/106).[35]

There is a certain irony that the changes brought about to the parole system by the Convention in order to protect fundamental rights should eventually operate as a restriction on the progression of common law domestically. This paradox has its origins in the limits of the ECtHR (as analysed above) in their ability to analyse and interpret domestic legal institutions and can result in a tendency to circumscribe rights identified.

The contrasting decision of *R (Smith)* v. *Parole Board*[36] where the Board was found to be failing in its duty of fairness by not convening oral hearings for recalled determinate prisoners demonstrates not only how the common law can proceed ahead of Convention rights, but also how the designation of the Parole Board as a court has consequences for its other activities. The *Smith* decision was reached through two routes. The first was that on an analysis of the standards of common law fairness, recalled prisoners were not receiving a sufficiently rigorous review of their cases. Fairness in this context, the Lords decided, would very often require an oral hearing to allow disputed facts to be assessed. In this regard the decision can be seen as another step in the progression of general administrative law principles when applied to fundamental rights such as liberty. The Lords were not content to leave their analysis at this point and went on to analyse the position under the Convention. Their decision confirmed the long-standing view that Article 5(1) rights were fully met by the trial and initial sentencing process, but nonetheless went on to find there was a breach of Article 5(4). This was explained by Lord Hope in the following terms:

> It is not enough to satisfy the requirement of article 5(4) that the lawfulness of the detention must be decided by a court to point simply to the Board's independence and to its impartiality. It is, of course, possible to say that the Parole Board is an appropriate body to conduct the review because it is impartial and independent of the executive. But article 5(4) requires that the proceedings themselves must be conducted in the way a court would be expected to conduct them. From this it follows that, to satisfy article 5(4), the Board's procedure for conducting reviews must embody the procedural

---

[35] This judgment relies heavily on a long line of domestic and ECtHR authorities which have limited the applicability of Article 5(4) to release only, the most recent being *Blackstock* v. *UK* (2006) 42 EHRR 2.

[36] [2005] UKHL 1.

fairness that the common law requires of a court. Procedural fairness is a requirement of the common law. It is not in itself a Convention requirement. But it is built into the Convention requirement because article 5(4) requires that the continuing detention must be judicially supervised and because our own domestic law requires that bodies acting judicially, as a court would act, must conduct their proceedings in a way that is procedurally fair. As Lord Bingham has explained, the common law duty of procedural fairness required that the appellants be offered an oral hearing into their representations against revocation of their licences. As this was not done, the review of their detention was not conducted as a court would be expected to conduct it, so there was, in my opinion, a violation of their article 5(4) Convention rights.[37]

This construction of the Article 5(4) right has a degree of circularity. The apparent source of the right lies not in the nature of the proceedings themselves but in the nature of the body conducting the review. It is not easy to see how either Strasbourg or the domestic courts could make a finding that Article 5 was re-engaged independently of the procedural process of the review. Domestic decisions had previously been very firm in rejecting the contention that any new Article 5 issues could arise within the currency of a determinate sentence and the ECtHR has been fairly consistent in rejecting the concept that parole licences were anything more than an executive act of clemency.[38] There is a fairly surprising implication in the Lords' judgment that Article 5(4) is only engaged because of the identity of the decision-maker. If, for example, the Parole Board had never been required to take on this role, or if the government chose to regulate recalls through an administrative process at the Home Office, there would appear to be no breach of Article 5(4).

The application of Article 6

Underlying this focus on Article 5 is the question of whether Article 6 applies to the oral hearings that the Board is required to conduct. Given that the procedural requirements of Article 5 guarantee access to a court-like body, it might seem that there would be nothing further to be gained by the application of Article 6, either as criminal or civil proceedings, to oral hearings before the Board. The domestic courts have consistently found that parole reviews do not engage the safeguards of the criminal law under Article 6 on the grounds that the parole process

---

[37] Ibid. para. 75.
[38] For example: *Hogben* v. *UK* 46 DR 231; *Grava* v. *Italy* (10 July 2003) App No. 43522/98.

is protective and not punitive.[39] In relation to the civil limb of Article 6, the judicial view has been that this would not add anything of substance to the procedural guarantees of Article 5 and so it remains undetermined.[40]

Although there is a certain pragmatic sense to this approach, this does mask the extent to which the Board is granted a dispensation from the true rigours of a judicial process as a sacrifice necessary for it to fulfil its primary role of protecting the public. The allowances made for the Board to ensure it has adequate flexibility to receive all of the evidence that might conceivably be relevant to the process of risk assessment have ranged from the admissibility of contested hearsay evidence to make good findings of serious criminal wrongdoing[41] through to the adoption of the Special Advocate scheme to enable the Board to hear evidence which is not disclosed to the prisoner.[42] The majority of the Lords who permitted the Special Advocate procedure to be imported into the parole process founded their decision on the need for the Board to protect the rights of victims and witnesses as well as those of the prisoner. In his dissent, Lord Steyn indicated quite how unbalanced this balancing act had become and how stark the consequences are for the prisoner when he remarked that: 'In truth the special advocate procedure empties the prisoner's fundamental right to an oral hearing of all meaningful content.'[43] In contrast, the Lords imposed a far more restrictive role on the use of Special Advocates in criminal trials, where Special Advocates are not permitted a role before the tribunal of fact and are limited to arguments on pre-trial issues of disclosure.[44] Presumably, a decision to empty criminal trials of all meaningful content was a step too far whereas the special flexibility afforded to Article 5 proceedings persuaded the majority of the Lords that it was a legitimate step to take in the parole context.

Conclusions

The hybrid nature of the Parole Board and the piecemeal manner by which it has come to take on its powers has left it marooned in relation to other tribunals performing similar functions. The Comprehensive Review of Parole and Lifer Processes published in October 2001 stated it was 'unclear how far public or prisoner concerns about the Board's

---

[39] See, for example, Lord Bingham in *Smith* [2005] UKHL 1 paras 38–41.
[40] Ibid. para. 44.
[41] *R (Brooks)* v. *Parole Board* [2004] EWCA Civ 80.
[42] *R (Roberts)* v. *Parole Board* [2005] UKHL 45.
[43] Ibid. para. 96.
[44] *Re H* [2004] UKHL 3.

independence are a problem in practice, rather than theory'.[45] This seriously underestimates the disquiet among prisoners and those advising them on this issue. The wider progress in formalising the independence of the tribunal system from the executive resulted in the launch of the Tribunals Service in April 2006, a service which includes the Mental Health Review Tribunals. The history to the introduction of the Tribunal Service is strongly rooted in the requirement for these bodies to have genuine independence from the executive and legislature, both as a matter of form and substance. The initial review of the system by Sir Andrew Leggatt in 2003 which provided the basis for the changes was prefaced by the Lord Chancellor commenting that there had been a strong demand for tribunal reform, identifying the need 'for greater clarity over rights, procedures and decisions.'[46] The Lord Chancellor did not mention independence in his introduction to the review, even though this appears to have been one of the central areas for investigation by Sir Andrew Leggatt and has been identified as the key issue by Peter Hancock, the inaugural chief executive of the Tribunal Service:

> Until now our major tribunals have been managed in a disparate way, generally attached to the central Government department responsible for the policy and initial decision that is now being referred to or challenged. Although all of these tribunals have independent judiciary, administration and service delivery infrastructures, they have not been seen as truly independent of their parent structures.[47]

This focus on the need for tribunals – some of which perform functions directly comparable to the Parole Board – to be perceived as independent in order to ensure the delivery of justice is difficult to reconcile with the judicial approach to this problem in litigation against the Board, whether in Strasbourg or domestically.

The culture in which the Board operates does have an impact upon the perception of its duties by government agencies and the public but also on the effective policing of those duties by the courts. The recent Rice report investigated the decision-making process that enabled a discretionary life sentenced prisoner, convicted of sex offences, to be released only to commit a sexually motivated murder very shortly thereafter.[48] The report focused on inadequacies in the provision of

---

[45] See: http://www.paroleboard.gov.uk/pdfs/comp_parole_rev5.pdf.
[46] The report can be found at http://www.dca.gov.uk/consult/leggatt.
[47] http://www.tribunals.gov.uk/publications/documents/tribunals_service_business_plan.pdf, p. 5.
[48] HM Inspectorate of Probation (2006b).

information between various agencies in the criminal justice system and the extent to which human error played a role. However, special criticism was reserved for the oral hearing system which authorised the release, with the report suggesting that the balance of 'rights' has shifted too far in favour of the prisoner:

> This whole process is additionally complicated by human rights considerations which have grown in importance following a series of Court judgments. Prisoners are now legally represented at parole hearings, often by counsel, who also have recourse to judicial review. It is a challenging task for people who are charged with managing offenders effectively to ensure that public protection is not undermined by human rights considerations.[49]

And again, when considering the licence conditions that the Parole Board advised should be imposed upon Mr Rice, the report criticises the role of due process in reaching the final decision: '... We find it regrettable that attention to effectiveness and enforceability was undermined by the attention devoted to issues of lawfulness and proportionality.'[50]

These comments are quite extraordinary in the context of a government-sponsored inquiry into the parole system. They make explicit the theme which is implicit in many of the court judgments which have allowed the Board such flexibility in procedural and evidential matters. The absurdity of criticising the existence of due process and legal representation in judicial proceedings before a court-like body is self-evident but gives voice to the populist view that prisoners, and lifers in particular, should not retain residual rights.[51]

It may be possible to dismiss these comments as ill informed, but to do so is to ignore the importance of the problem they identify. While there is an ongoing debate about the relationship between the nature of the fundamental rights for the criminal trial process and the victims of crime, it is a debate which recognises the problematic that arises when the rights of a defendant are restricted and redrawn. This is, in part, informed by the recognition of the courts as the protectors of rights and the arbiters of justice. In contrast, the comments made by the Chief Inspector of Probation suggest that the parole system has been unbalanced by the introduction of due process and procedural fairness. The reality of the situation is that the parole process remains skewed strongly

---

[49] Ibid para. 1.3.5.
[50] Ibid para. 8.3.12.
[51] See, for example, the *Daily Mail*, 1 July 2006, pp. 14–15 which investigated 'The full extent of the scandal of early release for lifers ...'

against the prisoner, with the procedural and substantive rights that currently exist having been grafted onto a system which originally did not recognise the existence of any rights in this context. When Padfield and Liebling assessed the effectiveness of the DLP system in the late 1990s, they were struck by the failure of the parole system to recognise the additional rights which accrue to post-tariff lifers and the difficulty the system had in balancing those rights with the duty to protect the public:

> When panels are considering the statutory test [for release], they are primarily (and rightly) concentrating on the rights of possible victims. They therefore, rightly, operate on the assumption that the post-tariff status of the prisoner is not very important. But the ECHR forced the creation of DLPs to provide a *judicial* (court-based) protection for offenders' rights at the post-tariff stage. Continued vigilance to ensure due consideration of the right to be released, together with due consideration for the protection of the public, constitute the dual task at the hearing. (Emphasis in original)[52]

Interestingly, when Padfield revisited this area earlier this year, she was still struck by the number of tasks the Board had to perform and the failure to distinguish between its many roles, and her conclusion that 'the rights of those detained have to be scrupulously defended and vigilantly upheld'[53] is a depressing echo of those earlier concerns.

The Board remains central to the feasibility of the current criminal justice system. With the ever increasing focus on the use of protective sentencing and the corresponding rise in the numbers of prisoners serving life and indeterminate sentences, the Board will not only have a greater workload but is also moving from the periphery of how prison sentences are administered to a far more central role in determining how long prisoners should spend in custody. Although there appears to be a strong body of case law suggesting that the Board retains sufficient independence – indeed, the very case which led to the Board taking on a judicial role appears to provide the definitive answer to that issue – those cases must be viewed with a note of caution. The nature and role of the Board has changed beyond recognition in the intervening 20 years and careful consideration now needs to be given to allowing the Board to make the break with its past. Careful consideration needs to be given to allowing the Board to finally leave the Home Office and follow other tribunals to the Tribunal Service at the DCA to formalise its independence. The dual functions of the Board to direct release and to advise the

---

[52] Padfield and Liebling, with Arnold (2000: 125).
[53] Padfield (2006: 22).

Secretary of State also need to be reassessed as this leads to conflict and uncertainty. Logically, as a court-like body the Board should have directive powers in all cases referred to it by the Secretary of State. The alternative to a considered and thought-out resolution to these conflicts is the inevitability of these changes being brought about piecemeal through judicial intervention. Neither the Board nor the Home Office were prepared for the ECtHR decision to overturn 40 years of orthodoxy in relation to the mandatory life sentence,[54] although in retrospect, the logic of this decision was inevitable. It will be a lost opportunity if action is not taken now and the change in this area is also forced rather than planned as this will only serve to increase the prospect of a chaotic outcome.

---

[54] *Stafford* v. *UK* (2002) 35 EHRR 32.

Chapter 9

Current practice and future changes: a judicial member's perspective

*Anthony Thornton**

Introduction

The Parole Board is the body with statutory responsibility for deciding whether life sentence prisoners who have served their minimum term may be released on life licence and whether those lifers who have been recalled following a breach of their licence may be re-released. These functions are two of the most significant of the Parole Board's functions and they arise because Article 5(4) of the European Convention of Human Rights requires the lawfulness of the continued detention of those serving life or indeterminate sentences once the minimum term has expired to be determined by a court-like body. In this paper, I consider whether the Parole Board complies with the minimum requirements for such a body imposed by both the common law and the ECHR.

Indeterminate sentences

An indeterminate sentence is imposed for the most serious offences involving violence with or without a sexual element. A mandatory life sentence is imposed for murder. Other indeterminate sentences comprise

*The views expressed in this paper are personal to the author.

discretionary and automatic life sentences,[1] detention at Her Majesty's pleasure, custody for life[2] and sentences of imprisonment for public protection (IPP). There are currently about 7,500 lifers within an overall prison population of nearly 80,000[3] and their number is growing rapidly now that the IPP sentence provisions are in force.[4] All indeterminate sentences consist of an initial punishment period which must be served in prison and a subsequent period which involves living in the community on licence once the Parole Board considers that it is no longer necessary to detain the prisoner for reasons of public protection. Once released and during the currency of the licence, a lifer is liable to be recalled for breach of the terms of the licence or because his dangerousness has increased unacceptably. Following recall, the lifer will not be re-released until the Parole Board is again satisfied that it is safe to do so. The punishment period of the sentence is now known as the minimum term but is still popularly called the tariff. It is now fixed by the court when the sentence is imposed.[5]

A lifer's time in custody

All lifers' time in custody is subject to the same regime which differs markedly from other prisoners serving determinate sentences. This

---

[1] The 'two strikes' sentence introduced by the Crime and Disorder Act 1988 was replaced, with effect from April 2005, by the more widely available IPP sentence (ss. 225–226 of the Criminal Justice Act 2003).

[2] Those convicted of murder committed when under 18 are sentenced to be detained at Her Majesty's pleasure (s. 90, Powers of Criminal Courts (Sentencing) Act 2000) and those convicted of murder who are aged between 18 and 20 at the date of sentence to custody for life (ibid., s. 93).

[3] Lifers are predominantly male adults. On 31 May 2006, of 7,124 prisoners serving indeterminate sentences, 6,139 were old-style lifers and 985 were IPP lifers. Of these, 219 were women and 368 were young offenders. On the same date, there were 1,579 life licensees under active supervision by the Probation Service. In the year to 31 March 2006, 353 indeterminate prisoners were released and 140 life licensees were recalled. By March 2007, the number of IPP lifers had risen to over 2,000.

[4] The sentence must ordinarily be imposed where a person is convicted of a serious violent or sexual offence and the court is of the opinion that there is a significant risk to members of the public of serious harm occasioned by the commission by him of further specified offences. Court of Appeal guidelines for the imposition of IPPs are set out in R v. Lang [2005] EWCA Crim 2864 approving the recommendations set out in the Guide for the Sentence of Public Protection issued in June 2005 by the National Probation Service.

[5] Since the tariff of mandatory lifers was fixed by the Home Secretary until 2003, the CJA contains machinery for all such lifers to apply to a High Court judge to fix his tariff judicially in s. 269(5) and Sched. 21 of the CJA 2003. For pre-CJA mandatory lifers, the court is guided by the Sentencing Advisory Panel Sentencing Guidelines issued in 2002. For tariffs imposed since 2003, the sentencing judge is required to take into account the much longer statutorily recommended tariff imposed by the CJA 2003.

regime is covered by the detailed provisions of PSO 4700 (the Lifer Manual). The regime was developed for mandatory lifers and it has been extended over time to cover all lifers. It is ill-suited to the needs of automatic and IPP lifers whose minimum terms are too short to allow for a satisfactory progression in the approved manner. Indeed, it is not possible at present for any lifer to obtain release within less than three years of his sentence even though many IPP minimum terms are less than that period.

After conviction and sentence a lifer will be moved to a first-stage high-security category B prison where a Life Sentence Plan (LSP) will be completed.[6] This plan includes an appropriate risk assessment. For sex offenders, this will include an assessment for the Sex Offender Treatment Programme (SOTP). The LSP will be based on the home supervising probation officer's report and a Multi-Agency Lifer Risk Assessment Panel[7] assessment and it will identify the lifer's risk areas. This method of analysing a lifer's risk by reference to specific areas of risk has been adopted because much of the offending behaviour work provided in prisons to assist in a lifer's risk reduction is cognitive-based and moreover, much of it involves interactive group work devised and overseen by psychologists that focuses on specific risk areas. The course reports, coupled with statistically based risk assessments which assess a lifer's static risk, involving previous offending, and his dynamic risk, involving current and on-going risk, provide the two principal sources for the risk assessments prepared by prison and probation staff that are provided to Parole Board panels to assist in their determination of whether and when a lifer may be released.

A lifer will usually spend at least 18 months in a first-stage category B prison and while there will begin appropriate offending behaviour work. At an appropriate time, a lifer will be transferred to a second-stage training prison which is either a lower security category B or a category

---

[6] All whole-life tariff lifers and the most dangerous of the other lifers, except those in high-security mental institutions, are located in category A conditions, where they will usually also have been located while on remand. These prisons are top-security prisons where those who are highly dangerous to the public, to the police or to the security of the state are located no matter how unlikely they are to escape. Category A prisons are, in effect, prisons within the prison system and decisions as to the re-categorisation of category A prisoners are taken by a separate unit within the Home Office. The number of lifers located in category A conditions is not published but if a lifer located there is post-tariff, regular lifer oral review hearings will take place within the category A prison, often under conditions of extreme security.

[7] Multi-agency public protection arrangements (MAPPAs) arise out of ss. 325–326 of the CJA 2003 and are set up in each police and probation area by the police to make arrangements for the supervision of and sharing of information and intelligence about offenders who have been or are to be released into the community. Each MAPPA operates under detailed guidance issued in PC 54/2004. Most lifers' supervision in the community is subject to MAPPA arrangements.

C prison while a significant amount of work remains to be done, particularly in relation to violence, sexual offending, cognitive skills, drugs and alcohol. In a training prison, a lifer will eventually become eligible for, and will undertake, supervised day visits to local towns so as to enable the long and difficult reintegration into the community to begin. The objective is to enable the lifer to complete all necessary offending behaviour work assisted by effective sentence planning, detailed and realistic target setting, close observation and monitoring and constructive feedback. The seconded probation officers located in each prison play an important role in attempts to fulfil these objectives.

The final stage of a lifer's time in custody is usually spent in category D or open conditions. PSO 4700 stipulates that a lifer should usually spend at least two years in open conditions prior to release in order to develop his release plan, to acquire the necessary basic skills that will be required in order to survive in the community and to show that he has sufficiently reduced his risk and has acquired the necessary coping skills to avoid being a risk once released. While in open conditions, a lifer will make unescorted visits out of the prison to local towns and for the purpose of temporary resettlement leaves at the intended resettlement address and to work in the community in voluntary and paid employment. It follows that the decision to transfer the lifer to open conditions is a crucial one that usually lies on the critical path to release. The decision is taken by the Home Secretary, through the Parole and Public Protection Policy Section of the National Offender Management Service (NOMS), which is the agency within the Home Office which manages and is in overall directional control of the Probation and Prison Services. However, the Home Secretary is committed to seeking the advice of the Parole Board as to whether a lifer's risk is sufficiently lowered to allow him to be transferred. Until recently, the Parole Board's advice that a lifer is suitable to be transferred has been accepted in most cases but recently there has been a significant reduction in the acceptance of such advice.[8]

It follows that most lifers are released from open conditions. The Parole Board can only direct release if it is satisfied that it is no longer

---

[8] The reference is made under s. 28 of the CJA 1991. The Home Secretary regards such references as being made outside the reference to the Parole Board acting as a court-like body concerned with questions of release and as being made, instead, to the Parole Board acting as an executive body notwithstanding that the decision whether to release is taken at the same hearing and following a consideration of the same evidence as the decision whether to recommend a move to open conditions. The Home Secretary is considered to have an unfettered discretion to accept or reject the Parole Board's recommendation. Until May 2006, the Home Secretary was thought to accept about 95 per cent of the recommendations for a move but, following the publication of the Rice Report (HMIP 2006), this figure is thought to have dropped to about 50 per cent (unofficial estimates provided to the writer by the Parole Board secretariat).

necessary for the protection of the public that the prisoner should be confined.[9] The Court of Appeal, in a number of cases, has explained that this test involves the Parole Board in deciding that it is satisfied that the risk to the public or release would not be substantial.[10] However, the Home Secretary has directed the Parole Board that it must only release a lifer if the risk he poses to the public, if released, is no more than minimal.[11] The Parole Board has released a number of automatic and IPP lifers from closed conditions but this practice is deprecated by the Home Secretary.

A principal component of the parole review in open conditions is the release or resettlement plan prepared by the lifer's nominated home probation officer who will supervise him in the community on release. The Home Secretary's Directions expressly advise the Parole Board to consider this document before directing release.[12] This plan will deal with where a lifer will live on release, what supervision arrangements and life licence conditions he will be subject to and what further offending behaviour work must be undertaken in the community. Supervision plays a major part in a lifer's lifestyle in the early years of his release since a lifer's ability to harm others on release is governed by his dangerous characteristics, his ability to self-manage these risks and the ability of supervision to manage his remaining risks. Most released lifers will initially move into a bail hostel or Approved Premises run by the Probation Service or into similar accommodation run by private agencies or charities. Such accommodation is in short supply and, particularly for sex offenders, long waits for available places occur. During temporary home leaves from open conditions, the lifer will spend up to seven nights in any one period residing in the intended release premises. This first phase of release should normally last for between three and six months.

There is an acute shortage of funding and resources for all aspects of the parole system, entrenched and unenlightened attitudes of many

---

[9] Section 28(6)(b) of the Crime (Sentences) Act 1997 (CSA).

[10] See *R* v. *Parole Board (ex parte Lodomez)* [1994] 26 BMLR 162, CA following *R* v. *Parole Board (ex parte Bradley)* [1991] 1 WLR 134, DC. This is the 'life and limb' test. This was the applicable test for discretionary lifers, the only lifers whose release could be directed by the Parole Board at that time. Once the Parole Board's jurisdiction to direct release was extended to all lifers, this test is now applicable to all lifers since the basis of the extended jurisdiction was that all lifers had to be treated in the same way and all are now susceptible to the test provided for in s. 28 of the CSA.

[11] Paragraph 4 of *Directions to the Parole Board for the Release and Recall of Life Sentence Prisoners (2004)*. See below for a further discussion on the release, or life and limb, test and for the effect of the important recent decision of the Court of Appeal in *Girling* v. *Secretary of State for the Home Department & Anor* [2006] EWCA Civ 1779 (21 December 2006) which removes the Home Secretary's powers to issue mandatory directions and replaces them with powers to issue non-binding guidance and prohibits them entirely in relation to the life and limb test.

[12] Ibid., para. 7(b).

working at all levels in the lifer system, an acute shortage of offending behaviour programme places in many prisons and areas and an even more acute staffing shortage of appropriately qualified staff to deliver them. The lifer system, moreover, is catering with immature and institutionalised people, many of whom are suffering from mental and personality disorders without family connections and no means of obtaining employment, housing or outside support. It follows that the release decision must take into account a whole range of factors that will potentially affect a lifer's risk to the public if he is released.

Functions of the Parole Board

The Parole Board as a body and its involvement with lifers has changed and its functions have widened immeasurably since the Parole Board was set up in 1967. These changes have occurred largely as a result of the impact of the European Court of Human Rights' interpretation of the effect of Article 5(4) of the European Convention on Human Rights on indeterminate sentences. These decisions have established conclusively that continued detention following the expiry of the tariff is purely for public protection purposes for all indeterminate sentences and that any post-tariff continued detention can only be justified on such grounds. Such detention has to be reviewed regularly by a court-like body which is both independent of the executive and the parties and is impartial, and which has the power to direct the release of any prisoner who it determines no longer has to be detained in order to protect the public.

The Parole Board had already been established for 24 years before it was given the first of its decision-making roles in relation to lifers. This extension occurred following the ECHR's decisions in *Weeks* v. *UK* and *Thynne, Wilson and Gunnell* v. *UK*[13] concerned solely with discretionary lifers. This role was extended to young offenders serving a mandatory indeterminate or Her Majesty's pleasure sentence in 1997,[14] to automatic lifers in 1998,[15] to mandatory lifers in 2003[16] and to IPP sentences when these were introduced in 2005.[17]

---

[13] (1988) 10 EHRR 293 and (1991) 13 ECHR 666 given effect to by s. 34 of the Criminal Justice Act 1991.

[14] Following the ECHR decision in *Hussain* v. *UK* and *Singh* v. *UK* (1996) 22 EHRR 1 given effect to by s. 38 of the Crime (Sentences) Act 1997 which repealed s. 34 of the CJA 1991 and reintroduced its provisions in an extended form.

[15] By an extension to s. 38 of the CSA 1998.

[16] Following the ECHR decision in *Stafford* v. *UK* (2002) EHRR 32 given effect to by s. 275 of the CJA 2003 further extending s. 34 of the CJA 1991.

[17] By ss. 225(4) (for adults) and 226(4) (for those under 18) of the CJA 2003 further extending s. 34 of the CJA 1991.

Before 1991, the Parole Board had purely advisory functions in making recommendations to the Home Secretary in relation to those indeterminate and determinate sentences that the Home Secretary chose to refer. For mandatory lifers, the Home Secretary had an unfettered discretion as to when first to fix a lifer's tariff, which then meant the period that had to be served before a lifer was first considered for release, as to the length of the tariff and as to the release of a lifer on licence. The only statutory role of the Parole Board was that a lifer's potential release had to be referred to it since, following the abolition of capital punishment in 1965, the Home Secretary could not release a lifer unless he had first received a positive recommendation for release from the Parole Board. However, the Home Secretary was not bound by that recommendation and could refuse to release without giving reasons.[18] It followed that the Parole Board in such cases acted as a purely executive body, it had no tribunal functions and it reached all its recommendations on papers supplied by the Home Office which were not disclosed to the prisoner without publishing any reasons.[19]

The first ECHR cases concerned with indeterminate sentences related to discretionary lifers. These were lifers whose indeterminate sentences had been imposed because the sentencing court considered that the offence was grave, the prisoner would be likely to repeat it and the consequences of such a repetition were likely to be grave.[20] The government had considerable difficulty in deciding how to respond to the unexpected declaration by the ECHR that it had to establish an independent court-like body with the power to direct release and, at a late stage in the passage of the Criminal Justice Bill 1991, announced that the Parole Board would be established for this purpose. It is clear from the Home Secretary's speech in the House of Commons when introduc-

---

[18] The roles of the Home Secretary and the Parole Board are explained in *R* v. *Secretary of State (ex parte Hanscombe)* (1988) 86 Cr. App. R 59, DC (for discretionary lifers) and in *In re Finlay* [1985] 1 AC 318, HL (for mandatory lifers).

[19] There was an apparent exception to the Parole Board's executive advisory functions provided by s. 62(5) of the Criminal Justice Act 1967 which required the Parole Board to decide whether recalled lifers should be immediately released. The Parole Board had no further powers to consider and direct the release subsequently of those recalled lifers whose immediate release had not been directed. In the early days, very few lifer recalls occurred and this power was always considered as being similar to, and was operated in the same way as, all the other functions of the Parole Board.

[20] *R* v. *Hodgson* (1967) 52 Cr. App. Rep 113, CA. This was the first judicial definition of a dangerousness or life and limb test and the ECHR developed its jurisprudence relating to the difference between the punishment and the public safety parts of an indeterminate sentence largely from the *Hodgson* test for imposing a discretionary life sentence. Until *Stafford*, the ECHR and the English courts regarded the entirety of a mandatory life sentence, including its post-tariff part, as being part of the original sentence imposed for punishment purposes.

ing the necessary clauses that the Parole Board, when acting as a court-like body considering release at an oral hearing, was to be regarded as a different body from the body acting in an executive advisory manner for all other functions.[21]

Thus, as each gradual extension of the Parole Board's functions in relation to lifers occurred, that extension was treated as being a further minimal expansion of its court-like function without affecting its principal role as an advisory body. The Home Office continues to regard the Parole Board as a body exercising executive non-tribunal functions with a limited parallel role in relation to lifers. This view is no longer tenable in relation to any functions of the Parole Board. In the light of a series of cases including the *Stafford* and *Clift* cases[22] and also in the light of the CJA, the Parole Board is acting as an Article 5 court-like independent tribunal in relation to all its functions including those concerning lifers and determinate release and recall decisions whether taken following an oral hearing or on paper at a so-called paper panel.

The relevant changes to the Parole Board's original functions have occurred gradually. The first of these changes occurred when the Home Secretary delegated to the Parole Board the power to decide which determinate prisoners serving sentences of between four and 15 years could be released on licence having served half their sentence.[23] Further changes occurred when the Parole Board was given the power to decide on the re-release of recalled determinate prisoners in all cases and with the introduction of the Extended Sentence in 1998 when the Parole Board was given the power to decide on both release and re-release following recall. The Parole Board is now required to provide an oral hearing for all Extended Sentence recall cases and in a growing proportion of determinate recall cases.[24] It also has a discretion, which is rarely exercised, to hold an oral hearing in determinate release cases. Automatic release on parole for all determinate prisoners serving between four and 15 years was introduced by the Criminal Justice Act 2003. Thus, once all prisoners sentenced to determinate sentences of between four

---

[21] See the speech of the Prisons Minister, Mrs Angela Rumbold, introducing the relevant clauses as an amendment to the Criminal Justice Bill during the Commons consideration of House of Lords Amendments, HC Debs, 25 June 1991, cols 903–904).

[22] *R (on the application of Clift)* v. *Secretary of State for the Home Department* [2006] UKHL 54.

[23] Section 35 of the CJA 1991 as amended using the powers provided by s. 50 by the Parole Board (Transfer of Functions) Order 1998. This was considered by the Home Office as the grant of executive decision-making powers to a previously advice-giving body. As the Parole Board's tribunal functions and status has evolved, it is now better regarded as the grant of executive decision-making powers to an independent judge-like tribunal required to exercise those powers with appropriate standards of procedural fairness.

[24] *R* v. *Parole Board (ex parte Sim)* [2003] EWHC 152 (Admin) (for ESP cases) and in *R* v. *Parole Board (ex parte Smith and ex parte West)*, HL, [2005] 1 WLR 350 (for determinate cases).

and 15 years between 1991 and 2003 have been released, the Parole Board will have no role in the initial release decision of any determinate prisoner, save for those serving extended sentences when it will continue to take that decision.

The Parole Board, therefore, now functions entirely as a body exercising tribunal functions and it will in time become a recognised body with exclusively tribunal functions. It is exclusively concerned with the release of lifers and the recall of all prisoners.[25] It retains limited advisory functions dealing with those cases referred to it by the Home Secretary where its advice is sought. Advice is usually sought as part of a reference involving the Parole Board's decision-making functions and, in such cases, the Parole Board is acting as a tribunal both when reaching its decision and when giving advice since an independent tribunal cannot during the same reference act simultaneously as a decision-making tribunal and an executive advice-giving body. It is no longer a matter of serious debate as to whether or not all of its other decision-making functions are subject to Article 5(4) but, for any that are not, the Parole Board must function in accordance with common law requirements of independence and fairness. Although an oral hearing is not required in all non-lifer cases, these common law requirements, tailored appropriately to the individual case, must be observed in every reference including its paper panel hearings.

Minimum procedural standards required by law

In functioning as a judge-like body or tribunal in indeterminate cases, the Parole Board must comply with the statutory requirements directing how the Parole Board should function in such cases, with the Parole Board Rules, with the Home Secretary's Directions in lifer cases, with the requirements provided by Article 5(4) of the ECHR for the court-like body required to determine a post-tariff lifer's continued detention, with s. 6(1) of the Human Rights Act 1998 which makes it unlawful for a public authority to act in a way which is incompatible with a Convention right, and with the common law requirements that a court should be independent, impartial and make its decisions in a fair manner.[26] The

---

[25] The Parole Board has been described as a tribunal in a series of non-lifer cases. Particular examples are *Smith and West, R v. Roberts* and *R v. Parole Board (ex parte Giles)*, HL, [2004] 1 AC 1. The Parole Board's Statement of Purpose describes the Parole Board as 'a judicially independent tribunal that determines the lawfulness of the detention of prisoners and that protects the public'.

[26] The relevant statutory provisions are s. 26 of the CJA 1991, s. 28 of the CSA 1997 (as amended) and s. 239 of the CJA 2003. The CJA 2003 re-enacts s. 26 of the CJA 1991 but, currently, both the CJA 1991 and the CJA 2003 remain in force. When s. 26 of the CJA

effect of these provisions is that the Parole Board must act independently of the executive and the parties, must be impartial and must have the power to give a legally binding decision concerning a lifer's release. A lifer must be provided with a speedy hearing at the expiry of his minimum term and at regular intervals thereafter and he must have ready access to the Parole Board for such hearings. Procedurally, the Parole Board must provide appropriate procedural guarantees to the lifer which should not be markedly inferior to those applicable to procedures in the criminal courts. The procedure should provide equality of arms to the lifer and the state as parties and should ensure equal treatment to both parties and be truly adversarial. Finally, the procedure adopted must allow for an oral hearing and the state must enable the lifer to be legally assisted at that hearing.

The essential ingredients, therefore, of a fair hearing in lifer cases are that the Parole Board must be and must function as a court-like body, it must be independent and impartial, it must have the power to decide all relevant issues associated with the lawfulness of a lifer's continuing detention and it must provide appropriate procedural guarantees.

Court-like body or tribunal

The Parole Board is an incorporated Executive Non-Departmental Public Body or ENDPB, sponsored by the Home Office through its Parole and Public Protection Section which is within one of the key Directorates or Services of the Home Office. It is funded by a grant-in-aid from the Home Office and is subject to the accounting directions of the Home Secretary. The Chief Executive is appointed as the Parole Board's statutory Accounting Officer. The Parole Board's membership comprises a part-time Chairman, who is a non-lawyer and who sits on an occasional basis as a member, and a part-time Vice-Chairman, who is a High Court judge. There are currently overall 156 members of the Parole Board comprising the Vice-Chairman and two further High Court and 41 circuit judges, 13 psychiatrists, 10 probation officers, 4 criminologists and 77 independent members. All but three of the independent members are part-time. The Parole Board is managed by a Management Committee which has overall responsibility for Parole Board policy and strategy, representing the views of the Parole Board membership, advising on

---

1991 is repealed using the repealing powers of the CJA 2003, there will be no substantial difference in the powers of the Parole Board. In R (on the application of Clift) v. Secretary of State for the Home Department [2006] UKHL 54, the House of Lords decided that the Parole Board is acting as an Article 5 independent court-like body in all its functions including early release decisions and recommendations referred to it by the Home Secretary. See, in particular, paragraph 23 of Lord Bingham's speech.

overall strategic questions, overseeing the delivery of planned results and receiving audit reports. There is a Review Committee which reviews every case where a prisoner who was released on licence by the Parole Board then commits, or is suspected of committing, a further violent or serious sexual offence. This review seeks to assess whether the original parole decision was defensible and to establish learning points for the future. There are also committees concerned with Performance and Development and Quality Standards chaired by two of the full-time independent members that are answerable to the Management Committee.

The number of lifer and Extended Sentence recall cases considered by the Parole Board in 2004–2005 at oral hearings was 1,341. Of these, 90 were lifer recall hearings. The Parole Board projects an oral hearings case load for 2006–2007 of 2,300 cases.[27] These figures may appear low, particularly given the – albeit erroneously – suggested high cost of mounting a single oral hearing.[28] However, most of these oral hearings involve difficult questions of law, fact, opinion and assessment and all involve fundamental questions concerning the liberty, safety and lawful detention of the prisoner and, additionally, fundamental questions concerning public safety.

The structure of the Parole Board was established when the Parole Board was incorporated in 1994 and became an ENDPB in 1996. This structure is not an appropriate one for a tribunal for which a Tribunal Non-Departmental Public Body status is appropriate. The ENDPB status was fixed at a time when the Parole Board only acted as a tribunal in discretionary lifer cases but since 2003 that status is no longer tenable given that all the Parole Board's core functions, and a growing majority of its work generally, consists of oral hearings. The Parole Board's first ENDPB Quinquennial Review published in 2001 suggested that the Parole Board's sponsorship by the Home Office should be reconsidered once the major changes in the Board's role arising from what became the Criminal Justice Act 2003 took effect.[29]

---

[27] Parole Board Annual Report 2004–2005 and Parole Board Business Plan 2006–2007. The statistics do not distinguish between oral lifer and oral ESP recall cases and do not include one-member 'Smith and West' panels hearing DCR recall cases where the prisoner requested an oral hearing.

[28] The estimated, somewhat notional, figure provided by the Parole Board as the cost to the Parole Board of each case at an oral hearing is £1,511 for 2004–2005 (Annual Report, p. 27). The estimated cost of providing legal aid for each such oral hearing was just over £2 million for the same period (*Guardian*, 20 May 2006). This averages out at about £900 per case. Both are low figures given the difficulties that arise in most oral hearings cases and in their administration.

[29] *Comprehensive Review of Parole and Lifer Processes* (2001). All NDPBs are expected to be subject to quinquennial reviews by the Home Office and this was the Parole Board's first such review. The recommendation as to future sponsorship is contained in para. 5.4.7.

The result of these structural arrangements is that the Parole Board functions as an executive agency and not as a tribunal. The principal features of a tribunal, as these have evolved in England over the last 50 years and that are lacking within the Parole Board, include the following. A tribunal will be chaired by a working tribunal chairman, usually a judge, who will sit regularly and will hear and issue judgments in many of the major cases which will be published and used as guideline judgments in subsequent cases. Each panel or division of the tribunal will have judicial independence in deciding cases and will not be bound by, but will treat as authoritative, earlier decisions of the tribunal, particularly those of its chairmen. The tribunal will publish practice directions, through the chairman, and will have procedural rules drafted by a Rules Committee on which its members play a major role. These rules will be drafted using the guidance provided by the Council on Tribunals.[30] The tribunal will not be subject to any other influence. Once the Tribunals Bill, currently before Parliament, becomes law, tribunals will come under the administrative direction of the Tribunals Service which will operate independently of the executive and of the government departments whose acts or decisions the tribunal is concerned with. The internal administration and budgeting arrangements are run separately from the tribunal's judicial functions by a board chaired by the chairman which has no power to direct, advise or control individual panels or members when acting in a judicial capacity. The tribunal is funded by a block grant which it has autonomous powers to allocate and spend on tribunal functions.

None of these arrangements apply to the Parole Board. The chairman is an executive chairman who very occasionally sits on panels but whose role is to act as the principal link with the Home Office, being the Parole Board's sponsor. No guideline judgments or decisions are produced or published and general policy to be followed by panels, such as that relating to deferrals and adjournments or as to the risk test to be applied, are published internally by the Management Committee in an Oral Hearings Practice Guide. The Parole Board Rules are made and published by the Home Secretary without reference to a Rules Committee or to outside guidance and the Home Secretary also has the power to issue Directions which provide guidance as to the manner in which decision-making should be structured and oral hearings conducted. The Home Office can also direct how the budget should be spent and can therefore influence how hearings are conducted. For example, since oral hearings were introduced for determinate recall cases in 2005 following the decision of the House of Lords in the *Smith* and *West* cases, such panels are required to comprise only one member even though release decisions in similar recall cases decided by a panel on paper are decided

---

[30] Council on Tribunals Guide to Drafting Tribunal Rules (November 2003).

by a panel of two members. This decision was taken on purely financial grounds.

A further unusual feature of Parole Board oral hearings is their lack of transparency. Hearings are held in private in prisons since the Home Office is not prepared to make courts available and to transport prisoners to the courts for a public hearing on grounds of cost. Furthermore, all decisions are private and are not allowed to be published, even on a dedicated website. The ostensible reason is that privacy is required by data protection and human rights legislation but recent case law has established that there is an exception to this legislation for court and tribunal decisions on the grounds of public interest.[31]

Access

It is an obvious requirement of a court-like body that all parties served by that body should have free and unhindered access to it. This is not the case for lifers in two important respects, in relation both to initial access and to the Parole Board's advice-giving functions. A lifer is entitled to a Parole Board review at tariff-expiry and at regular intervals thereafter. In *Stafford*, the ECHR suggested that that period should ordinarily be no longer than one year between reviews. The relevant legislation, however, provides that the Home Secretary must initiate any review by first referring the lifer's case to the Parole Board and that the interval between reviews will ordinarily be of two years. There is no good reason why a lifer cannot initiate a review himself and that, in any case, the review period should ordinarily be no longer than one year in length. The Home Secretary's gatekeeper role and his power to limit reviews to a bi-annual cycle was accepted as being lawful in the two cases of *Clough* and *Day*[32] on the grounds that the Home Secretary is obliged to refer a lifer's case every two years to the Parole Board and because the court was informed that there was a procedure whereby a lifer could apply to the Home Secretary for an earlier review. In fact, there is no published or transparent procedure for such applications which depend on a lifer applying informally and, ordinarily, receiving a brief rejection letter. Furthermore, there is much to be said for Sedley LJ's views in the later Court of Appeal case of *Murray* to the effect that the Home Secretary's internal procedures by which the lifer can request a review do not meet the standards set by Article 5(4).[33]

---

[31] See *R (on the application of Stone)* v. *South East Coast Strategic Health Authority* [2006] All ER (D) 144, Davis J.

[32] *R (on the application of Clough)* [2003] EWHC 597 (Admin) and *R (on the application of Day)* [2004] EWHC 1742 (Admin).

[33] *R (on the application of Murray)* [2003] EWCA Civ 1561, para. 20.

A further restriction faced by lifers is that they may not seek the advice of the Parole Board on such matters as the timing of a review, their re-categorisation, any of the many issues associated with the availability of or necessity for particular offending behaviour work that is associated with the system of risk reduction that they are subject to or the contents of assessments considered to be erroneous or unfair. All these matters directly affect the risk that a lifer is considered to pose and his ability to obtain his release and, therefore, should be susceptible to review by the same court-like body as considers the release decision itself.

The Parole Board's judicial independence and impartiality

In the context of a court, court-like body or tribunal, the requirements of independence, impartiality, fairness and transparency are particularly onerous and they require the Parole Board, as such a body, to ensure that it rigorously and continuously maintains all these characteristics. In the context of lifer hearings, I would summarise the Parole Board's obligations in this way:

1. The Parole Board must be free from any influence, whether direct or indirect, from the government, the executive or the parties when carrying out its judicial functions.
2. Every Parole Board panel member must be free from outside influences which may, consciously or unconsciously, influence the decisions that they must make. These decisions must be made solely on the basis of the evidence and arguments adduced before the panel which both parties have had a fair opportunity of dealing with.
3. The Parole Board's structure, working methods, procedures and contacts must be such that the Parole Board is not only judicially independent and impartial but is perceived as being judicially independent by an objective non-party observer.
4. The Parole Board's work, working methods, rules, working practices and decisions should, so far as is practicable, proportionate and commensurate with the rights of third parties, be transparent, undertaken in public and readily accessible to both the public and the parties appearing before it.
5. Each panel member must be free from peer-pressure from other members or from those concerned with the Parole Board's management or administration.

These principles are potentially compromised in a variety of ways. The starting point in any consideration of the Parole Board's independence and impartiality is the role of the Home Secretary. He is a party to all proceedings of the Parole Board and the member of the executive concerned with prisons and prisoners. He appoints the members of the Parole Board, determines their terms of office and is responsible for their discipline and dismissal if appropriate. He employs, directly or on secondment, many of the staff of the Parole Board. He sponsors the Parole Board and, as such, has considerable influence in the policies and procedures operated by the Parole Board. He provides the Parole Board with its funding and has considerable influence on how that funding is spent and on required savings affecting its procedures and working methods. He can direct reviews of individual decisions in controversial cases to be conducted by the Chief Inspector of Probation. Finally, he has exclusive power, without the need for taking advice, to promulgate the Parole Board's procedural rules and may, exceptionally for a tribunal, issue directions as to the matters to be taken into account in discharging its functions.[34] Finally, he employs most of those who give evidence to Parole Board panels since these are largely probation or prison staff employed by or contracted to NOMS, and he provides guidance to panels in the form of his written view as to each case being considered which is read out at the start of a hearing. In advice cases, such as those concerned with a possible move to open conditions, having fully participated in the oral hearing, he then is free to reject the Parole Board's advice on the basis of a paper review without considering the oral evidence adduced to the panel and, if necessary, on different grounds or evidence to that presented to the panel.

There are many examples of how this symbiotic relationship between the Home Secretary and the Parole Board creates, or at the very least appears to create, a perception of bias or lack of independence and impartiality. It is clear that this relationship, in all its facets, will be the subject of judicial review proceedings in the near future and the twin questions of sponsorship and tribunal status for the Parole Board are also likely to be considered by the Home Office as part of its reconsideration of parole processes.

---

[34] In *R (on the application of Girling)* v. *Parole Board* [2006] 1 WLR 1917, Walker J held that it was unlawful for the Home Secretary to issue directions in lifer cases. This decision was overturned on appeal in *Norman Girling* v. *Secretary of State for the Home Department* [2006] EWCA Civ 1779 but on grounds which, in fact, indicated that the Home Secretary's powers to issue directions are even more limited than suggested by Walker J. The Court of Appeal held that the directions that the Home Secretary may issue in any case decided by the Parole Board, and not merely in lifer cases, must be only guidance, are not mandatory and are merely matters which the Parole Board panel must take into account when reaching its own independent decision.

Fair procedure

In deciding on questions of release or in giving advice on a possible move to open conditions, the Parole Board must carry out a risk assessment on the lifer. This involves the assessment of a noumenon, that is the assessment of a phenomenon or object of intellectual intuition.[35] This assessment is left to the subjective good sense of an individual panel calling on the varied expertise of its individual membership of three Parole Board members, one of whom is a judge, one usually a psychiatrist or psychologist and one an independent member appointed for his or her experience of violent offending and its effects on the public. The panel must be satisfied that it is no longer necessary for the protection of the public to confine the lifer, a decision that is taken on balancing subjective perception rather than factual probabilities. The procedure is an inquisitorial one in the sense that the panel decides what reports, documents and evidence it will receive and itself carries out much of the questioning of the witnesses. However, panels allow lifers full opportunity to call evidence, examine witnesses, know the case to be met and to participate fully in the proceedings.

Many lifers and their representatives complain that the procedures followed by panels are unfair. This unfairness arises, or is perceived as arising, in a number of ways. Legal aid is available to fund representation before panels but it is limited in scope and many prisoners feel that their legal representatives are unfairly constrained in commissioning independent risk assessments, obtaining access to security and other information held on prison files, being able to meet the panel's inquiries as to past offending behaviour relevant to their risk and in fully learning in advance the case as to their risk that they must meet if they are to secure their release.

These complaints are largely the result of the very deficient Parole Board Rules, which fail to cover adequately such questions as discovery of documents, rights to representation, preparation and service of the dossier containing the documents and reports to be used at a hearing, and enforceable powers relating to procedural directions issued by a panel given the frequent non-observance of these directions by the parties. These deficiencies can only be satisfactorily addressed by the promulgation of a completely new set of Parole Board Rules which address all the issues set out in the Council on Tribunals Guide and provide the Parole Board with appropriate powers to conduct fair inquisitorial reviews and sanctions which can be imposed on both

---

[35] See the speech of Lord Diplock in *Attorney-General* v. *English* [1983] 1 AC 116 as interpreted in *R (on the application of Hirst)* v. *Parole Board* [2002] EWHC 1592 (Admin), para. 83.

parties in the event of non-compliance with the Rules or with procedural directions made under them by panels.

Decision-making

There are two significant difficulties about the present decision-making process in lifer cases. The first is that the release test the Parole Board is directed to apply by the Home Secretary does not appear to coincide with what it is required to apply by statute. The Home Secretary's directed test is that a panel should not direct release unless it is satisfied that the lifer's risk to the public is not more than minimal. The statutory test, as interpreted by a series of cases, is that the Parole Board may not release if the risk to the public is greater than substantial which must mean more than merely perceptible or minimal. In other words, the Parole Board must be the decider of the appropriate level of risk and that level will vary within broad parameters depending on the circumstances of the lifer, the index offence, the nature of the risk he poses, the risk reduction he can demonstrate and the nature and effect of his lifestyle and the supervision and monitoring he will receive in the community on release. That is the appropriate test enshrined in the statutory formula as explained by the relevant case law.[36]

Further potentially unlawful constraint on a panel's decision-making is provided by Rule 20 of the Parole Board Rules 2004 which states that a panel's reasons should only make reference to matters which the Home Secretary has expressly referred to the Board. This rule is intended to preclude a panel from commenting on the timing of the next review, on offending behaviour work which should or which need not be under-taken before the next review or on suitability for re-categorisation from category B to category C. These matters often cause difficulty and dispute and a panel should be able, in appropriate cases, to comment on and make recommendations about them since they are intimately associated with both suitability for release and with whether it remains lawful to detain a lifer on public protection grounds. There is also a clear implied power for the Parole Board to comment on these matters in its

---

[36] R v. *Secretary of State (ex parte Benson)*, unreported, 9 November 1988, DC; R v. *Parole Board (ex parte Bradley)* [1991] 1 WLR 134, DC; R v. *Parole Board (ex parte Gittens)*, unreported, *Times* 3 February 1994, DC; R v. *Parole Board (ex parte Lodomez)*, (1994) 26 BMLR 162, DC; R v. *Parole Board (ex parte Watson)*, unreported, 16 October 1995, DC; and R v. *Secretary of State (ex parte Stafford)*, [1998] 1 WLR 503, CA and [1998] 2 AC 38, HL 28 and Girling's case in the Court of Appeal at paragraphs 29–31. The *Stafford* case in the ECHR (2002) 35 EHHR 32 should also be considered.

decision letter.[37] The Home Secretary cannot remove that implied power by procedural rules, particularly since his power to issue such rules is limited to matters 'with respect to the proceedings of the Board'. This statutory limitation confines the Home Secretary's power to make rules to procedural matters. Rule 20 goes much further and seeks to limit the Parole Board's jurisdiction and its implied power to do anything incidental to its release decision-making function.[38]

Conclusion

It is suggested that the Parole Board, to fulfil its statutory function in connection with lifers in accordance with both ECHR and common law requirements, should no longer be sponsored by the Home Office. Instead, it should be transformed from an ENDPB to a Tribunal NDPB, should join the Tribunal Service once this has been fully established and should for the future be run and administered as a tribunal. It should also be provided with appropriate rule-making powers and procedural rules particularly now that it is no longer to be subject to the mandatory directions of the Home Secretary.

---

[37] The Home Secretary informs panels in lifer recall hearings that he is not asking the Panel to consider a move to open condition, even though this is sometimes desirable. LRRS complains to the Parole Board if a panel considers it necessary to exercise its implied power to comment notwithstanding the terms of the reference.

[38] See also para. 1(2)(b) of Sched. 19 of the CJA 2003 which provides that the Parole Board has the power to do such things as are incidental to or conducive to the discharge of its functions in relation to lifers. This power cannot be circumscribed save by primary legislation. The decision of Sullivan J in *Mills, R (on the application of)* v. *Parole Board* [2005] CO/2315/2005 does not conclusively decide to the contrary since, although the Home Office's view of Rule 20 was upheld, the decision was not concerned with, nor did it consider, a case where a Parole Board panel decides that it is necessary, in deciding a case, to make reference to one of the prohibited matters such as a move to open conditions utilising these statutory powers. For the Parole Board's wide implied powers, see *Roberts* v. *Parole Board* [2005] UKHL 45, HL.

Part III
The particular challenges caused by recalls

Chapter 10

The recall and re-release of determinate sentence prisoners

Jo Thompson

Introduction

This chapter focuses on the current provisions for the recall and re-release of offenders on licence in the community from a determinate sentence. It looks at the contribution these provisions have made to the steady rise in the prison population and, importantly, the context within which National Offender Management Service (NOMS) staff in the Probation Service and the Home Office must operate: the demands of constantly changing legislation, ministerial priorities and agency policy, standards and culture.

The steady rise in the prison population to the level of 77,421 on 25 November 2005[1] has caused concern and debate within the Criminal Justice System, the government, the media and the general public. The *Observer* newspaper on Sunday, 8 October 2006[2] quoted the Prison Officers' Association as saying that prisons in England and Wales were now full; the official population stood at 79,843 on the evening of Friday, 6 October: 210 below officially accepted maximum capacity. These figures were contained in a front-page article which reported an interview with the Lord Chief Justice, Lord Phillips of

---

[1] Population in Custody, November 2005 (London: Home Office, Research and Development Section, National Offender Management Service (NOMS), 2005).
[2] 'Madness of Dustbin Jails' – by Lord Chief Justice. Mary Riddell and Jamie Doward, *Observer*, 8 October 2006.

Worth Matravers. Lord Phillips had personally tested a session of community punishment/community payback within a community order, and expressed his acute concerns about the size and make-up of the prison population.

The changes in the sentencing framework, their effect on the prison population and the changing law on recall have been well documented.[3] The system of early release on licence and the law on recall, introduced by Part II of the Criminal Justice Act 1991, represent a seminal change in the work of the Probation Service: by the nature of their sentences more seriously convicted offenders became an increasing part of the caseload of probation staff. Part II of the Criminal Justice Act 1991, and in particular s. 39 on recall, was repealed by s. 303 of the Criminal Justice Act 2003. The new release arrangements for standard determinate sentence prisoners (who committed their offences on or after 4 April 2005), and the new recall provisions introduced by the Criminal Justice Act 2003, Part 12, Chapter 6 have compounded the prison population issue and have set those who practice in the field of release and recall a number of challenges which are the subject of this chapter. The new automatic release arrangements for all those sentenced to a standard determi-nate sentence,[4] where offenders remain eligible for recall to the sentence expiry date, coupled with the new executive recall provisions will, in practice, lead to a rise in recall and a higher prison population.

Legislative provisions

Sections 254 to 256 of the Criminal Justice Act 2003 introduce the new recall provisions for determinate sentence prisoners. They are in place for any breach of licence initiated by the National Probation Service on or after 4 April 2005. Section 254 enables executive recall by the Secretary of State which in practice means that recall decisions are taken, following a recommendation by the National Probation Service, by caseworkers in the Release and Recall Section (RRS) of NOMS, acting on behalf of the Secretary of State. The same section contains the duty to refer the case to the Parole Board following the offender's return to custody. Section 255 relates to the power of the Secretary of State to recall offenders who breach the conditions of the Home Detention Curfew Scheme, and s. 256 gives the Parole Board the power to re-release an offender following recall.

---

[3] Padfield and Maruna (2006).
[4] The Criminal Justice and Court Services Act 2003, s. 244.

The effect of these provisions is to clearly separate the recall and review functions: the Parole Board no longer has responsibility for the recall decision; its role is in reviewing the decision and acting as the appeal body against such decisions.

The recall process in practice

Guidance to probation staff on the use of additional conditions and the recall and re-release process was issued to staff under a Probation Circular.[5] It contained a template report[6] to be completed on each recall. Previously, probation officers completed a short form itemising the licence condition that had been breached, and either recommending recall or in some circumstances requesting no revocation of the licence. The new provisions demand that, in the case of all breaches on or after 4 April 2005, a much more detailed report is submitted. The first part provides information on the circumstances of the breach, a history of compliance with supervision and a risk assessment that explains the offender's risk of reoffending and level of risk of serious harm. It is intended to evidence the recommendation for recall and to enable the Release and Recall Section to make appropriate decisions. The second part of the report containing the risk management or release plan and a recommendation on release must be completed in all cases and arrive at the establishment holding the offender within 14 days of the offender's return to custody. This part of the report is essential for the Parole Board to enable them to make appropriate release decisions. The process demands good communication, and a shared commitment to making the process work, between: the Prison Service, the Probation Service, the Parole Board, the Release and Recall Section (RRS) and the police. It also represents a large increase in workload for all concerned in the process.

The objectives of the new recall provisions

The recall processes are designed to meet the legislation and what are seen as the objectives of the new provisions: public protection, procedural fairness and the use of recall as a flexible risk management tool. The period on licence is seen as an integral part of the sentence, enforcement is thus a priority and the protection of the public is best served by a swift return to custody of those offenders on licence whose behaviour indicates an increased risk of reoffending. The revocation of

---

[5] PC 16/2005: Criminal Justice Act 2003 – Early Release and Recall.
[6] Ibid.: Annex B.

licence to the offender a matter of days after return to custody; every decision to recall is reviewed by the Parole Board; offenders may make representations against their recall; and s/he can request an Oral Hearing to consider his/her representations. It was thought that the new recall provisions, with the option of re-release before sentence expiry date, could be used in more flexible risk management: at a point when the offender was close to reoffending, or indeed their risk of serious harm was increasing, recall could be used within a risk management plan. This would enable the Probation Service to put other measures in place in order to manage the offender, who could then be re-released. When recall was requested because of a breach of the contact requirement of National Standards[7] and there were no specific risk reasons to keep the offender in custody, the Parole Board could re-release him/her immediately. The Parole Board has not been re-releasing offenders in the numbers envisaged.

The figures on recall show a steady upward trend that is set to continue, adding 4,000 to the prison population at any one time; the Parole Board are not re-releasing recalled offenders to balance the numbers entering establishments. Behind the figures is a process which entails large increases in workload that are bound to stretch resources, particularly when endeavouring to ensure that due process is followed.

Table 10.1 shows the Recall Caseload set out by the Release and Recall Section at September 2006. This table includes the increasing number of recalls following breach of Home Detention Curfew (HDC) conditions. The Crime and Disorder Act 1998[8] inserted new sections into the Criminal Justice Act 1991 to provide for the release of short-term prisoners on HDC. This was implemented in January 1999 since when the rules have changed and the scheme has grown, resulting in a concomitant rise in recalls for breach of HDC.

I intend to concentrate on the reasons for the rise in recall for breach of other licence conditions, since it does seem reasonable to contend that this lies not in the behaviour of the offenders themselves, but in the legislation and the professional practice of those involved in the processes.

Reasons behind the increase in recalls

Legislation

I have already noted the 1991 Criminal Justice Act and the new licences for short- and long-term prisoners.[9] Section 39 of the Act provided for

---

[7] PC 15/2005: National Standards 2005, SS9.1, SS9.10–SS9.13.
[8] The Crime and Disorder Act 1998, ss. 99–100 inserted new ss. 34A, 37A and 38A into the Criminal Justice Act 1991.

Table 10.1 Recall caseload

	Recall following breach of licence	*Recall following breach of Home Detention Curfew conditions*	*Total*
2000/2001	2,457	725	3,182
2001/2002	4,369	717	5,086
2002/2003	6,323	2,065	8,388
2003/2004	8,133	3,082	11,215
2004/2005	8,262	2,819	11,081
2005/2006	8,678	2,632	11,310

the recall of long-term prisoners by the Parole Board but in order to set in train the process of recall for short-term prisoners, the Probation Service had to apply to the court. This drawn-out process often meant that offenders reached the end of their licence before the case was heard. It was not meaningful to the offender because of the time lapse between his/her behaviour and enforcement, and gave no incentive to the Probation Service to initiate breach proceedings. Section 103(3) of the Crime and Disorder Act 1998 therefore made a real impact by amending s. 39 of the Criminal Justice Act 1991 to include short-term prisoners and provided for the rollout of executive recall from 1 January 1999. In addition s. 104 provided for the extension of supervision to sentence expiry date for those recalled and re-released at licence expiry date: the licence prolonged to end of sentence made them eligible for recall a second time.

As well as the more obvious changes in the law affecting the recall provisions and thus the rate of recall, the legislation introducing the Multi-Agency Public Protection Arrangements (MAPPA) had an effect on practice. The Criminal Justice and Court Services Act 2000, ss. 67 and 68 put the MAPPA and the sharing of information between criminal justice agencies on a statutory footing. During the 1990s, the police and probation services had been working together to manage offenders in the community whom they assessed as posing a risk of serious harm. The notification requirements in the Sex Offender Act 1997 for the first time gave the police a role in the monitoring and management of offenders

---

[9] A short-term prisoner is one who is sentenced under the CJA 1991 to between 12 months and under four years; s/he is released at the halfway point on Automatic Conditional Release (ACR) and supervised to the three-quarters point of sentence. Long-term prisoners are those who are serving four or more years and are eligible for release by the Parole Board after half their sentence has been served. Those not released by the Parole Board on discretionary conditional release (DCR) must be released at the two-thirds point and remain on licence to the three-quarters point.

post conviction and in many areas police and probation practitioners were working in teams together to identify, monitor and manage offenders. The Criminal Justice Act 2003, s. 325 reinforced the working together principles and also placed a duty to cooperate with the police, probation and prison services (as the 'Responsible Authority') on a number of agencies and authorities, including housing, children's services and health providers. Formal processes for sharing information have led to probation practitioners reassessing the risk of reoffending or the risk of serious harm that offenders pose and then initiating recall as a preventative measure.

The public protection agenda

Public protection has become the priority for the Probation Service. Alongside legislation that has public protection at its heart, the risk of harm agenda has been growing in the Probation Service. In the last 30 months in particular there has been an increasing focus on the need to improve practitioners' abilities to assess and manage risk of serious harm. The Offender Assessment System (OASys) tool for the assessment of risk and need began to roll out in 2001. Chapter 8 of the OASys Manual, giving guidance on the 'Analysis of Risk of Serious Harm Section', has just been revised and reissued under a Probation Circular.[10] In June 2005 the Director of Probation launched the ten-point Risk of Harm Action Plan[11] in a bid to improve practice and De Montfort University were contracted to produce training materials for NOMS (probation and prison) staff. The 'Risk of Harm Guidance and Training Resources' pack was launched on 8 June 2006, and all probation areas were required to audit their risk of harm training needs and devise a training implementation plan for their staff[12] ready for the issue of the pack.

This agenda, within which practitioners are working, has also been driven by high-profile serious further offences by offenders under licence to the Probation Service and the Reports by Her Majesty's Inspectorate of Probation (HMIP) that have followed. In particular the HMIP Report into a serious further offence case which concerned the murder of John Monckton and the attempted murder of his wife Homeyra by Damien Hanson, an offender on licence, led to 31 practice recommendations in an action plan for probation areas,[13] an independent review of the

---

[10] PC 36/2006: OASys – Revised Chapter on Risk of Serious Harm (Chapter 8).
[11] PC 49/2005: Assessment and Management of Risk of Harm Action Plan.
[12] PC 22/2006: Implementation of the Risk of Harm Guidance and Training Resource Pack.
[13] PC 15/2006: Guidance on the Implementation of Practice Recommendations arising from an HMIP Independent Review of a Serious Offence Case, February 2006.

information on which the Parole Board make decisions and an Oral Ministerial Statement by the Home Secretary Charles Clarke on 23 April on Public Protection. As a result the risk assessment and management skills of the Probation Service moved centre stage.

It could be argued that all this has made both practitioners and their managers much more risk averse. In some cases it is fair to say that offenders' risk of serious harm levels are assessed as higher; practitioners lack support and confidence and consequently err on the side of caution, resulting in more recalls. It is vital that practitioners use their professional judgment when they consider whether a failure to comply with licence conditions represents an *unacceptable* failure: whether the act of recall would increase an offender's risks by destabilising him/her, interrupting what is otherwise positive compliance with the sentence plan, or by losing accommodation or employment or the support of family and friends. Professional judgment should be based on the evidence produced by the assessment tools and interpreted for a particular individual. In a climate where staff are inclined to watch their backs rather than use their judgment, more offenders are likely to be recalled.

A performance culture

National Standards for the Probation Service were introduced in 1995 and are set by the Home Secretary. Since then, the shift has been to a performance- and target-led culture within the Probation Service. Improvement in enforcement performance in respect of licences is the key determinant of the increase in recalls.

The National Probation Service (NPS) Performance Targets and Measures 2006–2007 issued under Probation Circular 28/2006 contains the Performance Targets and Measures set by ministers, after preparatory work done by the National Probation Directorate (NPD) and the NOMS Strategy and Performance Section. Government allocates the resources that the NPS has available to meet the targets. They relate directly to the NPS Key Priorities: 'Although the goal is to maintain a stable set of targets and measures throughout the year, adjustments may be necessary if circumstances change e.g. ... because of changes in government priorities.' Enforcement is a ministerial priority. It is a target in the 'weighted scorecard'.

The weighted scorecard measures the performance of each of the 42 probation areas according to a set of performance targets and measures that are included in it. These are weighted in relation to their importance and are classed for descriptive purposes as the Key Performance Indicators (KPIs). Performance on each of the KPIs against target is aggregated to produce a single score upon which areas can be ranked.

The main aim of the scorecard has been to facilitate performance improvement. It has achieved this by enabling the NPS to 'create a performance-oriented culture'. Performance Target 6 concerns enforcement in line with National Standards; it includes licences and the target is 90 per cent of cases. In 2005/6 the target for licence enforcement was exceeded and reached 93 per cent.

There is a target in the weighted scorecard for compliance, but this concerns the number of appointments attended in the first 26 weeks by an offender; three performance measures not in the scorecard also concern compliance; one such measure is the percentage of orders/ licences reaching the six-month stage without requiring breach action. This reached 91 per cent for licences, which is a measure of the successful engagement of offenders during the earlier stages of their licence supervision. The successful completion of the licence is a compliance measure, not a target.

In July 2006 the Home Office published its criminal justice review,[14] and in Chapter 2, 'Putting law-abiding people and communities first', it stated a commitment to speed up the recall to prison of offenders who breach their licence and to introduce a tough new target for serious offenders (para. 2.45). The probation, police and prison services and Home Office departments had worked together to produce a Joint Protocol[15] in January 2005 to ensure the sharing of information and the swift return to custody of offenders in breach of their licence (in particular those who posed a high risk of serious harm to the public) but there were no targets set for the end-to-end process, from the decision to breach and recommend recall to return to custody. An end-to-end target, covering individual police, probation and RRS targets, is being developed within the community penalties enforcement arena; there will be an overall or 'end-to-end' target set for the return to custody of all offenders, and one for those who present a higher risk of serious harm. Enforcement of licences therefore is part of the wider development within the NPS to achieve targets and measures set by ministerial priorities and practice standards.

The recall system: challenges for NOMS

Caseworkers within the Release and Recall Section and practitioners in the Probation Service are all part of NOMS. They are equally exercised

---

[14] *Rebalancing the Criminal Justice System in Favour of the Law-Abiding Majority* (Home Office 2006a).

[15] PC 03/2005: The Joint National Protocol: Supervision, Revocation and Recall for Prisoners Released on Licence.

by the challenges thrown up by the recall provisions, the public protection and performance-led culture and their desire to do a good job in terms of the offender and the public.

The system demands swift enforcement action by probation and by caseworkers in RRS. This demands that probation staff are using their professional judgment properly in a pressured environment, acting appropriately according to National Standards and enforcement targets, meeting what will be an end-to-end enforcement target and working within the aims of the Joint National Protocol and with the protection of the public as their number one priority.

RRS caseworkers must ensure procedural fairness; they must ensure that the offender is notified swiftly of the reasons for recall and their right to appeal; they must also ensure that the offender has a full understanding of their rights. To mitigate problems in informing offenders of the reasons for recall in a timely fashion, a process has been devised whereby all prisoners should be handed a letter when apprehended by the police, informing them of the reasons for recall and their right of appeal. Of course when an offender is arrested outside their home police/probation area this letter will not be available. This leads to problems in informing offenders, but also in the identification of prisoners as recalled offenders, with consequent delays in the process of review and re-release. Offenders are required to show this letter to reception staff at the prison establishment to aid identification. It is only when the offender is identified as a recalled offender and RRS is notified that the process can begin. Too many offenders have been returned to custody without notification to RRS. To ameliorate the situation, regular checks are made by NOMS staff of those offenders listed as unlawfully at large (UAL), i.e. their licence has been revoked.

The time-scale for the process is daunting, given the numbers of recalls. In too many cases return to custody following recall takes too long, and the offender must serve the time, no matter how long s/he is unlawfully at large. Targets for the police may ease this situation. There is also a commitment to continue to improve performance in issuing recall dossiers to prisoners.

There are serious challenges for the Prison Service in delivering a service to recalled offenders. There needs to be due attention paid to the management of the heightened suicide and self-harm risk of recalled prisoners through identification, support and advice; recalled prisoners also need to access regime activities and have a sentence plan that means they do not sit in custody biding their time, but have access to accommodation, benefits and employment advice at least.

The biggest challenges lie in ensuring the swift review of recall decisions by the Parole Board and the provision of high-quality reports to the Board with risk of serious harm and risk of reoffending assessments and recommendations on release in every case to enable the Board to make appropriate decisions. It is clear that managers within the Probation Service at senior level need to understand the recall provisions and the 'whole organisation' responsibility for risk assessments and risk management plans that are fit for purpose. Alongside this there needs to be an awareness by the Parole Board that not all offenders need the same intensity of supervision and management on release; the current propensity to be risk averse is not limited to the Probation Service.

The House of Lords judgment in the case of *Smith*[16] has set NOMS and the Parole Board a further set of challenges. The National Probation Directorate issued further guidance on oral hearings in 2005[17] to explain the nature of the oral hearing, the roles of the participants and how the hearings should be conducted. There has been a mixed experience by probation practitioners, and it is clear that the Probation Service needs to have practitioners trained, supported and equipped to perform effectively at Oral Hearings. It is some time since probation officers routinely appeared in court to present contentious Pre Sentence Reports (PSRs) and thus there are few staff members now with experience of appearing in a court setting, other than perhaps Crown Court Liaison Officers. In addition, the Secretary of State's Representative is not present at 'Smith and West' Oral Hearings, usually heard by a one-member panel. Often, representation from the Secretary of State could be seen as too passive, and there may need to be new measures established to ensure that the public protection is clearly articulated at the Panel Hearing.

Although there is a commitment to procedural fairness and high-quality professional practice in the assessment of offenders, in order to enable the Parole Board to release offenders appropriately there is an equal desire to provide an explanation of the victim impact and concerns.

Conclusion

The increase in recalls is thus set to continue if nothing changes in terms of legislation; the processes necessary to implement the law, including quite appropriately human rights legislation, the performance-led culture within NOMS and, importantly, policy that is led by the need to respond to media pressures. The response from the media, and not just the 'red tops', to high-profile sentences and serious further offences

---

[16] Judgments – *Regina* v. *Parole Board, ex parte Smith* and *Regina* v. *Parole Board ex parte West* [2005] UKHL 1.

[17] PC 76/2005: Oral Hearings: Further Guidance.

committed by those already under the supervision of the Probation Service is alarming. Reports are uninformed, inflammatory, accusatory and assume that 'we' can have – indeed are entitled to – a risk-free society. These cause insurmountable problems when they force changes in policy that leave agencies unable to put measures in place to manage offenders in the community; they inhibit discussion about what might really work, and make offenders and staff vulnerable.

The standard determinate sentence implemented for offences committed on or after 4 April 2006 is set to compound the problems of recall; with longer licences there are more chances of failure and more recalls. Government has also stated a commitment to extend the licences of those offenders sentenced under the Criminal Justice Act 1991 to their sentence expiry date: this will undoubtedly have an impact on the recall caseload. The roll out of the indeterminate sentence of Imprisonment for Public Protection (IPP) is causing problems in the management of the prison population with issues of prisoner movement and location. Recalled prisoners should return to their nearest local prison; if they are moved there are problems in ensuring that the recall dossier reaches them swiftly and that the probation report reaches them on the occasions when changes to the risk management plan really do need to be discussed.

With the size of the prison population, the number of recalls, and the number of departments, agencies and procedures needed to process recall, it is sometimes surprising that so much goes right rather than wrong.

The reasons behind the rate of recall present us with the most serious challenges in offender management. There are more offenders on longer licences with more chances of recall; the recall provisions enabling re-release call for more comprehensive reports of a high quality, with risk assessments and risk management plans needing to be updated and revised through OASys. National Probation Service Performance Targets on enforcement and 'end-to-end' targets published by government drive professional practice, particularly in a world leading to contestability. Prisoners are returned to prison and the Release and Recall Section are not notified; the process of review cannot start and frustrations build up. The 28-day timetable from notification of return to custody to review by the Parole Board is hugely difficult to meet.

When reports do not meet the standard needed to make decisions, the Parole Board is forced to set a further review date, i.e. to defer the decision for more information etc. Often, when a further charge is part of the behaviour causing an increased risk of reoffending or an increased risk of serious harm and more information is sought, nothing can be resolved speedily. Sometimes the Parole Board is looking for measures in a risk management plan that simply cannot be provided – usually these concern accommodation and drug and mental health services in the community. The increase in oral hearings following the Smith and West judgment compound the resourcing problems.

The challenge then for NOMS, the Parole Board and the police lies in having enough staff at appropriate levels, each with an understanding of the task and the training, skills, confidence and experience to carry it out while taking into account both the rights of the offender and the victim. The tragedy is that the problematic size of the prison population militates against good practice and the number of recalls exacerbates the problem of the prison population.

Chapter 11

A consideration of discretion, offender attributes and the process of recall

*Helen Collins**

The numbers of offenders being recalled back to prison in the United Kingdom has more than trebled in the last five years (Prison Reform Trust 2005) with recalled prisoners now accounting for almost 11 per cent of local prison populations (HMIP 2005b). It is suggested that this increase is not a reflection of increased reoffending but because of a decline in the use of professional discretion within the Probation Service:

> For the last four years, probation staff have been obliged to follow strict national standards on enforcement. Previously, there was greater professional discretion. The clear consequence of the change in policy has been a huge rise in the number of recalls and breaches, and, therefore, the prison population. (Fletcher 2003: 1)

From the 1980s onwards the criminal justice system has been increasingly subject to the principles of managerialism which highlights, among other things, performance targets and national standards, one of the associated effects being a restriction on the amount of discretion which professionals are able to use (Loader and Sparks 2002). A restriction in

*Comments, observations, etc. on this paper are welcome at: helen.collins42@btinternet. com.

the use of discretion can be beneficial as it avoids the potential for discrimination, which as Holloway and Grounds (2003) note is of real concern when this involves loss of liberty as in the case of recall. However, I would suggest that the use of discretion can also provide positive outcomes in that it allows for the use of 'mercy' (Hawkins 2003).

In addition to the rise of managerialism during the 1990s the Probation Service embraced a specific public protection agenda moving closer toward the assessment and management of risk. The resultant effect of this is that risk assessment and management has tended toward 'precautionary' or 'defensive' practice (Kemshall 1998a), 'there are few prizes for taking risks with offenders, only penalties' (Tuddenham 2000: 175). The new context for decision-making appears therefore to be one of decreased professional discretion, tighter guidelines and standards, and an emphasis upon risk management and public protection. Certainly the figures contained in the Annual Parole Board Reports for England and Wales (see Table 11.1) give credence to the argument that the dramatic rise in recall is not because of increased reoffending. For example, in the period 2003–2004, only 7 per cent of parolees were recalled for committing further offences and in 2004–2005 the corresponding figure was 6.5 per cent (see Maruna 2004 for a discussion of the issue in California).

Before routinely accepting this explanation, however, one must give consideration to research which shows how professionals working in other areas of the criminal justice system similarly affected by the principles of managerialism continue to use a level of discretion. For example, discretion has been highlighted within police officer decision-making indicating discriminatory practice in relation to ethnicity and decisions to stop and search people (Jones et al. 1986), in the courtroom in relation to gender and ethnicity (Hood 1992), in prison officer decision-making (Leibling and Price 2001) and within Discretionary Lifer Panels where cultural and personal factors seemed to influence decisions (Padfield and Liebling 2000: x). It is therefore quite feasible to suppose that probation officers continue to use discretion when making recall decisions within the confines of guidelines and standards.

Table 11.1 Recalls

	2001–2002	2002–2003	2003–2004	2004–2005
Number of recalls	4,885	7,246	9,031	9,320
Percentage increase from previous year		48%	24.6%	3.2%

Source: Parole Board Annual Reports 2003–2004, 2004–2005.

When reviewing previous research surrounding this subject conducted in the United States one finds contradictory conclusions. For example, Simon (1993) explored decisions relating to the revocation of licences and argued that agents were able to use discretion and resist the 'waste management model'. However, he concluded that while parole agents do have discretion at the local level they rarely exercise it. In contrast Lynch (1998) concluded that workers in parole resisted the trend towards managerialism and retained an individualistic approach to the supervision of offenders. Clear et al. (1992) concluded that 'substantial variation' existed in terms of officer responses to violations of supervision indicating that discretion was indeed in operation. The latter suggested that responses to violations were shaped by two factors, namely organisational policy, the agencies' formal rules and procedures and organisational tradition introducing the importance of organisational culture into the analysis. Similarly Reitz (2004) points to the 'sensitivity' of the supervision system which can be influenced by a number of factors, including the institutional culture of the field service. As part of my Cambridge Masters degree this was to be my starting point. I wanted to know if officers were utilising a level of discretion or simply following a mechanistic process, and if there were any correlations in terms of officer attributes and decisions reached.

The current research methodology

This study was conducted in County Durham Probation Area, an area largely rural in its geographical make-up. Two methods of data collection were used, namely questionnaires and an analysis of files. The questionnaires distributed to 63 officers asked for basic demographic information such as gender and length in service which allowed an examination of any correlations associated with decisions made. Two hypothetical cases were presented. Case One concerns an offender subject to Discretionary Conditional Release (DCR) who is in breach of his licence for being charged with a further unrelated offence. Case Two concerns an offender subject to Automatic Conditional Release (ACR) who is in breach of his licence for technical violations in the form of failing to attend appointments.

The rationale for examining two different types of breach of licence was to see if there was any difference in officers' responses, drawing on the premise that there would be more of a uniform response to Case One which involved further offending. The types of enforcement action which the officers were able to initiate were Expedited Recall, Non-Expedited Recall, Assistant Chief Officer Warning (ACO), Formal Warning, Home Visit (prior to taking action) and Other.

Also contained in the questionnaire were some open questions, one of which requested information about previous decisions and consequences, the aim being to identify whether 'risk aversion' was influential. In other words, had the officer made a previous decision not to recall which had negative consequences, the assumption being that had this been the case then the officer would be more likely to err on the side of caution and initiate the most severe enforcement sanction. A total of 29 completed questionnaires were returned which provided a sample of 65.5 per cent probation officers and 34.5 per cent probation service officers and 41.4 per cent males and 58.6 per cent females, while 89.7 per cent of all officers had been involved in a decision to recall a licence. The officers' length in service and age can be seen in Tables 11.2 and 11.3.

The data derived from the questionnaires was then inputted into the Statistical Package for the Social Sciences (SPSS) and analysed using descriptive statistics, chosen because of the small sample size. Phi and Cramers V tests were used to measure the association between variables to ascertain whether this was significant at the level .05 or lower, meaning least likely to be attributable to chance.

In addition data was collected from the case files of a sample of offenders supervised on licence between 1 January 2004 and 31 October 2004. This time period avoided any potential impact of the Criminal Justice Act 2003 recall and revocation procedures, and the revised National Standards for supervision of licences. In total 66 case files were examined, comprising 33 successful completions and 33 recalls. Details of supervising officer, variables such as type of licence and information

Table 11.2 Length in service

Years	Frequency	%
–5	14	48.3
5–10	9	31.0
11–15	3	10.3
16–20	1	3.4
21 +	2	6.9

Table 11.3 Officer age

Years	Frequency	%
–25	2	6.9
25–35	7	24.1
36–45	11	37.9
46–50	2	6.9
50 +	7	24.1
Total	29	100.0

derived from the OASys assessment tool were collected and analysed in the same way as the data derived from the questionnaires. Each case file has within it a contact log, which is an account of all the interactions with the offender. I was able to identify from reading the case file log whether a breach of licence had occurred and what the officer's response was. Of course in reality the use of discretion is constrained by National Standards and licence conditions. However, discretion is a choice within the rules, and was measured and reported to have been used if an offender did not comply with the noted conditions and standards but the officer initiated an alternative course of action other than recall, also if an officer followed the process, for example issued a warning letter, but accompanied this with another response, such as a home visit, to attempt to re-engage with the offender.

The case file analysis provided a sample of offenders the majority of whom were subject to Automatic Conditional Release for offences of either a violent nature or for theft and dishonesty as can be seen in Tables 11.4 and 11.5.

Methodological limitations

Both methods of data collection employed have limitations which it is useful to acknowledge at this point. While questionnaires are a relatively

Table 11.4 Type of licence

	Frequency	%
Young Offender Institute (YOI)	25	37.9
Automatic Conditional Release (ACR)	33	50.0
Discretionary Conditional Release (DCR)	8	12.1
Total	66	100.0

Table 11.5 Current offence

	Frequency	%
Drug	7	10.6
Violence	25	37.9
Sexual	1	1.5
Motor vehicle	8	12.1
Theft/dishonesty	24	36.4
Other	1	1.5
Total	66	100.0

cheap and efficient method of collecting data respondents may not have accurately reported their beliefs, particularly as I occupied a higher level of grade to the respondents. It may be that the findings were influenced by a socially desirable response bias (Robson 2002). In other words the respondents may have indicated that they would initiate a more lenient or punitive response to the breach in order to present more favourably. Also problematic is the size of the sample. Just under half of the questionnaires sent out were returned, meaning that the results may not be representative and readily generalisable to officers in both County Durham and the service in general. Moreover, file analysis is notoriously difficult since files are often incomplete and, of course, were constructed for purposes other than research (Garfinkel 1967). The level and quality of recording varied in the files and did not always give an indication of the process which the officer went through in terms of decision-making. One must allow for the fact that alternative courses of action other than recall may have been considered but not recorded. Also when interpreting the data collected from OASys one must also bear in mind that actuarial risk assessments are not entirely objective and are produced through the judgment of the assessor. This means that the data is subject to the officers' interpretation and that different officers could produce different assessments on the basis of the same information (Rex 2001; Stephens and Brown 2001).

The findings

As noted, two hypothetical cases were presented to officers within the questionnaire. Enforcement action taken in relation to Case One varied considerably. Only one officer initiated Expedited Recall, three initiated Non-Expedited Recall, 16 initiated an Assistant Chief Officer Warning, seven initiated a Formal Warning, and one initiated a Home Visit prior to any enforcement action being initiated (see Table 11.6).

In Case Two the enforcement action initiated varied more widely. As can be seen in Table 11.7, seven officers initiated Non-Expedited Recall, 11 an Assistant Chief Officer Warning, one a Formal Warning, and nine a Home Visit.

All officers in the sample received exactly the same hypothetical case scenarios. The findings therefore fail to identify any real consistency among officers in their response to offender behaviour, and showed that they were not all responding in a simple mechanistic way thus supporting the findings of Clear et al. (1992) and Lynch (1998). Taking the analysis further and exploring any correlations between decisions made and the demographic variables of the officer, gender, grade and age were found to be non-significant. Interestingly the qualification which officers held was also found in this study to be non-significant.

Table 11.6 Distribution of responses – Case One

Response	Frequency	%
Expedited Recall	1	3.4
Non-Expedited Recall	3	10.3
ACO Warning	16	55.2
Formal Warning	7	24.1
Home Visit	1	3.4
Other	1	3.4
Total	29	100.0

Table 11.7 Distribution of responses – Case Two

Response	Frequency	%
Non-Expedited Recall	7	24.1
ACO Warning	11	37.9
Formal Warning	1	3.4
Home Visit	9	31.0
Other	1	3.4
Total	29	100.0

A probation officer can qualify via the following means: Certificate of Qualification in Social Work (CQSW), Diploma in Social Work and Diploma in Probation Studies. One might have expected that the officers who qualified via the more traditional social work route of CQSW to have been more lenient in their response, given the orientation of this training to resist the more controlling aspects of enforcement (Raynor 2003). However, this expectation was not borne out by the results which do not support previous findings suggesting that training in a social work discipline appears to be related to a less punitive orientation (for example, see Brennan and Khunduka 1970).

Length in service was found in this study to be statistically significant in both Case One and Two, showing that more officers in service for 11–15 years initiate the most severe sanctions and are less likely to conduct a home visit prior to making a decision (see Tables 11.8 and 11.9). This supports the findings of Eskridge (1979) who found that, regardless of initial orientation or level of education, officers become more conservative. The finding may mean that the longer an officer is in service the more likely they are to operate a level of risk aversion. However, it is also common practice for the more experienced officers to

Table 11.8 Length in service – Case One

Enforcement action		–5	5–10	11–15	16–20	21+
Expedited Recall	Count	0	0	1	0	0
	% within length in service	0.0	0.0	33.3	0.0	0.0
Non-Expedited Recall	Count	1	0	1	0	1
	% within length in service	7.1	0.0	33.3	0.0	50.0
ACO Warning	Count	7	7	1	1	0
	% within length in service	50.0	77.8	33.3	100.0	0.0
Formal Warning	Count	6	1	0	0	0
	% within length in service	42.9	11.1	0.0	0.0	0.0
Home Visit	Count	0	1	0	0	0
	% within length in service	0.0	11.1	0.0	0.0	0.0
Other	Count	0	0	0	0	1
	% within length in service	0.0	0.0	0.0	0.0	50.0

be allocated the more complex and higher-risk cases which could account in some way for their response. A note of caution must be exercised with this conclusion given the fact that only three officers in the sample had 11–15 years length in service.

In terms of risk aversion I began from the premise that if an officer had taken a decision not to recall previously and that this had resulted in

Table 11.9 Length in service – Case Two

Enforcement action		–5	5–10	11–15	16–20	21+
Expedited Recall	Count	0	0	0	0	0
	% within length in service	0.0	0.0	0.0	0.0	0.0
Non-Expedited Recall	Count	3	3	3	0	0
	% within length in service	21.4	33.3	33.3	0.0	0.0
ACO Warning	Count	6	2	1	0	2
	% within length in service	42.9	22.2	33.3	0.0	100.0
Formal Warning	Count	0	0	0	1	0
	% within length in service	0.0	0.0	0.0	100.0	0.0
Home Visit	Count	5	3	1	0	0
	% within length in service	35.7	33.3	33.3	0.0	0.0
Other	Count	0	1	0	0	0
	% within length in service	0.0	11.1	0.0	0.0	0.0

negative consequences, then they may err on the side of caution and initiate the most severe sanction. Again this factor was not shown to be statistically significant and contrary to my original thoughts did not suggest that risk aversion is in operation.

In summary the only factor which was found to be statistically significant was length in service, though a note of caution must be exercised with this result. Furthermore, factors which in this analysis are shown to be non-significant may in fact have a very significant bearing on decision-making, but do not emerge as such because of such a small sample size. Future research may benefit from using a larger sample and also from combining in the analysis factors such as individual personality traits of officers. The use of a professional orientation survey such as the Klofas-Toch (1982) which measures characteristics such as punitive orientation may be beneficial.

The supposition that officers would use professional discretion within the standards and guidelines is further supported by the findings from the case file analysis which comprised 13 officers supervising licences. From the analysis it was not possible to ascertain whether four officers in the sample utilised discretion in their decision-making. This does not necessarily mean that they did not, as one must allow for the fact that alternative courses of action may have been considered but not recorded. However, the evidence from an analysis of both recalls and successful completions of licences illustrated that nine officers in the sample did use a level of discretion in their responses by initiating an alternative course of action other than recall or another action alongside the process. In terms of the demographics of the officers again no clear patterns were found which I was able to correlate with the use of discretion, with variations in gender, grade, qualification, length of service and age. In summary this study found that the majority of officers are not responding to breaches of licence in a purely mechanistic way but are utilising a level of discretion within the confines of standards and guidelines, a finding which I view positively. However, given the wide variation, particularly in terms of the hypothetical breaches, and in order to avoid discrimination and injustice, managers and Assistant Chief Officers must actively review cases before the final checks and balances are provided by the Parole Board.

In this sample out of the 33 cases just over half were recalled for committing further offences[1] (see Table 11.10).

This finding does not correspond to the national trend showing that the majority of offenders are recalled for technical violations of their

---

[1] It should be noted that a significant number of those offenders recalled for further offences were also failing to attend appointments but the further offence was taken as the main reason for the recall. In fact a number of those offenders were remanded in custody.

Table 11.10 Reason for recall

Reason for recall	Technical[2]	Further offences
Number	16	17
Per cent	48.5%	51.5%

licence (Annual Report and Accounts of the Parole Board for England and Wales 2003–2004) and could be interpreted in a number of ways. For example, the reasons for recalls could correlate solely with the reoffending rates of offenders in the area. However, it would be difficult to accept that offenders living in County Durham are reoffending significantly more than offenders resident in other parts of the country. Alternatively it could be argued that the police in the County Durham area are more effective at detecting and prosecuting. Certainly the percentage of recorded offences brought to justice for 2004–05 was 26.8 per cent, which is noted to be well above the nearest equivalent force average of 20.8 per cent (Durham Police Authority Annual Report 2004/2005). My own hypothesis, however, is that the pattern captured in this study provides further support for the supposition that officers continue to use a level of discretion which is strongly influenced by the organisational culture of the service in Durham. The service promotes a 'culture of compliance' (Bruce 2003), and I would suggest that the 'basic assumptions' held by staff are that recall is a last resort. This is perhaps best illustrated by the compliance data collected nationally. For instance, in the period April to September 2005 Durham had, along with Warwickshire, the country's highest compliance rate of 90 per cent (Home Office 2005/06). In order to promote a more tolerant and individualised approach to recall I would suggest that a focus on the organisational culture of the service is necessary and critical to an understanding of discretion and decision-making.

In terms of correlations with offender attributes type of licence was not found to be statistically significant with only slightly more young offenders being recalled than those subject to either Automatic or Discretionary Release. Current offence was found to be significant at the level .025. Offenders on licence for offences of theft or dishonesty were more likely to be recalled, 62.5 per cent, followed closely by violence at 56 per cent. This finding lends support to research which identifies that property offenders are more likely to fail on probation, the general theme being that they reoffend more quickly than those offenders convicted of

---

[2] Technical breaches were unacceptable absences, entering exclusion zones and failing to notify of a change of address.

Table 11.11 Current offence and drug use

OASys drug use		Current offence: theft/dishonesty
−4	Count	3
	% within current offence	12.5%
+4	Count	20
	% within current offence	83.3%

violent offences (see Petersilia 1985). However, I propose that it is the level of drug misuse and the link with acquisitive crime (South 2002) which is the significant factor rather than the type of current offence. As can be seen in Table 11.11, 83.3 per cent of offenders subject to licence for offences of theft or dishonesty have drug use identified as a criminogenic factor.

Risk of reoffending was found to be significant at the level .006. Only 35.3 per cent of those offenders assessed as being at medium risk were recalled as opposed to 62.8 per cent of those assessed as high risk, a finding which could be used to lend support to the predictive power of actuarial risk assessment tools such as OASys. Risk of harm was not found to be significant with broadly the same number of offenders recalled falling within each category. I had expected that recall would be initiated more often in the cases of those offenders who were assessed as presenting a higher risk of harm to the public. The reason that this was not the case could be linked to the fact that those offenders who were assessed as presenting a higher risk of harm to the public were not subject to licence for offences of theft or dishonesty who, as shown previously, are significantly more likely to be recalled. Similarly, whether or not the offender had dependants and their level of alcohol use were not found to be statistically significant in relation to being recalled.

Those factors which did correlate as being statistically significant are outlined in Table 11.12. For example, 93.9 per cent of those offenders recalled had education identified as a criminogenic need, a finding which supports previous research showing that the higher the level of education the more likely the offender would succeed on probation (see Morgan 1994). This could be related to the fact that the more educational qualifications a person has the more likely they are to secure employment, a factor which was found in this study to be least likely to be the product of chance and a factor consistently associated with successful probation outcome (see Sims and Jones 1997). The findings also indicate that offenders who are in a long-term relationship are less likely to be recalled again supporting previous studies showing a positive correlation between stable relationship and probation success (Sims and Jones

Table 11.12 Criminogenic factors correlated with recall

Identified criminogenic need	% of offenders recalled	Statistical significance
Education	93.9	.005
Employment	97.0	.001
Drug	81.8	.003
Accommodation	69.7	.003
In relationship over one year	12.1	.050

1997). While I have been unable to find any previous research which looked at the correlation between an offender's accommodation and outcome of supervision, the finding that 69.7 per cent of offenders recalled had identified problematic accommodation is perhaps unsurprising. It stands to reason that if an offender has stable accommodation then they are more likely to be able to comply with the requirements of licence supervision.

Some conclusions and implications for practice

Offenders sentenced to prison often have a number of complex needs such as drug dependency, low educational attainment, limited employment opportunities, homelessness and debt. Imprisonment exacerbates the disadvantaged circumstances which many offenders face prior to their incarceration: 'A third lose their accommodation, two-thirds lose their employment, over a fifth come out facing increased financial problems, over two-fifths lose contact with the families' (Morgan 2004: 4). While one must bear in mind the danger of making conclusions about spurious relationships and accepting that correlation does not equate to cause, the present study found that those offenders more likely to be recalled were also the most disadvantaged. This I would suggest provides more reason to rethink the current strategy for the management of post-release licences: that a return to prison should be reserved for those offenders who pose a risk of harm to the public rather than automatically returning all offenders to an overcrowded prison system only to release them again often to the same set of circumstances in place prior to the recall. Certainly research, again conducted in the United States, suggests that the use of prison recall is an ineffective and costly means of reducing crime (Re-Entry Policy Council 2005), sentiments echoed in this country by organisations such as the Prison Reform Trust. Perhaps when one considers the actual treatment of offenders recalled back to prison the debate becomes even more acute. In a recent HMP

Thematic Inspection (HMIP 2005b) it was found that recalled prisoners often have limited understanding of their situation which, after consideration of the fact that some offenders are recalled because of some 'personal setback' (HMIP 2005b), does raise concern:

> Mr B was sentenced initially to an eighteen-month custodial period and a period of four years on extended licence. He was released having served nine months of the eighteen-month custodial element. His licence was revoked three months later after he wrote a farewell note to his ex-partner with whom he was banned from communicating under the terms of his licence. The following day the police arrested him in the early hours of the morning. His re-release date was calculated to the end of his extended licence, which was over four years later. A slip containing this information was sent to Mr B through the prison's internal postal system and was received three days after his return to prison on a Saturday when staffing was at a reduced level. The slip gave no other information. The recall dossier containing the reason for recall and information about the right to appeal arrived in the prison the day after Mr B hanged himself. (HMIP 2005b: 16)

HM Inspectorate of Probation recently highlighted serious failings on the part of the Probation Service in the management of two offenders, including non-adherence to National Standards (see HMIP 2006a). While I am not proposing a deviation from standards and reiterate that a recall to custody is the only defensible option for those offenders whose behaviour indicates a potential risk of serious harm to the public, what I am suggesting is a more considered response to breaches of licence conditions. Where there is no indication of a risk of harm to the public rather than adopting a 'blanket' approach, the application of professional discretion and a more graduated response to recall I believe would be more beneficial. For example, the processing of those cases not deemed to pose a risk of harm to the public could be administered through the courts which would allow the application of the same enforcement procedures to licences as with community penalties. 'Criminological theory, along with a limited body of evidence, suggests that swift, certain, graduated responses, when coupled with immediate offender accountability, can help increase compliance with supervision and may provide a more cost-effective approach than re-incarceration' (Re-Entry Policy Council 2005: 29). This study and the recent Thematic Inspection identified significant numbers of recalled offenders who have identified problematic drug misuse. I would suggest that the model set by the review courts in relation to drug treatment and testing orders, which require the judge and all other interested parties to work together to monitor the progress of the offender, is worth considering (Senjo and Leip 2001). When an offender breaches their licence the court could give consideration to recall or alternatively deal with the breach by way of the imposition of a further sentence, for example a drug rehabilitation requirement to run alongside their licence. Alternatively, for some offenders a warning by a member of the judiciary and an additional punishment such as a specified amount of unpaid work may effect a successful completion of the licence. This graduated response to breaches of licence is already in operation in some US states. For example, in Utah, Community Review Boards can respond to violations of parole by instructing the offender to complete a specified number of community service hours, to comply with treatment referrals or to undertake some form of restorative justice to the victim. Certainly positive outcomes have been shown to result from this response in the US state of Georgia; successful completions of parole licences increased from 61 per cent to 72 per cent in the period 1998–2002 (Re-entry Policy Council 2005). Recent developments have seen closer alignment of the National Standards for supervision of offenders on licence and community orders based on the premise of tiering (Home Office 2005).

For instance all offenders subject to both community orders and licences now report a minimum of weekly for the first 16 weeks of supervision. Similarly the recently published *Rebalancing the Criminal Justice System* (Home Office 2006a) proposes consideration be given to providing probation staff with the power to vary punishment for breaches of orders without having to return the offender to court. Aligning the sanctions available for breach of licence to those available for breach of community order would simply continue this development. While the operation of two tandem systems for dealing with breaches of licence would require a whole reconfiguration of the current system, it is not inconceivable and is currently in operation with respect to young offenders subject to licence. Recently Anne Owers, Chief Inspector of Prisons, stated: 'There is an urgent need for NOMS, together with relevant prison and probation managers and the Parole Board, to undertake a wholesale review of recalled prisoners status and needs and to consider how best to manage them' (HMIP 2005b: 5). Perhaps if the steep rise in the numbers of offenders recalled is to be halted then a radical rethink of the whole process and policy is necessary and consideration of a graduated response worthwhile.

I conclude in the hope that this small-scale study has furthered our understanding of the factors associated with recall and gives some impetus for future research and discussion.

Chapter 12

Recalls: contested facts and risk assessment

Hamish Arnott

Introduction

Prisoners will necessarily have experienced the normal criminal court process before they come before the Parole Board. The experience of the procedural and evidential safeguards of the criminal process can lead to unrealistic assumptions about how the Board will approach its task of deciding whether the prisoner poses a sufficiently low risk to be released. This is especially so where issues of contested fact arise. Although, while serving a sentence, prisoners will be subjected to a wide range of administrative decision-making where the most basic standards of procedural fairness apply,[1] there often remains an expectation that if a matter has not been the subject of a formal prison disciplinary hearing (where the standard of proof and exclusion of hearsay evidence, at least in theory, mirrors that in the criminal courts) it should not be taken into account in any formal decision-making process. This concern is at its highest in the parole process, particularly when offenders are recalled to prison from liberty in the community facing allegations of criminal or other conduct in breach of their licence.

---

[1] For example, in decisions affecting security category and the prisoner's level on the incentives and earned privileges scheme.

Although the Parole Board is part of the machinery for managing sentences imposed by the courts, it is still often required to resolve issues of disputed fact. These can relate to matters that occur while the prisoner is serving the sentence (such as whether an assault was committed), but most obviously when offenders are recalled to custody. It is where such contested facts are in issue that the degree to which the Board provides a sufficiently adversarial procedure[2] is most questioned, as in the vast majority of recall cases the existence of the disputed facts will be determinative as to whether recall is justified. The need for the fair consideration of disputed facts was one of the key reasons the House of Lords decided that oral hearings would in most cases be necessary to determine whether fixed-term prisoners should be recalled.[3]

There is a tension between the task of deciding facts and assessing risks. This paper seeks to examine this in the parole context by reference to other legal contexts where these issues arise. It will then examine some of the practical issues this tension gives rise to and suggest ways in which procedures should be adopted to ensure fairness in the recall process involving both determinate and indeterminate sentences.

Assessing facts/assessing risks

The core Parole Board function of assessing risk to the public (of dangerousness for those serving indeterminate sentences and of committing further offences for fixed-term prisoners) is of course very different to deciding whether a defendant has committed a criminal act. In the recall context the role of the criminal courts in considering whether an offender should be recalled was limited to short-term prisoners under the Criminal Justice Act 1991 (those serving fewer than four years) and this role was removed from January 1999.[4] Risk has been held to be an object of 'intellectual intuition',[5] by its very nature not something that can be objectively determined. The notion of indefinite detention dependent on an assessor's 'intuition' raises alarm bells of arbitrariness, which is why the Convention when Article 5 is engaged requires an expert body acting as a court, such as the Parole Board, to provide a review 'wide enough to bear on those conditions which, under the

---

[2] Required when Article 5 is engaged: *Hussain and Singh* v. *UK* (1996) 22 EHRR 1, para. 60.
[3] *R (on the application of Smith)* v. *Parole Board* [2005] UKHL 1.
[4] By the Crime and Disorder Act 1998.
[5] *R (on the application of Hirst)* v. *Parole Board and another* [2002] EWHC 1592 (Admin) para. 83.

ECHR, are essential for the lawful detention of a person in the situation of the particular detainee'.[6]

But even with such a body, there remains for prisoners something very 'un-legal' about the process of risk assessment, and there is often bewilderment that lengthy periods of imprisonment are consequent on expressions of what amount to 'mere opinion' (including a wide range of reports from non-experts in parole dossiers). The problems that legal processes have with 'being' rather than 'doing' was recently explored in a concurring judgment of Judge Zupančič in the European Court of Human Rights, where the French system of providing for aggravated sentences for those identified as recidivists was examined:

A status cannot be properly litigated. If we speak of the status of 'being' a drug addict, murderer, robber, arsonist etc., both the major and the minor premises of the syllogism are fuzzy, vague and indistinct. Such fuzziness – for example, because it is not subject to controversy – is permitted in a medical diagnosis. In law, the vagueness reduces to nothing both the procedural and the substantive safeguards.[7]

This of course casts the issue in a rather stark light and there are many instances beyond the parole context where English courts and tribunals are charged with determining status (such as whether an asylum seeker is a refugee, or whether a patient is suffering from a mental disorder sufficient to warrant detention), or with deciding whether someone poses such risk as to warrant the imposition of preventative measures (such as anti-social behaviour orders, sex offender prevention orders and football banning orders).[8]

However, the fact that a court or tribunal is tasked with assessing risk to the public does often result in a blurring of the functions of fact-finding and risk assessment. Laws LJ has observed in the context of a case involving national security:

... our law is no stranger to the prevention of risk. Its processes are not limited to the allocation of legal consequences on proof of facts. This is unsurprising. The prevention of risk may be a very powerful

---

[6] *Smith* above, note 3.

[7] *Achour* v. *France* ECtHR App. No. 67335/01 29/3/06, where reference was also made to the Supreme Court case of *Robinson* v. *California*, 370 US 660 (1962), where the criminalisation of the *status* of being a drug addict was held to be unconstitutional.

[8] The 'legislative technique' of these measures was described as 'the use of the civil remedy of an injunction to prohibit conduct considered to be utterly unacceptable, with a remedy of criminal penalties in the event of disobedience' by Lord Steyn in *R (McCann)* v. *Crown Court at Manchester* [2002] UKHL 39, para. 17.

imperative; powerful enough, in reason, to justify the imposition of legal sanctions or burdens where there is no conventional proof that this or that has happened or will happen. It is true that in the instances I have mentioned relating to personal injury and crime, a case will at least have first been proved against the defendant before he has to pay for unproved risks. He will have been shown to have been negligent, or to have committed the crime in question, according to the appropriate standard of proof. The sanction imposed upon him for the prevention of risk – additional damages, longer imprisonment – is not the whole substance of the case against him.[9]

Context, as always, is important in determining the degree to which the court or tribunal should be required to make findings of fact. In the asylum context the purpose of the proceedings is to ensure that asylum applicants are not returned to face torture or other persecution in their countries of origin. Accordingly it would be inappropriate to fix a burden on the asylum seeker of establishing the facts of his/her case to, for example, any particular standard. Sedley LJ has stated:

> The question whether an applicant for asylum is within the protection of the 1951 Convention is not a head-to-head litigation issue. Testing a claim ordinarily involves no choice between two conflicting accounts but an evaluation of the intrinsic and extrinsic credibility, and ultimately the significance, of the applicant's case ... Such decision-makers, on classic principles of public law, are required to take everything material into account. Their sources of information will frequently go well beyond the testimony of the applicant and include in-country reports, expert testimony and – sometimes – specialised knowledge of their own (which must of course be disclosed). No probabilistic cut-off operates here: everything capable of having a bearing has to be given the weight, great or little, due to it. What the decision-makers ultimately make of the material is a matter for their own conscientious judgment, so long as the procedure by which they approach and entertain it is lawful and fair and provided their decision logically addresses the Convention issues. Finally, and importantly, the Convention issues from first to last are evaluative, not factual. The facts, so far as they can be established, are signposts on the road to a conclusion on the issues; they are not themselves conclusions. How far this process truly differs from civil or criminal litigation need not detain us now.[10]

---

[9] *A and others* v. *Home Secretary* [2004] EWCA Civ 1123, paras 157–159 – the challenge in the Court of Appeal to the indefinite detention of foreign national terror suspects.

[10] *Karanakaran* v. *Home Secretary* [2000] 3 All ER 449, CA, para. 18.

At the other extreme and perhaps more problematically, in the national security context when charged with deciding whether a person should be deported on national security grounds Lord Hoffman has stated that the question as to whether deportation was justified 'cannot be answered by taking each allegation [of past conduct] seriatim and deciding whether it has been established to some standard of proof. It is a question of evaluation and judgement'.[11] This decision was explicitly set in the context of the deference the courts will accord to the executive in national security issues. But the approach does result in a concern over the 'fuzziness' of the legal process involved when the outcome may have such serious consequences for the deportee (although of course the counter-argument is that a wrong decision the other way would have catastrophic effects for society).

The asylum and national security contexts are at opposite ends of the spectrum in terms of how the individual is treated by the state but the approach appears to be the same. The drastic consequences of getting a decision wrong lead to an approach where an holistic evaluative approach to determine the question in issue replaces a forensic approach to fact finding.

But different legal contexts will require different approaches. As noted by Lord Nicholls in a childcare case:

> The legal context may permit, or require, the decision maker to take into account a real possibility that a past event occurred, or even a mere possibility. Rationality does not require that only past events established on a balance of probabilities can be taken into account. Or the context may require otherwise. The range of matters the decision maker may take into account when carrying out this exercise depends upon the context. This, again, is a question of legal policy, not logic.[12]

Recalls and disputed facts

In the parole context, as noted above, the starting point of the risk assessment process is the conviction itself, made after the sentencing court has ascertained the relevant facts. But the approach of the Board when considering the initial release of a prisoner must differ to that when recall is in issue. Although the ultimate test, that is whether the offender poses such a risk as to justify further detention, is the same as

---

[11] *Home Secretary* v. *Rehman* [2001] UKHL 47, para. 56
[12] *In re O and N* [2003] UKHL 18, para. 13.

that which pertains on original release,[13] the offender is in a significantly different position when returned to custody from the community. Since the creation of the Board in 1968 this has been recognised by the granting of directive powers of release in recall cases even when this had not been held to be required by the Convention.

All indeterminate prisoners will already have been assessed by the Board as posing a sufficiently low risk to the public to warrant release. Fixed-term prisoners may similarly have been released by the Board, or are in the community because of a statutory presumption that they can be managed in the community. Accordingly, while the sentence provides the legal basis for redetention, recall will only occur after adverse developments in the community. As Bingham LJ (as he then was) noted when confirming the ultimate test for release remained the same for recalls as for initial release:

> If a prisoner has been released because the Board was satisfied [the statutory test for release was met], and nothing has changed, it would be absurd and oppressive if, following recall and review [under the relevant statutory powers] the board were not entitled to direct immediate release. There must in practice be some relevant new material to justify the board's reconsideration of the substance of the case.[14]

This clearly calls for a distinct two-stage approach by the Board, namely to decide whether the facts giving rise to recall are made out, and then to decide whether the risk threshold is met for redetention. While the impact of the Parole Board getting a decision wrong must never be underestimated this is a very different situation to that which pertains in asylum or national security deportation cases.

There are examples of this two-stage approach being adopted in other contexts where the ultimate aim of the court or tribunal in question is to prevent risk to the public. Where courts are deciding whether to impose ASBOs, for example, firstly the court has to decide whether someone 'has acted in an anti-social manner' and then whether an ASBO is necessary to protect the public 'from further anti-social acts'.[15] The House of Lords has decided that while proceedings imposing ASBOs are civil, the facts determining whether a person meets the threshold for their imposition need to be established to the criminal standard.[16]

The example that has maybe been most cited in the parole and mental health contexts is how the courts are required to approach the decision

---

[13] R v. Parole Board ex parte Watson [1996] 1 WLR 906.
[14] Watson above, note 13, 916D.
[15] Section 1(1), Crime and Disorder Act 1998.
[16] McCann above, note 8.

as to whether to make a care order in respect of a child. The power only arises if the court is 'satisfied' that the child 'is suffering, or is likely to suffer, significant harm'. The House of Lords has held that this requires the court to be satisfied to the civil standard of proof (with the more serious the allegation more cogent evidence being required) of facts to establish the threshold condition for imposition of the care order.[17]

The approach in care order cases has recently been examined in the mental health context. It has been held that in deciding whether to discharge patients detained under the Mental Health Act that the proper approach is the same as determining the facts in childcare cases:

> If there is some specific allegation of past conduct which is being relied upon then the Tribunal must decide as a matter of fact, and applying the ordinary civil standard of proof, whether the allegation has been proved. If it is not proved then it cannot of itself be the basis for any continuing detention of the patient.[18]

Oral hearings before the Parole Board were of course modelled on the Mental Health Review Tribunals. One key difference from the parole context is that the tribunal will be the first occasion on which there has been a judicial determination of the issues. Accordingly the Convention requires that the burden of proof (to the extent that this will make a difference) is on the state to justify the need for detention under Article 5.[19] This is different to how the courts have interpreted the burden of proof issue in parole cases (see below) even though the courts have often held that the two legal processes provide perhaps the closest analogy.

The care order approach to contested facts has been relied upon in challenges to recall decisions. In one case which examined the extent to which the Board is entitled to take into account hearsay evidence the judge considered that the care proceedings analogy was 'remote from this jurisdiction'.[20] However, in a case involving a discretionary lifer recalled in relation to an allegation of rape, the Board adopted the approach and this appeared to be endorsed by the Court of Appeal, Wall LJ stating:

---

[17] *In re H (minors) (Sexual abuse: standard of proof)* [1996] AC 563 – when assessing the probabilities the court will have in mind as a factor, to whatever extent is appropriate in the particular case, that the more serious the allegation the less likely it is that the event occurred and, hence, the stronger should be the evidence before the court concludes that the allegation is established on the balance of probabilities.

[18] *R (AN) and another* v. *MHRT (Northern Region) and others* [2005] EWHC 587 (Admin), para. 114, a decision upheld on this point by the Court of Appeal [2005] EWCA Civ 1605.

[19] *R (H)* v. *MHRT North and East London Region and another* [2001] EWCA Civ 415.

[20] *R (Sim)* v. *Parole Board* [2003] EWHC 152 (Admin), para. 60.

The way in which the Board went about its task followed the overall approach laid down in *Re H* namely (1) it looked at the totality of the evidence; (2) it assessed that evidence critically in order to decide what facts were established on the *Re H* balance of probability/standard of proof test; and (3) it then, on the basis of the facts it found, made its assessment as to whether or not it was any longer necessary for the protection of the public for the claimant to be detained. There is no rationality attack on the reasons, nor in my judgment could there be.[21]

Burdens of proof/default positions

Although it is clear that the Board will apply the civil standard of proof when deciding facts,[22] the degree to which parole hearings are required to be 'adversarial' is also tied up with the issue of whether there is in truth a burden of proof and also the quality of the evidence upon which the Board is entitled to rely. The House of Lords has held that the determination as to whether an offender should be recalled to prison does not amount to a 'criminal charge' within the meaning of Article 6 of the Convention, essentially as the purpose of recall is preventative not punitive.[23]

The courts have also been resistant to the notion of there being any burden of proof in parole cases. However, this has been decided in the context of the core task of assessing risk. In relation to indeterminate sentences the rationale for this is that they are either imposed after a finding of dangerousness by the court, or by a finding of guilt of such a serious offence that it is reasonable to expect the prisoner to displace the presumption.[24] Similarly it has long been held in relation to indeterminate sentences that the threshold of dangerousness found by the Board to warrant post-tariff detention may be lower than that required to justify the imposition of the life sentence – accordingly the degree of risk sufficient to detain a lifer post-tariff is merely one that is substantial.[25] This marks a distinction from the mental health context where the Court of Appeal has recently held that the civil standard of proof should not just apply to the establishing facts, but also to the 'predictive' role of the tribunal, although this might not actually make much difference 'given the limited role that the

---

[21] *R (Brooks)* v. *Parole Board* [2004] EWCA Civ 80, Wall LJ para. 78.

[22] *Brooks* above, note 21, para. 28.

[23] *Smith* v. *Parole Board* above, note 3.

[24] See *R* v. *Lichniak* [2003] 1 AC 903, para. 15; *R (Henry)* v. *Parole Board and another* [2004] EWHC 784 (Admin).

[25] *R* v. *Parole Board ex parte Bradley* [1991] 1 WLR 134.

standard of proof will have in relation to matters of judgement and evaluation'.[26]

However, as noted above, the presumption of necessity for detention is to an extent reversed in recall cases (in the case of extended sentences the court has gone so far as to hold that the Board should approach even the question of risk in recall cases on the basis that the 'default position' is liberty).[27] This must impact upon the way in which the Board in practice decides whether the fresh factual matrix warrants recall.

In the parole context there is a distinction between the applicable standard of proof and the quality of evidence that can be taken into account when establishing whether facts are made out. Accordingly, given its ultimate task is assessing risks, hearsay evidence is generally admissible with the long-stop position that there may be 'circumstances where the evidence in question is so fundamental to the decision that fairness requires that the offender be given the opportunity to test it by cross-examination before it is taken into account at all'.[28]

The distinction between the standard of proof in relation to disputed facts in parole cases and the quality of evidence is the area where most practical difficulties are thrown up by recall cases and where the degree to which the Board adopts a sufficiently adversarial approach arises.

The role of the Probation Service, Lifer Review and Recall Section and the Release and Recall Section

Where proceedings are required to become more adversarial because of the need to resolve disputed facts, the role of the Home Office departments with responsibility on behalf of the Secretary of State for the recall decisions and management of the cases before the Board (Release and Recall Section (RRS) and Lifer Review and Recall Section (LRRS) for fixed-term and indeterminate prisoners respectively) is thrown into greater relief. The Parole Board Rules 2004 make repeated references to duties of the 'parties' to the hearing and confirm that the parties are 'the prisoner and the Secretary of State'.[29]

Before the Secretary of State's involvement one concern in relation to the Probation Service is the degree to which recall recommendations make appropriate distinctions that apply to different sentences (the test for recalls is different for indeterminate sentences where the risk is of serious harm, and fixed-term sentences where the risk is of committing

---

[26] See note 18 above, para. 104 of Court of Appeal judgment.
[27] *R (Sim)* v. *Parole Board* [2003] EWCA Civ 1845.
[28] *Sim* above, note 27, para. 57.
[29] Parole Board Rules 2004, Rule 2(2).

further offences or unacceptable licence breaches). The Probation Service National Standards state that breach action may be initiated where there has been 'one unacceptable failure' to comply with licence conditions[30] without making a distinction between determinate and indeterminate cases.

When a recall recommendation arrives at the Home Office so that consideration can be given as to whether the licence should be revoked it has been held that there is no duty to make further inquiries beyond what is contained in the recommendation.[31] This can compound problems where the probation request itself contains little detail or source material regarding the allegations leading to recall. There is sometimes concern that in relation to life sentenced offenders, insufficient scrutiny is given to the issue as to whether the conduct giving rise to the recall request has a genuine 'causal link' with the original sentence (in a recent example a lifer whose sentence for murder arose as he was a secondary party to a terrorist murder, who had no history of violence but was recalled in relation to offences for dishonesty to fund a drug habit developed in prison).

The absence of any need to inquire behind the face of the Probation Service recommendation tends to be mirrored once a revocation decision has been made by a failure by the Home Office to do anything to ensure that proper evidence of allegations is put before the Board. Recall dossiers disclosed by the NOMS departments will include the probation report leading to the recall, the reasons for the revocation of the licence, any provisional Parole Board decision and material from the dossier leading to initial release. The probation recall request will usually be the only document relating to the reasons for recall and may contain only the vaguest detail about the allegations. It may contain multiple hearsay. If the offender is to successfully challenge the allegations it is almost always necessary to seek directions from the Board for further disclosure and/or obtain witness evidence so that informed decisions can be made as to whether witnesses should be sought. Prisoners' representatives are therefore often required to do the running in terms of firming up the evidential basis of recall, only so that it can be challenged. The risk of not doing everything to try and ensure that the best evidence is before the panel, given the general admissibility of hearsay evidence, is that the Board will be able to proceed to rely on inferior evidence.[32]

Before any of these steps can be taken the initial reasons for recall and the associated dossier should be served on the prisoner but in many cases this does not happen for several weeks (this problem was most

---

[30] National Standards, GS9.
[31] *R (on the application of Biggs)* v. *Home Secretary* [2002] EWHC 1012 (Admin).
[32] *Brooks* above, note 21.

acute in relation to determinate sentence prisoners in the wake of the House of Lords decision that they were generally entitled to oral hearings to determine whether they should be released).

The role of the Parole Board

Although stress has been placed in this paper on the need for recall hearings to be sufficiently adversarial, it remains the fact that the Board is an expert specialist body ultimately making a decision as to risk to the public. Although it should be incumbent upon the Secretary of State's departments to make proper disclosure of the best evidence supporting recall, the Board clearly is entitled to consider of its own motion what evidence is needed to fairly consider the case.[33]

The Board has power to issue directions under Rule 8 of the Parole Board Rules 2004, and has also adopted Case Progression Requirements which are means of panel chairs managing cases to reduce the need for deferrals due to failure to obtain relevant reports. Use of these measures on the Board's own motion has improved management of recall cases in recent years. However, there can be problems where representatives request directions and such requests are not dealt with promptly, and there are also situations where directions are issued but not then served on the representatives.

The *Brooks* case demonstrated a number of the practical difficulties prisoners encounter in endeavouring to ensure a fair hearing of disputed facts in the recall context. The key issue was an allegation of rape that had not come before the criminal courts. It was evident when the matter was considered by the Court of Appeal the LRRS did not appreciate its responsibility to call witnesses to support the case for recall, it failed to act promptly in response to Parole Board directions and none of the parties were aware of the possibility of obtaining a witness summons under the Civil Procedure Rules to secure attendance before the board.

Further criminal charges

Where the offender faces fresh charges particular problems arise. Probation Service guidance on completing reports to NOMS recommending recall where fresh criminal charges are in existence states rather confusingly that probation officers should 'disregard the charge, the plea, and whether the offender has been remanded into custody' but focus on

---

[33] For example, there is power in the Parole Board Rules 2004 for the Board of its own motion to issue directions as to evidence (Rule 8(2)) and to call witnesses (Rule 15(2)).

the behaviour surrounding the incident giving rise to the charge and whether the new offence is similar to the one giving rise to the sentence, and whether it indicates any increased risk.[34] The Parole Board, in its Bench Book guidance on when deferrals are likely to be refused, states:

> The duty judge/chair should consider the reports and decide whether sufficient material is there about the alleged incident(s) to enable the panel to reach a decision, with the benefit of oral evidence, whether the risk of further offences is acceptable, regardless of whether a crime has actually been committed. Remember, the Board is not required to adopt the criminal standard of proof.

This is obviously problematic and in certain cases will clearly risk prejudicing criminal trials. There is clearly no problem in Article 5 terms in deferring a hearing at a prisoner's request so as to preserve the fairness of the hearing of the criminal charge under Article 6.

An opposite problem can arise in relation to recalls where there are anticipated charges. This happens when the Board fails to grasp the nettle and effectively sanctions pre-charge detention for unreasonable lengths of time where it appears charges are pending and the offender has been recalled (but not remanded). This appears to be one effect of the otherwise generally welcomed powers in relation to determinate recalls to fix a further date for review.[35] There have been instances where offenders have been recalled pending charges where there has been no remand and only very poor information about the charge. It would be wholly appropriate for the Board in these circumstances to expect the Release and Recall Section to justify detention; however, in one case, rather than convene an oral hearing to determine recall, the Board considered the case on the papers on three occasions over four months to allow the case to be established against him. In its decision deferring a decision the board stated:

> Mr [M]'s case was considered by a panel of the Parole Board on 21st November 2005. A previous panel had requested information regarding the serious charges Mr [M] was facing and a reassessment of risk by the Probation Service. Regrettably this information was not available to the last panel and they set a further review date for this to be provided.

This approach is clearly unacceptable, especially as it has been held that the existence of a charge in itself is insufficient to warrant recall.[36]

---

[34] Probation Circular 16/2005, para. 61.
[35] Section 256, Criminal Justice Act 2003.
[36] *R (Broadbent)* v. *Parole Board* [2005] EWHC 1207.

Decisions and reasons

As noted above, it is very important for those appearing before the Board that allegations relevant to risk, where these have not been determined by the criminal courts, are resolved by the Board. If recalls are upheld those managing prisoners, writing reports and carrying out further risk assessments that will go before future panels will need some certainty about the factual basis of a recall. However, the inconsistencies in the Board's decision-making process can be illustrated by two cases in which the representative had made similar legal submissions that the Board should proceed by initially deciding whether the facts were made out before making a risk assessment.

In the first, the recall allegation against the prisoner was that he had assaulted his wife (the original life sentence having been imposed for the murder of his partner). No finding was made but the panel commented:

> The panel considered that your risk areas should be assessed on the basis of you posing a risk to your wife and to any female with whom you were sharing a close personal relationship and that risk was heightened in circumstances of domestic or personal stress and where there was a personality difference or relationship difficulty.

The problem with such a finding is evident. The failure to make a finding of fact leads to uncertainty. The prisoner concerned was actually recalled again and in the probation report leading to the recall a comment was repeatedly made that the lifer had assaulted his wife prior to the first recall.

In the second decision the prisoner had been recalled for an alleged indecent assault on a minor which was strongly contested. The finding was that: 'The panel is not satisfied on the available evidence that you committed an act of indecent assault but the panel is quite satisfied that you were engaged in an inappropriate relationship with a young girl.' This finding enables those completing future reports on the offender to do so on a clear basis as to how risk should be assessed, and provides the offender himself with clarity as to what has been decided regarding his conduct.

Conclusion

Although there is some recognition by the Board that recall hearings will often need to be more adversarial than first release cases in order to determine disputed facts, in practice the Board's approach is very often not rigorous enough. This situation is not helped by the fact that in its reasons the Board often does not set out with clarity the approach it has adopted beyond recitation of the statutory test and it is very rare for decisions to refer to case law even when this is relied upon by prisoners' representatives. The judicial decisions and subsequent discussions on how the Board should approach the issue of burdens and standards of proof have often failed to differentiate between deciding facts and assessing risks. In relation to the latter the courts have consistently and over a wide range of areas confirmed that these issues have little relevance.[37] In all recall cases, however, it is not unreasonable for the Board in relation to its assessment of facts to adopt the approach that the 'default position' is liberty. This would then ensure that in the assessment of disputed facts the LRRS/RRS are required to demonstrate that recall is positively required to protect the public.

The Parole Board should, in relation to the key disputed facts that go to the issue of whether recall is justified, make clear findings of fact to the civil standard of proof, making it clear how the evidence has been weighed, including the need for more cogent evidence in relation to the more serious allegations (and should explicitly reject hearsay evidence where fairness so requires). Only then should a decision be made on whether the risk threshold for redetention is made out.

It is suggested that within the current framework the fairness of recall procedures would be improved (which would also ensure that the requirements of Article 5 of the Convention are met) if:

- the RRS and LRRS took proactive steps where appropriate to take further steps to obtain evidence beyond the Probation Service recommendation prior to revoking a licence;

- the RRS and LRRS, after making a decision to revoke a licence, reviewed the reasons for recall in order to determine what further evidence (with the aim to obtain first-hand evidence where possible) should be obtained in relation to the key allegations against the prisoner;

- similarly once a recall is referred to the Board a proactive case management approach should be adopted so that a duty chair can issue directions on evidence at the earliest opportunity, including giving clear timetabling. The Board should make it clear that it is for the Home Office, which has the duty to substantiate allegations, to obtain the best evidence available;

---

[37] Even in the mental health context where the Court of Appeal has in principle confirmed that the civil standard should apply to predictive issues, but then effectively disavowed its utility. See note 18 above.

- clearer procedures should be adopted for communicating case management decisions to avoid the situation where directions are issued but not communicated to all the parties and/or not acted upon promptly.

Part IV
Is predicting risk fair?

Chapter 13

Offenders' views on risk assessment

*Gill Attrill and Glenda Liell**

In recent years there has been an increasing interest in risk assessment, marked by a notable expansion in literature debating how risk assessment should be best approached, what tools should be used, how risk should be communicated and what ethical and legal issues arise. Yet virtually none of this literature has been written from an offender perspective or in collaboration with individuals who are the subject of risk assessment.

Therefore, in the run up to the conference 'The Role and Function of the Parole Board – Perceptions of Fairness', held in Cambridge in September 2006, the authors and a small number of colleagues held a series of discussions with offenders on their views and experience of risk assessment. Our aim was not only to better understand the perspective of those who are subject to risk assessment, but more importantly to offer them a voice for their views at the conference. The authors wish to emphasise that the chapter merely reflects what some offenders said during discussions and cannot be considered representative of all prisoners' views or a formal research study. In our usual role which is

*In particular we thank the offenders who shared their views for their thoughtfulness and willingness to help us. We hope we have done your views justice.

We thank Rachel Atkinson, Christine Bull, Carmen Corbett, Jacci Milsom, Rob Paramo, Vaneeta Patel and Mick Rochford for their help in gathering the views of offenders. We would also like to acknowledge the support and assistance of all staff at the sites, without whom we could not have completed this review.

developing treatment programmes, we have always found it incredibly useful to hear the views of offenders we work with.

This chapter reports some of the comments and views they wanted to share with professionals engaged in risk assessment and decision-making. We believe they offer an eloquent commentary on the meaning of risk assessment and what it is like to be risk assessed. We asked the offenders to draw on their experiences across different correctional settings and sentences so the following comments apply broadly to prison, health and community settings and the offenders' experience with a range of staff from different disciplines working independently as well as for particular services.

A total of 60 adult offenders took part in the discussions. Obviously this represents just a tiny proportion of the tens of thousands of offenders risk assessed each year in different UK forensic settings and was not a random sample. They came from different security settings ranging from a high security unit for dangerous and severely personality disordered offenders to a probation and bail hostel. The majority had committed a violent, sexual or drugs-related offence. Their current sentence ranged from a 12-month probation order to life sentence, which 29 had received, 23 for having taken a life. Although the range of determinate sentences was from one to 22 years, the majority were serving lengthy sentences, the average for the group being 9.5 years. Only six (10 per cent) of the offenders were women and we recognise their voice is unfortunately under-represented.

We intentionally did not define risk assessment in our discussions to elicit as broad a range of responses to the issue as possible. The response of the offenders to being asked to share their views was overwhelmingly positive. Many of them expressed appreciation for having their views heard and taken note of. Their thoughtfulness and desire to give clear and considered responses was impressive; many of them took particular care to ensure that their comments accurately expressed what was important to them.

The chapter structures their views in terms of their perceptions of the meaning and purpose of risk assessment, factors they felt influenced risk and the accuracy and fairness of risk assessment.

Offenders' understanding of the meaning and purpose of risk assessment

When asked to explain what they felt was the purpose of risk assessment, why it is done and what risk assessment really means, the majority of offenders talked about risk in terms of whether or not a person will commit another offence. For example:

It looks at you and your crime and assesses risk of reoffending. Risk is the likelihood of it happening again.

A few also spoke about risk assessment in terms of the level of security a person requires within an institution and monitoring in the community. A small number, particularly those who had been involved in some form of rehabilitative treatment, also described risk assessment in terms of understanding the factors which underpin an individual's offending and allocation to appropriate treatment.

Looking at the risk of you reoffending and how much harm you might cause, helps decisions on how much support you need and how much monitoring.

To see if an offender is a risk to society and if at risk of committing the same offence. See if they are doing anything which contributed to the offence or whether they've done work to address the behaviours which contributed to the offence.

Listening to the offenders it seemed they were echoing the pressure we suggest is often felt by professionals and decision-makers to evaluate and communicate risk in terms of predictions, quantifying how likely the person is to reoffend. Very few people spoke about risk assessment in terms of identifying specific risk factors or aspects of a person's functioning which if changed could reduce or manage their risk. Their understanding of risk often centred around public protection in simple terms: whether or not an individual might harm another. While this issue is at the heart of risk decision-making, there is a broader perspective which is important to understand. This includes a recognition that risk assessment may look at a range of different risks (for example risk to others, risk to self, risk of different types of offending behaviour); that it might focus on different time periods (over the next 24 hours, for the licence period, for the next five years); that it should consider severity and potential harm from reoffending, likely imminence, frequency, potential victims and circumstances and context. It has been argued that risk assessment should ethically be accompanied by risk reduction and risk management pathways for the individual (Logan 2003), yet few of the offenders articulated risk assessment in terms of a process whereby individuals understand their risk and how they can reduce it.

This perhaps links to a concern expressed by one offender that risk assessment can feel like something that is 'done to you', which you have little control of or input into. The need to feel consulted and be a participant in the process is discussed further in the section on perceptions of fairness. For this offender it was a particularly important issue:

> I want to communicate the pure fear that risk assessment has caused in me. The post-sentence report process was the hardest time of my life – it made me suicidal by leaving me in the dark and being so swift and out of my control.

Offenders' views on what increases and decreases risk

As a way of gauging what offenders understood and thought about risk we asked them to list factors which they felt would make an individual more or less risky.

Several offenders, particularly those who had been engaged in interventions to reduce their risk such as offending behaviour pro-grammes, talked about cognitive factors. Factors they felt increase risk included whether a person denies or minimises their offence, the belief that you have no other options, a lack of remorse, the belief that what you did was right and not wanting to stop. Several individuals felt that a preparedness to change and taking responsibility for your actions are important in reducing an individual's risk. A number of offenders talked about the importance of knowing what you have to change and that not knowing what makes you risky can lead to enhanced risk. This further emphasises the value of explaining risk to offenders so that they not only understand the type and level of risk they pose, but the range of factors which underpin their risk and what they can actively do to address these.

The offenders generally came across as positive about treatment programmes, seeing them as an important mechanism for reducing risk. Monitoring was also seen by some as a positive influence on risk. Several felt that drug use and contact with other anti-social people heightens risk. A small number believed that going to a hostel increases risk because of the people they are likely to come into contact with and availability of substances.

The most frequent answers tended to focus on situational factors and the context in which a person functions. They felt that where an offender lives, who is around them, the availability of drugs, housing, education, keeping friends, family and isolation from others all influence risk. They had insight into the difficulties facing risk assessors who evaluate individuals in controlled, structured environments and who are unable to influence or assess the full circumstances in which a person may function in the community. As one offender said:

How can you assess risk when you can't put the person in the situation which makes them risky?

Offenders' views on the accuracy of risk assessment

In general the offenders felt that risk assessment is fairly accurate, with the caveat that they also consider it difficult to make valid assessments of an individual's risk. We asked them how they would go about assessing risk in an offender and what factors influence accuracy. Some fairly typical comments were:

I think it's an almost impossible task, except in broad strokes.

Risk assessment is very difficult.

Nobody wants to take a risk.

The influence of external and changing circumstances was one of the reasons they felt it was difficult to accurately assess risk. Another was the need to understand the thinking and motivation of offenders and the likelihood that an offender will not give a full and honest account of their internal world unless they feel safe to do so without negative consequences. As three of the offenders said about assessing risk:

People think that if they open up they'll never get out and will be held back, so they don't tell them things and don't tell the truth.

It's human nature to make mistakes, no one is a mind reader.

You cannot be 100 per cent sure someone is/is not going to commit an offence as you don't know what's going on in their head.

This highlights the need for the offender to see the risk assessment process as meaningful and of some benefit for him or her. We believe offenders are more likely to share their views of the world if they feel the process is credible and collaborative and that through participating they gain useful information about how they can progress, reduce and manage their risk. The more we (whatever our role, be it risk assessor, case manager, decision-maker, etc.) are transparent about the risk assessment process and the choices and consequences that follow for the offender, the more likely they are to feel they have choice and control within the process and constructively engage (Harris et al. 2004; Heilbrun 1997). As one offender said:

It's important to make the process more open and friendly – give the prisoner an idea it's for his benefit as well as society's. Give the offender the chance to comment.

In discussing the accuracy of risk assessment some offenders also identified the type of offence the person has committed and whether they have committed previous offences as important factors. They felt that certain types of criminal behaviour are more difficult to assess accurately than others (examples given included 'white-collar offenders'), and that individuals with no previous criminal history are also hard to evaluate in terms of risk. This level of insight was interesting. It is true we know very little about what contributes to risk and how to effectively assess it in a number of areas, including arson and robbery. What might not be so clear is how well we communicate these limitations to offenders and others. Individuals with no previous convictions also present challenges to assessment. In some areas such as sexual offending there are limited risk assessment tools available to assess for risk unless the individual has a prior conviction or known incident relating to sexual offending.

A consistent finding during discussions was that offenders felt inaccurate or out of date information could be held in their files and subsequently used in assessment and decision-making. Some expressed concerns that they might not know if this is the case and that they would have difficulties in getting wrong information corrected. In the words of three offenders:

Be aware that mistakes are written down and are then taken as gospel.

I think that the basis of risk assessments is good but worry as to the quality of assessments that inform them.

Make sure you get the paperwork right – you can't get to know someone in 20 minutes, how can you decide on risk in that time?

In our experience as practitioners, we are aware that inaccuracies may creep into offenders' files across time and different contexts and sources. For example, inaccuracies may occur where an offender has reported an incident or past experience resulting in it being recorded as if a corroborated fact or observed behaviour. Over time opinion, evidence or conclusions can be repeated in new reports making it difficult to identify the original author, context or time it was written. There may also be the diminishing of importance over time of aspects of an offence identified at the time of sentencing as significant. Access to information and openness in reporting has dramatically improved in recent years and working in HM Prison Service we are aware of a real emphasis on transparency. It remains important, however, that we consider what processes we have in place to ensure information is gathered in as sound a manner as possible (McGuire 1997) and to check the validity of information, wherever we work and in whatever context.

Finally, two other factors offenders felt influenced accuracy were the degree to which the person making an assessment knows them personally and their level of training and skills. Comments on this included:

How can you judge me if you don't know me?

More money needs to be invested into Probation; people should simplify OASys and draw on a greater source of qualified persons when making reports and assessments. They should spend more time with offenders to get to know them.

They should know more about what goes on in prisons, they should come in and see it and see it's not a softly softly approach. They should sit in on some programmes and see exactly what people are doing.

This raises a dilemma facing professionals involved in risk assessment and other work with offenders. Good practice may suggest that you should have some contact and involvement with the offender, but how much is too much? In a recent independent review completed following a serious further offence committed by Anthony Rice (HMIP 2006b), it was suggested that staff heavily involved in the long-term treatment of an offender may weigh up evidence differently than those who have less personal engagement in the case. Within the recommendations section the report stated:

Someone not involved in delivering treatment is sometimes better able to see the recent progress made in a clearer perspective and in proper proportion to the size of the overall problem presented by the case as a whole. (p. 53, para. 10.1.6)

The inference is that significant involvement, particularly in delivering treatment, may lead an individual to judge evidence more favourably for the offender. This raises implications for practice, particularly in gaining better understanding of how we can train and maintain staff objectivity. It would also be helpful to explore further how type, degree, frequency and intensity of contact may impact on accurate risk assessment and how support and supervision may address these issues.

Offenders' perceptions of the fairness of risk assessment

The offenders we spoke with identified a number of ways in which they felt the fairness of risk assessment could be affected. This linked back to accuracy, in that several individuals commented that if information is not correct or was biased in some way then an assessment is less likely to be fair.

Several individuals also expressed frustration with being assessed on static factors, which are not amenable to change. Some comments which reflect this were:

Please don't pay too much attention to static risk.

For the rest of your lives, if you were judged on the two or three biggest and most regrettable mistakes you had made – would you release yourself into the community?

It's not fair –I'm pre-judged on what I did in the past, not what I am doing now.

Risk assessment isn't fair as I can't prove I have changed while I am inside a prison.

In talking with the offenders we gained the impression that some felt trapped by their past and the continual assessment of behaviours which may have occurred years ago. This may have reflected a lack of understanding or willingness to acknowledge how they could address their dynamic risk and resettlement needs. It is true to say, however, that static and actuarial risk assessments are not without some significant limitations. In particular, actuarial assessment, which attempts to help us quantify risk, says very little if anything about the risk posed by an individual and in what ways that risk may be influenced by a change in circumstance or change within the offender (Hart et al. in press). The best that we can draw from these approaches are inferences about group membership and possible comparisons with a group of people with similar characteristics but who might have been assessed in different countries or cultures or at a different time. We believe it is also important to remember that structured clinical risk assessment tools also have their limitations in applicability to offenders from different ethnic, cultural and geographical backgrounds as well as those who have important characteristics such as brain damage and low levels of intelligence.

Offenders also felt the fairness of assessments could be compromised by too great a focus on negative factors. For example, some offenders commented:

The Parole Board is fair, as long as it takes into consideration the negative and positive facts.

From my experience risk assessment isn't fair as it's just pure negatives that people look at, not positives.

They should take into account fully every attempt the individual has made to address offending behaviour and remain objective and consider all the main indicators. They should consider all the work he's done in prison and his intentions for rebuilding his life and the steps taken towards this – in prison.

These comments raise an interesting point about the degree to which we focus in risk assessment, treatment, management and research on the deficits, problems and risk factors an individual presents compared to their strengths and protective factors. In recent years there has been a move towards more motivational, strengths-based models of offender rehabilitation which take into consideration not just the reduction of risk but also the development of new fulfilling ways of living pro-socially (Ward and Brown 2004; McMurran and Ward 2004). Understanding and developing an offender's protective factors is not just a good risk reduction strategy it is also more motivational. Perhaps these comments serve as a useful reminder that at a time of intense public concern around risk, focusing predominantly on why someone is a risk may be attractive but comes at the cost of potentially important information about an offender's capabilities and strengths relevant to risk management.

Seeing the offender as a whole links to another theme we identified in discussions around fairness. Several offenders felt not being seen and treated as an individual reduced the fairness of risk assessment. For example:

I committed a crime that was terrible, that doesn't make me a terrible person. I can change and I have done work to do this. You shouldn't generalise; look at extraordinary circumstances. Look at people's achievements. Do not look at knee-jerk reactions to prominent serious offences.

Each offender should be seen as an individual case.

Involvement in the assessment process was also described as an important issue in terms of fairness. As discussed previously some offenders expressed concern about how accurate an assessment could be if they did not contribute to the process. They also discussed the importance of feeling they had an opportunity to comment and put their side across. This reflects a growing recognition of the advantages of a collaborative approach in risk assessment (Shingler and Mann 2005). This also links to the issue of how well you know the assessor. Interestingly, many offenders felt that their Personal Officer (the officer allocated to them for support and information) or a member of staff involved in their treatment would be the best person to assess them.

The Parole Board should have a more active role in prisons and the risk assessment process. Before a parole board meeting, they should meet the prisoner as you get a lot more information out of the person face to face.

One of the most important factors offenders felt influenced fairness was what they saw as political influence. Many appeared acutely aware of this, and expressed advice and comments including:

Don't be so media led.

Don't listen to the papers and don't write policy/practice according to the media. Everyone is bigger than their crime. Everybody deserves a second chance.

You shouldn't be influenced by public opinion and the media.

Stop listening to the media and listen to prisoners' needs.

Government and politicians shouldn't get involved with offenders when something goes wrong – it affects those already in. They should be concentrating on running the country effectively instead.

You should treat everyone as an individual, don't be swayed by media influence, don't assume that any offence necessarily links to certain risk.

One final area related to fairness was around clarity of communication. We have already discussed the importance for offenders of understanding the process of risk assessment, its complexity and limitations. The offenders also felt that having clear and consistent reports would increase a sense of fairness in the process:

Communication on risk assessment is not very good as everyone is so vague.

Please stop moving the goal posts, tell me exactly what I need to do to be released.

Conclusions

This paper provides just a snapshot of some offenders' perceptions of risk assessment and as previously stressed cannot be considered representative of all offenders' views. A more thorough investigation would undoubtedly be helpful in better understanding how we can improve risk assessment in terms of enabling the offender to engage in the process and see it as fair and meaningful. This is not just about individual rights and ethical practice. We argue that it is central to risk reduction. If an offender understands not just what type and level of risk (or indeed risks) he or she poses, but also how to reduce, monitor and manage that risk and what circumstances are likely to enhance and reduce it, then together we have a better chance of reducing that risk and protecting the public.

Through our discussions with offenders we learnt about the importance of communication and clarity and taking a collaborative approach to risk assessment and management. We identified how important it is for offenders to be recognised as individuals with unique experiences, deficits and strengths, and understanding the context within which they live their lives and attempt to settle into the community.

The views and comments made by the offenders we met were not unreasonable, unrealistic or naïve. What they often wanted was probably much the same as we do, as professionals involved in risk assessment and decision-making. They wanted accuracy, fairness and a chance to be involved in decisions about their future. In this, and many other things, we have common ground.

Finally, as ever, we are reminded that we have much to learn from offenders themselves.

Chapter 14

MAPPA, parole and the management of high-risk offenders in the community

Hazel Kemshall*

Introduction and context

The community management of high-risk offenders has attracted significant public, political and media attention (Thomas 2005). The murder of John Monckton by Damien Hanson raised concerns not only about the appropriate risk assessment of offenders prior to release, but also about their effective management once in the community (HMIP 2006a). The murder by Anthony Rice also highlighted tensions in the interface between the Parole Board and local MAPPA, and the appropriate balance between offenders and potential victims (HMIP 2006b). The Hanson Serious Incident Inquiry Report (HMIP 2006a) noted that there was a lack of clarity about how the Parole Board should respond to significant changes in release plans and release circumstances prior to the prisoner's release date. In essence, should prisoners be released if their risk management plan significantly changes or is undermined by changes in circumstances?

The incoming Home Secretary John Reid summed these cases up by stating that: 'Reasonable people would view the decision to release someone that appears to emphasise the rights of a convicted murderer over the rights of his potential victims as tragically and disastrously mistaken' (Home Secretary 2006: 1). The Home Secretary continued this theme by stating that: 'The public has the right to expect that everything possible will be done to minimise the risk from serious violent and dangerous offenders' (ibid.), an expectation that has been quickly translated into a 'dramatic overhaul of public protection arrangements',

*Thanks are extended to my colleagues Jason Wood, Gill Mackenzie and Bernadette Wilkinson for assistance with the various research projects drawn upon in this paper.

and a rebalancing of justice between offenders and victims (Home Secretary 2006; Home Office 2006a).

While it is difficult to measure the erosion of public trust in both the parole system and MAPPA there has been a swift political response to restore public confidence (Home Secretary 2006; Home Office 2006c, 2006d) and to put 'victims first' (Home Office 2006a). This has included acceptance of the main recommendations of the Serious Incident Inquiry Reports, proposals for a violent offender order and revisions to the parole system. In particular, recent proposals to 'rebalance the criminal justice system' (Home Office 2006a) refer to 'shocking recent incidents in which offenders who were under our supervision have committed serious crimes' (ibid.: 34), and outline the 'decisive action' required to improve the management of 'serious, violent and dangerous offenders following release from custody' (ibid.). Notably, this includes parole decisions being unanimous rather than by majority at panels of three to ensure greater assurance that they are safe for release, the use of violent offender orders to impose additional conditions of residency and restricting who offenders can associate with or visit with a breach penalty of up to five years imprisonment, and an increased emphasis upon public protection sentences (Home Office 2006a, 2006b, 2006c).

In respect of parole, the Home Secretary announced proposals to enhance the public protection focus of the Parole Board:

- to require unanimous verdicts on serious offenders;

- to improve public protection representation at oral hearings via the 'use of "Public Protection Advocates" who will represent victims' and society's views';

- to review whether supervision and the whole process is 'sufficiently joined up';

- to improve risk assessments (including the interviewing of offenders).

(See Home Secretary 2006: 1–5.)

The immediate response of the Parole Board to these proposals was to reiterate the extent of victim experience and familiarisation with victim views already held by Parole Board members (Parole Board 2006b), and to emphasise that current panel processes led to unanimous decisions in most cases (Parole Board 2006b; Hood and Shute 2000). The Corporate Plan 2004–2007 targets risk assessment as a key strategic aim (reiterated in the Annual Business Plan 2006–2007):

To make risk assessments which are timely, rigorous, fair and consistent and which protect the public while contributing to the rehabilitation of prisoners so that effective decisions about prisoners can be made as to who may safely be released into the community and who must remain in or be returned to custody. (Parole Board 2006a: para. 2.2)

This paper will examine the MAPPA–parole interface, considering it as part of a 'complex system' of risk management within which parole decisions are made. A complex system can be understood as a system comprising multiple parts with differing systems, procedures and processes, and where accountability and responsibility are often fragmented and on occasion conflict (Hood and Jones 1996). Risk management systems of this type have been much investigated and are viewed as a source of potential risk management failure (Hood and Jones 1996; Kemshall 1998a). Such systems are prone to error and faults, tensions and conflicts, and multiple and often differing objectives, and are subject to a degree of atrophy in their functioning. These failures are best understood as 'systemic faults' rather than as merely the faults of poor practice or the errors of individual workers (Kemshall 1998a). In essence, they require improved system management and greater integration of the constituent parts of the complex system rather than corrective action targeted at individual practitioners or single agencies.

What is MAPPA?

Public protection has become a key theme of much recent legislation and penal policy resulting in increased formal procedures and multi-agency structures to risk assess and manage the 'critical few' (Criminal Justice and Court Services Act 2000; Criminal Justice Act 2003; Home Office 2004c). Multi-Agency Public Protection Arrangements (MAPPA) were formally created by ss. 67 and 68 of the Criminal Justice and Court Services Act 2000, although they had evolved from multi-agency arrangements in the late 1990s for the assessment and management of sex offenders subject to the sex offender register. These arrangements were consolidated by the CJA 2003 which made Police, Probation and Prisons 'Responsible Authorities' and giving other agencies a 'duty to cooperate'. These arrangements place a statutory responsibility on the three main agencies to assess and manage high-risk offenders. MAPPA are concerned with three categories of offender:

- *Category 1* – Registered sex offenders who have been convicted or cautioned since September 1997 of certain sexual offences (s. 327(2), CJA 2003), and are required to register personal and other relevant details with the police in order to be effectively monitored. The police have primary responsibility for identifying category 1 offenders.

- *Category 2* – Violent and other sexual offenders receiving a custodial sentence of 12 months or more since April 2001, a hospital or guardianship order, or subject to disqualification from working with children (s. 327(3)–(5), CJA 2003). All these offenders are subject to statutory supervision by the National Probation Service and consequently probation is responsible for the identification of category 2 offenders.

- *Category 3* – Other offenders considered by the Responsible Authority to pose a 'risk of serious harm to the public' (s. 325(2), CJA 2003). Identification is largely determined by the judgment of the Responsible Authority based upon two main considerations:

  – The offender must have a conviction that indicates he is capable of causing serious harm to the public.

  – The Responsible Authority must reasonably consider that the offender may cause harm to the public. The responsibility of identification lies with the agency that deals initially with the offender.

  (Home Office 2004c)

MAPPA also has a three-tier pyramid structure, aimed at targeting resources at the highest level of risk or the 'critical few'.

- *Level 1 offenders* ('ordinary risk management') – Where the agency responsible for the offender can manage the risk without the significant involvement of other agencies; only appropriate for category 1 and category 2 offenders who are assessed as presenting a low or medium risk.

- *Level 2 offenders* ('local interagency risk management') – Where there is 'active involvement' of more than one agency in risk management plans, either because of a higher level of risk or because of the complexity of managing the offender. Responsible Authorities should decide the frequency of panel meetings and also the representation and quality assurance of risk management.

- *Level 3 offenders* (Multi-Agency Public Protection Panels (MAPPP)) – Those offenders defined as the 'critical few' who pose a high or very high risk, in addition to having a media profile and/or management plan drawing together key active partners who will take joint responsibility for the community management of the offender. Level 3 cases can be 'referred down' to Level 2 when risk of harm deflates.

  (Home Office 2004c: paras 111–116)

Multi-Agency Public Protection Arrangements (MAPPA) best reflect what Connelly and Williamson (2000) have termed the 'community protection model'. This model is embedded in the criminal justice system and is characterised by the use of restriction, surveillance, monitoring and control, compulsory treatment and the prioritisation of victim/ community rights over those of offenders. Special measures such as licence conditions, tagging, exclusions, registers, selective incarceration and, more recently, satellite tracking are all extensively used (Kemshall 2001, 2003; Kemshall et al. 2005). Risk management plans are devised and delivered by statutory agencies in partnership (Home Office 2004c) with Police and Probation as key drivers (Nash 1999; Kemshall 2003), more recently joined by the Prison Service as a statutory partner (Criminal Justice Act 2003).

The MAPPA–parole interface

Given the remit and target group of offenders for MAPPA, high-risk parolees should fall within the boundaries of MAPPA. However, this in itself poses something of a conundrum – parolees must be high risk of committing an offence of serious harm to be managed by MAPPA, but if they are that risky should they be released on parole? Conversely, it could be argued that it is the management and monitoring arrangements of MAPPA that reduce the risk to acceptable levels to enable release into the community – a position stated by the Chief Inspector of Probation in the Rice report.

In essence, high-risk, MAPPA level 3 prisoners may still be released if the plan provided by local MAPPA is good enough to manage them safely:

> In our view it may be helpful to emphasise that these 'levels' are not describing 'inherent qualities of the offender', but instead are describing the level of restrictive intervention required in order to keep to a minimum the offender's Risk of Harm to others. (HMIP 2006b: para. 6.9.6, p. 20)

Such a system is, however, dependent upon the appropriate identification and referral of such offenders to the MAPPA. This is more problematic than might at first appear, and takes place within a 'complex system' (Hood and Jones 1996), in which critical information is provided by various personnel within Prisons and Probation, an independent Parole Board panel makes a decision about release and crucial risk management resources may be provided by MAPPA.

Risk management within complex systems

Research into complex systems from a number of fields[1] indicates a number of threats to effective risk management. In brief these are:

- *Clashes of work-based cultures, conflicts of value-base and professional ideologies* (Hood and Jones 1996; Horlick-Jones 1998; Kemshall 2000; Lynch 2000). As Macgill (1989) and Lupton (1999) have argued, risk perceptions are rooted in personal experience, social networks, group interactions and immediate locale. Risk perceptions can be deployed in accordance with the worker's preferred value base (Kemshall 1998a; Maynard-Moody et al. 1990), and can also be strategically deployed, for example to avoid agency/personal blame and censure in the light of potential negative outcomes. Agencies that have been the subject of a 'Serious Incident Inquiry' are likely to be more 'precautionary' in their risk decisions, at least initially.

- *Routinisation and occupational survival.* Workers tend to routinise complex tasks over time, particularly in the face of high volume and professional stress (Lynch 2000; Satayamurti 1981), and risk is no exception (Kemshall 1998a). Worker compliance with risk procedures can be mistaken for ownership, and without vigorous and repeated enforcement it can fall. Hence procedural compliance declines over the long term as shown by numerous 'disaster' inquiries (Cullen 1990; Fennell 1988; Hidden 1989; Health and Safety Executive 1988). An investigative stance is lost (Prins 1988), and judgment is weakened. The consequences of this can be severe. For example, workers may fail to see signs of escalation (as in the case of Hanson – HMIP 2006a), or indeed operate contrary to risk procedures in order to 'get the job done' as in the Piper Alpha fire (Cullen 1990), the Challenger Shuttle disaster (*Report of the Presidential Commission* 1986; Starbuck and Milliken 1988; see also Runciman 1993 for examples in healthcare) and of course the Chernobyl nuclear disaster (USSR State Committee 1986). The case of Anthony Rice illustrates how once a decision (in this case to release) has gained momentum it is difficult to undo, even in the face of significant risk information (HMIP 2006b). Indeed the Chief Inspector noted that the Parole Board gave 'insufficient weight to the underlying nature of his Risk of Harm to others' and that this happened for a number of reasons including (unreal) optimism, lack of information, a momentum towards release and prioritising offender rights over risk to the public (HMIP 2006b: para. 1.3, p. 5).

---

[1] These include the nuclear industry, the oil industry, railways, health, social work and social care, and probation.

- *Fragmentation of accountability*. This can also erode the effectiveness of risk systems. This has been notable in early multi-agency child protection case conferences and procedures (Parton 1986) and in mental health inquiries into case management failures (Blom-Cooper et al. 1995; Sheppard 1996). The most significant flaws are the failure to exchange critical information, the failure to communicate changes in risk status, divisions between those who risk assess and those who risk manage resulting in a failure of risk management delivery as intended, and a lack of accountability for decisions made and subsequent failures to act. The case of Hanson, for example, illustrates failures to communicate between prison, home area and Parole Board, and within the London Probation Area (HMIP 2006a), and the case of Anthony Rice illustrates the misperception about appropriate responsibilities and accountability within a complex system of risk management (HMIP 2006b – see, for example, paras 6.9.6, 10.3.1, 10.3.17).

These are significant threats to the risk management process of the parole system, although they do not always occur and risk decisions within parole generally have a good record (Hood and Shute 2000). In their research into parole decision-making Hood and Shute noted that 'there was a strong and statistically significant correlation between actuarial ROR [risk of reoffending] for a serious offence while on parole and parole decisions so far as non-sex offenders were concerned' (ibid.: xii).

In other words, Parole Board members were more actuarial and predictively correct than they (or indeed the Home Secretary) might realise, although Hood and Shute noted a tendency to 'overestimate the degree of risk posed by many prisoners' (ibid.: xvii). However, since this research conducted in 1998, the Probation Inspectorate has noted that figures from the Lifer Review and Recall Section indicate that there does appear to be a slight increase in reconvictions since 2003 (HMIP 2006b: 13). It is important to recognise that many risk failures, while often attributed to the actions of individual workers, can have their roots in the systemic faults inherent in complex systems (Hood and Jones 1996), and in essence failures have been created and 'incubated' within the system itself (Perrow 1984).

Other problematic conditions

The interface of this complex system with MAPPA is also framed by some problematic conditions. These can be categorised as historical, organisational and contextual. Historically MAPPA developed with only minimal contact with the Prison Service and little (if any) connection to the Parole Board (there were notable exceptions such as Durham) (Maguire et al. 2000). The Prison Service was not initially a statutory partner and therefore did not establish the processes, systems or key networks to link with MAPPA (Kemshall et al. 2005; Mate 2006). The inclusion via the CJA 2003 was an attempt to deal with the problems arising from this initial omission.[2] However, direct links to the Parole Board and panel processes were not established. As Mate puts it:

> The Act imposed new responsibilities upon the Prison Service (from April 2004) to establish regional and local strategic arrangements with key partner agencies, and to ensure the exchange of key information with those agencies through the MAPPA structures. It was recognised that the Prison Service had a key role to play in the planning for the release of identified high-risk offenders, and in the contribution to the risk-assessment and risk-management of those offenders. (Mate 2006: 50)

Mate's research, conducted between September 2004 and March 2005, examined the Prison Service's response to MAPPA, and the development of systems and processes to deal with the additional requirements laid out in Home Office MAPPA Guidance (2004c). These were:

- To help address the discontinuity of public protection work (often occurring when offenders enter and leave custody).

- To retain offenders in custody, help them to address the causes of their offending behaviour and assist their successful resettlement.

- To contribute to the 'operational functions' of MAPPA (i.e. the identification of priority offenders in custody, early notifications of release, delivery of regime programmes, contribution to risk assessment and management of priority offenders, and communication of the above to external partner agencies).

(Home Office 2004c)

While Mate identified variation and inconsistency, best practice was evidenced in those areas where prisons had appointed local public protection leads at senior management level. These personnel could advise on prison practice, key processes, local and regional offending behaviour programmes and specialist facilities (such as psychiatric services). These leads were forging positive links between Prison Service

---

[2] The CJA 2003 had an implementation date of April 2004 for the Prison Service to become a Responsible Authority. Until this change the Prison Service had a 'duty to cooperate' under the CJCS Act 2000.

regions and local MAPPA, and were influential in facilitating pre-discharge preparation, particularly by ensuring prisoner location close to the home release area. According to Mate, the regional aspect has been particularly beneficial in providing comparison of local MAPPA practices, regional access to prison offender programmes and services, and early preparation for release.

Organisationally the MAPPA–parole interface presents some difficulties. The Parole Board decides release but on the risk assessment information presented by others, and does not directly control the risk management packages delivered by either MAPPA or by single agencies (such as probation). The consequence of this is to divide responsibility for the release decision from the responsibility for risk management. It separates the key decision from the delivery decision (not unusual in risk work) but it is known to be a source of failure as it fragments responsibility and accountability (as discussed above) (see Adams 1995; Cullen 1990). In this context, it has already led to blurred responsibility for recall and enforcement decisions between MAPPA and the Parole Board (e.g. the Anthony Rice case – HMIP 2006b). More broadly, this set-up requires parole panels to rigorously test the evidence on risk versus release, and to consider the quality and likely success of the risk management plan proposed – a key recommendation of the Rice report (HMIP 2006b: para. 10.1.7, p. 53).

Testing the evidence of risk at a parole panel requires knowledge of actuarial and clinical risk factors and a working knowledge of key risk assessment tools such as OASys and the main sexual and violent offender assessment tools. (Interestingly, Hood and Shute's earlier research found parole board members were less actuarial and less predictively accurate about sex offenders.) It also requires full knowledge of the risk management plan proposed and a working knowledge of what makes community risk management effective. This can be provided by the training of Parole Board members, decision guide procedures and mechanisms to quality assure panel decisions.[3] Comparison to other parole systems may also help. For example, the Risk Management Authority (RMA) in Scotland is tasked with ensuring the appropriate assessment and management of high-risk offenders subject to the Order for Lifelong Restriction (OLR) in Scotland. As part of their remit they have developed the following to assist RMA members and practitioners:

- *An audit and rating document of risk assessment tools.* This provides accessible information about the main tools and a rating of their

---

[3] Some of this is already in place or is planned. See the Annual Business Plan 2006–07 (Parole Board 2004b) and the Corporate Business Plan 2004–07 (Parole Board 2006a).

reliability. This enables both practitioners using them and also panel members utilising their scores to understand their predictive accuracy and fitness for purpose (RMA 2006a).

- *Guidance on the preparation of risk assessment reports.* While this predominantly covers the preparation of risk assessment reports for the initial making of an OLR it has applicability to the preparation of parole reports and sets a high standard for the preparation and presentation of evidence of risk to courts and panels (RMA 2006b). NOMS, in conjunction with the Parole Board, could usefully compile and publish such a document to cover the risk work of prison, probation and MAPPA personnel.

- *Standards for judging the effectiveness and fitness for purpose of risk management plans prior to release under an OLR.* This work is currently taking place and involves an effective practice review based on existing research, a fieldwork exploration of current best practice and the use of expertise from an Advisory Group.

Contextually the MAPPA–parole interface operates in a very difficult climate. In brief, this can be described as risk averse, highly politicised and subject to constant and immediate scrutiny. The Home Secretary summed this up succinctly by stating that 'independent bodies are ultimately accountable to the public and more accountable than ever before' and that 'decisions are profoundly more transparent and as a result those that take decisions are profoundly more accountable' (Home Secretary 2006: 3). He also noted that the public are more educated, more informed and as a consequence both more demanding and more questioning than ever before. This can result in precautionary and defensive practice, avoiding risk, blame and censure (Kemshall 1998a). It is important to respond to such challenges with defensible practice, based upon criteria set for a defensible decision (Kemshall 1998b):

- All reasonable steps have been taken.

- Reliable assessment methods have been used.

- Information has been collected and thoroughly evaluated.

- Decisions are recorded (and subsequently carried out).

- Policies and procedures have been followed.

- Practitioners and their managers adopt an investigative approach and are proactive.

(Kemshall 1998b; reproduced in Probation Circular 54/2004;
HMIP 2006b)

The Chief Inspector of Probation has stated that 'the public is entitled to expect that the authorities will do their job properly, i.e. take all reasonable action to keep risk to a minimum' (HMIP 2006a: 4), a position reiterated by the Home Secretary John Reid. To ensure this, Probation Circular 82/2005 poses the following questions as essential to quality risk practice:

- Is there *sufficient* assessment and planning in the sentence plan and risk management plan to address the risk of the offender causing serious harm to the victim(s) of the offence?

- Is there *sufficient* assessment and planning in the sentence plan and risk management plan to address the risk of the offender causing serious harm to the public?

- Is there *sufficient* assessment and planning in the sentence plan and risk management plan to address the risk of the offender causing serious harm to staff?

A further overall question is posed:

- Overall, is there sufficient evidence in the case file that throughout the period of supervision the risks of harm have been identified and assessed to the required standard and all reasonable actions have been taken to keep the offender's risk of harm to a minimum (i.e. the case would pass a Serious Further Offence management review)?

This could usefully be translated into minimum standards for a release decision. Such standards would be more challenging than achieving a unanimous decision. (It is of course possible to have a consensus that is wrong as well as a consensus that is right.)

In essence, this would create criteria against which the decision is tested and recorded, in addition to the current case summaries presented at panels. The criteria might cover:

- a review and checklist of the evidence presented;

- the panel's view on its adequacy and quality, e.g. what is missing, what it is based on (offender interviews, MAPPA risk assessment, etc.);

- actuarial risk tool used and score;

- identification of key risk factors;

- if appropriate, whether a referral has been made to MAPPA and information received from MAPPA including a risk management plan;

- adequacy of the risk management plan – does it meet the risk factors identified, how will it reduce the risk, how will it be delivered, how will it be reviewed, how will it be enforced?

- what the contingency plans for a risk management failure are;

- the recommendation of the board including use of conditions and licence requirements.

The panel chair could be tasked with ensuring that this pro-forma is used and completed, providing a focus, test and record for defensibility.

Conclusion and recommendations

This paper has attempted to demonstrate that it is important to understand the MAPPA–parole interface and the systemic flaws it may be prone to if we want to plan for them and avoid them. This requires a more systemic approach to risk management failure than the attribution of individual blame and corrective action at a system rather than practitioner level. Effective corrective action can only be achieved through strategic management of the system as a whole and greater integration of key objectives, policies and desirable outcomes. To a large extent MAPPA have achieved this already through the use of legislation, national guidance and local protocols to regulate their activities and ensure more national consistency (Kemshall et al. 2005), although this does not necessarily exclude the risk of local failure as the case of Anthony Rice illustrates. Despite the recent integration of the Prison Service into MAPPA, this has not necessarily translated into an effective interface between MAPPA and the Parole Board. This could be facilitated by joint guidance from NOMS and the Parole Board, and if necessary Secretary of State Directions on the status of MAPPA and their role in risk management planning, and greater clarity on roles and responsibilities between MAPPA, the Prison Service and the Parole Board for release planning and risk management subsequent to release.

At an operational level, parole release decisions for high-risk offenders may well be improved by the following:

- a more rigorous test of the evidence and information presented to parole panels – how 'trustworthy' and reliable is it?

- an increased and transparent use of actuarial risk factors;

- increased awareness of the key risk assessment tools;

- application of the key requirements for a defensible decision to release;

- a more rigorous test and interrogation of risk management plans for release, particularly whether restrictive conditions are adequate and likely to manage the risk effectively in the community.

The MAPPA–parole interface is a complex one, bringing together numerous agencies with differing remits under the broad umbrella of public protection. While it has been common-sensically assumed that this system is a 'good thing' and will automatically result in better practice it is important to recognise that it has a number of inherent flaws and may be *as* programmed to produce poor results as it is programmed to produce positive ones. The interface itself requires proactive management and recognition of the wider complex system within which it is operating. Recent case failures and serious incidents have alerted us to these potential flaws and it is time to think about strategic management of the system as well as individual censure of practitioners.

Chapter 15

The paradoxical effects of stringent risk management: community failure and sex offenders

Jackie Craissati

In England and Wales over the past ten years there has been a series of legislative changes which have addressed the problem of managing convicted sexual offenders in the community. The inception of the Sex Offenders Register in 1997 was followed by the introduction of the sex offender order (now sex offences prevention order) in 1998, and then ss. 67 and 68 of the Criminal Justice and Court Services Act 2000 which put the multi-agency arrangements for public protection on their current statutory footing. More recent guidance has confirmed that both the police and the Probation Service – supported by a range of other relevant agencies – are responsible under the auspices of MAPPA (Multi-Agency Public Protection Arrangements) for all registered sex offenders, a significant proportion of violent offenders being released from custody and, indeed, any other potentially dangerous offender who is resident within the MAPPA's geographical remit.

These legislative changes have necessitated a steep learning curve for a range of agencies, not only in their understanding of the differential risks posed by sexual offenders, but also in terms of forging ways of working together in partnership. The current management structure is generally considered to be a positive and progressive step, with England and Wales having high levels of compliance with sex offender registration (Plotnikoff and Woolfson 2000), and a relatively low rate of sexual reconviction (Friendship and Thornton 2000).

However, with a prevalence rate for sexual conviction estimated to be around 1 per cent of the general male population across a lifespan (Marshall 1997), MAPPA have had to prioritise resources, targeting the highest-risk offenders. In order to achieve this, simple but effective actuarially based tools for risk assessment have been devised by Thornton and colleagues in the UK and by Hanson and colleagues in N. America. The Risk Matrix 2000 (Thornton et al. 2003) is used widely in sex offending populations in England and Wales and can be derived from file information. It provides a simple baseline risk classification based on conviction data, adjusted at Stage 2 if two or more aggravating factors are found (for example, male or stranger victims). Two cross-validation studies tested the predictive validity of the scale in a short-term follow-up sample of treated sex offenders and a long-term follow-up sample of untreated sex offenders. The reconviction rates for the two- and 19-year follow-up periods in relation to the four risk categories are outlined in Table 15.1.

Although the predictive ability of the tool is statistically robust, the results immediately suggest four problems. First, they provide a stark reminder that the label 'high' or 'very high' risk is somewhat misleading as it relates to surprisingly low percentage figures – only the highest risk category over a risk period of almost twenty years suggests sexual reconviction is more likely than not. In saying this, it must be acknowledged that there is a universal agreement that the reconviction figures do not accurately reflect the actual reoffending rates. Thus the tool labels a substantial number of individuals as high or very high risk who do not apparently go on to reoffend (a false positive rate which is particularly problematic in the short to medium term). The third problem is also related, insofar as the figures suggest that the time-frame for risk management needs to be very long term indeed, which does not sit easily with the immediate priorities of the police and probation services. Finally, static or historical tools cannot help with the

Table 15.1   Re-defining 'high risk': Risk Matrix 2000

	2 Years (%)	19 years (%)
Low	1	8
Medium	1	18
High	6	40
V. high	17	60

question of which individuals within each risk categorisation will be the reoffenders.

Attempts to enhance risk prediction in more recent years have turned to dynamic (changeable) variables which appear to be linked to risk (see Beech et al. 2002; Craissati and Beech 2003; Thornton 2002), or to broader psychological features of an offender – such as personality functioning – which in turn overlap with concepts of dynamic risk domains. Although there have been various approaches to the question of dynamic risk predictors, there is a useful level of overlap between researchers in terms of core findings. Essentially, there appear to be broadly four domains of relevance: intimacy deficits, pro-offending attitudes, sexual self-regulation (including deviant sexual interests) and general self-regulation/ lifestyle. Dynamic domains describe the characteristics of sex offenders, identify areas of treatment need and determine – by various means according to the researcher – when risk concerns should be raised. The latter point has been particularly relevant to the identification of those particular individuals within the static risk groups who are most likely to sexually reoffend. However, dynamic risk domains have not been used to identify general failure in the community, that is violent or acquisitive offending as well as sexual offending, or breach/recall on statutory orders.

Using an alternative approach, Craissati and Beech (2005, 2006), in a series of publications, have demonstrated that key developmental variables – childhood experiences of abuse and neglect (sexual, physical and emotional), childhood emotional/behavioural difficulties and insecure attachments to primary caregivers – can potentially enhance the risk assessment process by contributing directly to a static measure. It is important to note that this model was highly effective in predicting those sex offenders in the community who were most at risk of reoffending generally (not specifically sexually) or being breached/recalled on licence, and in predicting those who were likely to engage in sexually risky behaviours (including sexual reconvictions or offences with a sexual element, as well as offence 'approach' behaviours). However, the model was unable to be tested against sexual reconvictions given the low base rate. Subsequent research (Craissati et al. 2006) has established that these key developmental variables are strongly associated with adult measures of personality dysfunction and could therefore be understood as historical psychological factors which underpin personality disorder in adulthood.

Why worry about adult personality disorder and community failure? First, it is clear that both the use of key developmental variables and dynamic risk domains point to pervasive psychological dysfunction as a core feature of aggravated risk. There is a well established interdependent relationship between:

- the diagnosis of personality disorder and increased risk ratings on a range of well known and validated risk prediction tools;

- failure on statutory supervision or in treatment and increased risk ratings on these tools; and

- personality disorder and increased likelihood to fail on statutory supervision (see Figure 15.1).

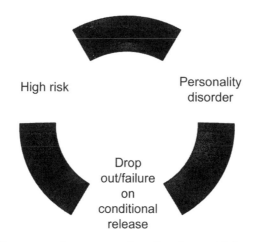

High risk

Personality disorder

Drop out/failure on conditional release

Figure 15.1   Why worry about personality disorder and failure?

Indeed, many tools contain items for both personality disorder and psychopathy (a subset of anti-social personality disordered individuals), thus double-counting the problem, as well as scoring for failure on prior conditional release/treatment. These three intertwined issues are particularly salient for community settings: although custodial settings often contain much of the behavioural expression of personality difficulties – impulsivity and emotional volatility – these problems are only too apparent in the community. Even if the base rate for sexual reconviction is low, at least in the short to medium term, there is a considerable benefit in being able to identify those offenders most likely to fail in their rehabilitative efforts in order to focus interventions.

Personality disorder is a complex and fairly controversial concept, with problems in achieving agreement between professionals regarding approaches to identification, causation and treatment. However, it can be reduced – with enormous simplification – into a few key ideas: what is personality disorder, where does it come from and can it be treated? Cooke and Hart (2004) described personality disorder in terms of the three Ps: pathological (significantly deviating from the social norms), persistent (from a person's twenties onwards) and pervasive (present within personal and social contexts across the domains of cognitive, affective and interpersonal functioning). The three Ps should result in either distress to the individual or others around him/her and *cannot* be exclusively related to a particular offending behaviour – either a single offence or a pattern of offences. The key element to personality disorder is its interpersonal impact. That is, it is often said that it is not possible, unlike other 'disorders', for personality disorder to be overtly manifest when a person is on a desert island; it is only when in an interpersonal context that a sense of self in relation to others can emerge. In terms of its origins, more recent research would suggest that there is growing consensus for a fairly integrative biopsychosocial aetiological model underpinning personality disorder (Paris 2000) in which inherited traits, early attachment experiences, trauma and abuse all play a part in its causation. The question of change over time remains controversial, the evidence suggesting that it is no longer tenable to consider personality disorder as unchanging and untreatable. Some studies (for example, Verheul et al. 1998) would suggest that between 10 and 80 per cent of individuals with anti-social and borderline personality disorder no longer meet the threshold for the diagnosis over a two- to ten-year period, that there is a natural maturational aspect to the disorder. Examination of these findings – together with the findings of treatment studies (Craissati et al. 2003) and research on psychopathy specifically – would suggest that there are fairly immutable core traits to a personality disorder (for example callousness, egocentricity or emotional sensitivity) but that the behavioural expression of such traits (impulsivity, temper outbursts, sensation seeking, substance misuse) can be responsive both to treatment and to maturational effects (Cooke and Hart 2004).

Having established the relationship between risk, pervasive psychological dysfunction and the increased likelihood of community failure, we now need to consider these issues in relation to current community management approaches. Summarising the current situation, there are encouraging signs that the sexual reconviction rate is fairly low overall, not all of which is related to problems with the prosecution of such offenders; high-risk sex offenders are not reoffending anywhere near the predicted rate, although they are recalled at fairly high rates (4–8 per cent a year of all registered sex offenders in the London area, and 2–4 per cent a year in more rural areas – London Probation 2005). Interestingly, it is the medium-risk offenders who now account for around 50 per cent of the few sexual (but also violent) reconvictions (Craissati and Beech 2005; Probation Inspectorate 2005). It seems reasonable to assume that higher risk sex offenders are being managed partly as a result of their own feelings of shame and fear and partly as a result of more efficient and transparent risk management arrangements. There must be little doubt that MAPPA are generally a good idea and may well be effective for a number of offenders in a way that registration and community notification in America does not appear to have been (Finn 1997; Zevitz and Farkas 2000).

However, it is worth examining in greater detail those aspects of a particular subgroup of MAPPA offenders – high-risk personality disordered sex offenders – which renders them particularly susceptible to community failure, and the ways in which the multi-agency process may ameliorate or exacerbate these difficulties. Such difficulties may take the professionals by surprise, having been successfully contained – or lain dormant – within the clear boundaried environment of a custodial setting, in which there are few ambiguities about the nature of relationships or the meaning of communication. The relationship between the MAPPA and the offender is well described by Davies (1996):

> The view is taken that professionals who deal with offenders are not free agents but potential actors who have been assigned roles in the individual offender's own re-enactment of their internal world drama. The professionals have the choice not to perform but they can only make this choice when they have a good idea of what the role is they are trying to avoid. Until they can work this out they are likely to be drawn into the play, unwittingly and therefore not unwillingly. Because of the latter, if the pressure to play is not anticipated then the professional will believe he is in a role of his choosing. Unfortunately, initially, only a preview of the plot is available in the somewhat cryptic form of the offence ... It is also important to comment that it is not only the offender's internal drama that professionals are called upon to enact but also those more explicit scripts of their own organisations and central government. They will also be under pressure from themselves to re-enact their own dramas ...

Although Davies draws on psychoanalytic ideas, there are complementary concepts derived from more cognitive models of psychological functioning. Padesky (teaching material) identifies – perhaps over simplistically but with helpful clarity – the core beliefs or schemas primarily associated with each type of personality disorder, and the way in which these are related to core views of the other, the expression of the core personality features and the interpersonal strategy. Some of these ideas are detailed in Table 15.2. For example, the anti-social personality disordered individual (the most commonly found within prison populations, and particularly prevalent in sex offenders with adult female victims) tends to hold a core view of himself as strong and a loner who perceives others to be exploitative and the world as a jungle; his strategy therefore in dealing with others is to deceive and to

Table 15.2 Activation of core beliefs

	Self	Others	Expression	Interpersonal strategy
Anti-social	Strong/alone	Exploiting	Impulsive	Deceive/manipulate
Borderline	Bad/vulnerable	Malevolent	Spasmodic	Attach/attack
Dependent	Weak/helpless	Overwhelming	Incompetent	Submissive
Paranoid	Right/noble	Malicious/intricate	Defensive	Suspicious

manipulate in order to gain the upper hand and survive. He will therefore perceive friendly and nurturing advances from a professional with mistrust and contempt, alert to deception (and mistakes) or signs of weakness; he may respond to frankness and moderate assertiveness with some grudging respect. Conversely, the individual with marked borderline personality traits believes him/herself to be bad and vulnerable in a malevolent world; his/her behaviour is chaotic and ever changing between strategies of extreme dependence and clinging to hostility and rejection. This results in confusion for the professional who invests hours of support for an offender who, for example, subsequently denigrates them to their senior colleague.

What might one then expect from personality disordered sex offenders in relation to the MAPPA?

- *Rule breaking*, not to achieve any conscious goal, but for the sake of it, because rules embody authority and authority (parents, carers, teachers and so on) has deceived and betrayed them in the past.

- *Excessive confiding or secretiveness*, without evident gain and often contrary to the offender's best interests, but always with the certainty that it will draw the other person (professional) into a seductive pursuit of the 'truth' in which they will be seen as interesting and worthy of attention.

- *Hypervigilance to any unfairness*, including the identification of illogical constraints surrounding risk management, because the world – and authority in particular – has often not played by the rules in their earlier experiences.

- *Emotional instability*, neediness swiftly followed by oppositional and hostile emotions, in which the offender attempts to regulate closeness while keeping control, with the other person being made to feel special then rejected, and of course then angry and rejecting in turn.

- *Impulsive behaviour*, often thinking one thing (not to reoffend) while doing another (attempting to offend), as though the offender lived simultaneously in two parallel worlds.

- *An inability to disentangle care from control*, arising from early experiences of abusive and/or neglectful care, in which the offender blurs the roles of therapist, policeman and housing officer.

- *Fantasy as a compensatory tool*, rather than an offence rehearsal, which regulates self-esteem, is an end in itself and does not need to be enacted.

- *Alliances with other sex offenders*, which are formed on the basis of their mutual 'unlovability'; relationships which may be sexual but have acceptance and companionship as their aim.

- *Inflexible cognitive styles*, and poor perspective taking, which are linked to core psychological deficits and may have only a tenuous relationship to risk, but nevertheless are highly provocative and irresistible to professionals as targets for change.

In turn, what should we expect from the MAPPA who, as Davies states so eloquently, are at risk of entering into the sex offender's unconscious re-enactment of their developmental dramas? There are likely to be arguments developing between agencies, often represented by the 'collusive' mental health worker and the 'punitive' police officer, to the point where the offender can perceive, triumphantly, that he has taken control and can 'slip through the net'. Professionals often mistake cooperation and compliance in the offender for the first year or two for a reduction in risk rather than a problematic personality trait and start to withdraw services; in doing so, they take their 'eye off the ball' and reinforce the offender's belief that there is nothing interesting or worthwhile about him other than his offending behaviour. Conversely, assuming that uncooperativeness and pushing boundaries equates to a higher risk situation – rather than a reflection of difficult personality traits – may lead to high levels of anxiety and coercive regimes which overestimate the actual risk posed. Responding to agency anxiety with excessive intrusion and control of the offender ultimately becomes persecutory and destructive. Commonly, agencies believe that 'more is better', and in imposing ever more controls eventually engage in seemingly meaningless gestures which are perceived – perhaps accurately – by the offender as more for the agency's benefit than his own. Ultimately this spiralling cycle of interactions inevitably results in the offender believing himself to have been deceived, encouraged to engage in a degree of trust and honesty with professionals for which he feels betrayed, and condemned to a high-risk script from which no one appears to want to release him.

Some of these ideas may be clear, others may seem quite abstract. They arise from the literature but also from clinical experience. Working with high-risk offenders in the community means that the question of potential failure is of immediate concern rather than subject to longer-term prediction. Attending to failures – scrutinising the paperwork, but also following up the offender and reviewing his/her view of the failure – arguably results in a sharper learning curve than focusing on success. The following three case examples provide a more vivid example of the ways in which offenders may, paradoxically, be drawn into community failure as they respond to stringent – often highly competent – risk management strategies. Graham, Paul and Jack (fictitious cases based on real examples but anonymised) are all rated as very high risk on the Risk Matrix 2000, and have a clear diagnosis of personality disorder; they have all spent more time in prison than living in the community throughout their adult life, but are now engaged with services at a time when they are seriously contemplating change – for their behaviour and their lifestyle. The contemplation of change is often taken lightly by professionals and by society, as though it would be obvious – as with a long-standing smoking habit – that change was simply a matter of deciding to stop an abhorrent behaviour in order to lead a decent life. However, for the high risk sex offender who wants to change, he is engaged in the predicament of contemplating relinquishing the sole reliable – if fleeting – source of pleasure in an otherwise emotionally barren life for the very uncertain returns of a socially acceptable – but possibly unattainable – community lifestyle. Finally, it is important to point out that all three cases were competently managed, with adherence to national standards; they do not represent failures of care.

Graham (a case of 'false confession')

> Graham is a 33-year-old man with a history of three separate violent assaults on post-pubescent boys; he has a diagnosis of paranoid and anti-social personality disorder, and has only managed to spend six weeks in the community over the past 15 years. Released on licence to a probation hostel, he was absolutely determined to find work, frantic in his efforts to assume a 'normal' life. He was therefore frustrated by the slow and cautious approach of professionals, the hostel curfews which limited his ability to seek work, and the requirement of appointments and self-disclosure (about which he was unusually suspicious). The probation officer became concerned as he felt he was losing control of the management of the licence: Graham was taking on many jobs via agencies, he accepted work as

a night-time labourer repairing roads, he was out of the hostel throughout the day, and commenced a relationship with a woman 25 years his senior. There were understandable concerns that the relationship was unsuitable, perhaps rather pathological, and attempts to refocus Graham on his licence and risk management only seemed to lead to a greater 'collusion' between him and his girlfriend. Graham began to experience the supervision arrangements as stifling; he became agitated and complained to hostel staff of nightmares. The probation officer visited him and had a lengthy session in which he tried to reassure Graham that he was doing well. The more reassurance provided, the more agitated Graham became, as though he felt he was not being properly heard. Eventually, he blurted out that he had committed a sexual assault on a young boy at the local leisure centre a week previously. This 'confession' resulted in Graham's recall to prison, although a careful investigation by the police strongly suggested that no such assault had in fact taken place (and Graham later retracted his confession).

Graham served a further three years in prison, and was released without any statutory obligations other than to register on the Sex Offenders Register. He refused any voluntary contact with probation, having decided – unreasonably – that his recall was the fault of the probation officer who was overly persecutory and controlling towards him. He did, however, remain in contact with his psychologist who had corresponded with him in prison; however, he was given control of the frequency and topic of sessions. He married his older girlfriend, found work and three years later appeared to be settled, having achieved a 'normal' life.

Although it is, of course, too soon to say whether or not Graham will reoffend in the longer term, it would appear that for an individual with his style of personality functioning, stringent risk management approaches were felt to be unbearable, and he has fared much better being left alone to a large extent.

Paul (a case of 'a visit to the seaside')

Paul is a 45-year-old man with a long history of sexual assaults on pre-pubescent boys. He has a diagnosis of borderline and dependent personality disorder. Paul was generally very isolated in the community and had poor social skills; however, he had forged a friendship with another sexual offender (a lower-risk 'incest' offender) who he had met in prison. Paul tended to be very disclosing to professionals – often contrary to his best interests – and on this occasion requested permission to go on a trip (already planned) with his friend to the seaside. His request was denied on the assumption that there was a high risk that the two offenders might target potential victims on the beach. The MAPPP [Multi-Agency Public Protection Panel] police were informed, and also a discrete word was had with the lower-risk offender, suggesting that his own rehabilitation might be jeopardised by his association with Paul. The refusal was handled courteously, but nevertheless Paul was disappointed. Within two weeks, Paul was presenting as significantly more sexually preoccupied – although he denied specifically fantasising about boys – and shortly afterwards, he was breached and returned to prison after approaching a boy in the park and engaging him in a conversation about masturbation.

Paul's own account to his psychologist regarding the visit to the seaside was that he had never seen the sea; his own childhood had been unusually deprived and abusive, and he was an unloved child who had been ostracised from the family from a young age. His fantasy of the seaside was of happy families going on day trips together, and he wanted to have a sense of what this might be like. His experience of the refusal – and his friend's subsequent distancing from him – was like a re-enactment of his own family's withholding of love and care from him. With an acute sense of emotional deprivation, he responded as he had always done – replacing the anxiety induced by his inner emptiness with a sexual excitement in which he felt he had control.

Clearly, Paul's account may not have been truthful (although it was psychologically compelling), or even if sincere, the agency fears may also have been entirely valid. Certainly, the risk to the institution/agency – that Paul might be identified by the media as having been given permission to gaze at boys on the beach – was very acute. Nevertheless, the sensible risk management response triggered an acute phase of relapse, which was very difficult to manage and led to failure.

Jack (a case of the 'condemnation script')

Jack was a 58-year-old offender who had committed a sadistic sexual murder on a female stranger 30 years previously. At the time of the index offence he had been diagnosed with a mix of narcissistic, schizoid and avoidant personality traits, although for many years it had been doubtful whether he met the criteria for any diagnosis of personality disorder. He made slow, but positive progress in prison, engaged constructively in treatment and behaved in an exemplary fashion during his extremely long and cautious release process. He managed well in open prison and spent 18 contented months in a pre-release hostel (which was surprisingly little supervised and he was subject to few constraints). His transition on release to a probation hostel with a stringent risk management plan was more difficult but he coped well with setbacks. He was particularly dismayed by the reaction potential employers displayed – understandably – to his disclosure letter, and the only useful work role he could foresee for himself was in relation to helping ex-offenders.

To the shock and dismay of all those involved in his management, Jack committed a further offence – a seriously violent attack, again on a female stranger – only a few days after he had participated in a risk management meeting. For this meeting, Jack had requested that his risk rating be reduced from high to medium in the light of his sustained good behaviour and progress, and he put forward some reasoned arguments as to why he should be allowed to undertake a short counselling course. Both requests were turned down, but in a sensitive fashion: a senior probation officer had reviewed his file and advised delaying a reduction in his risk rating; he had also been told that the Home Office were unlikely to respond positively to his request for the counselling course. In retrospect, Jack described how enraged he felt at the perceived injustice of the situation: not only had a 'stranger' judged him, but also there was a lack of illogicality in the thinking about counselling – his history suggested clearly that he posed a risk to strangers not to acquaintances; he was more of a risk wandering the streets than to other course participants.

Within days, Jack was engaging in high-risk behaviours, drinking, watching pornography and planning an offence. He consciously considered his well-rehearsed relapse prevention plan and deliberately decided not to ring his psychologist for help, preferring to offend. He felt that his main thought during this emotionally aggrieved state of mind was 'if they think I'm so high risk, I'll f***ing show them what high risk is'.

Clearly we can never be certain whether or not Jack was destined to reoffend regardless of the risk management plan. However, his case does exemplify the unexpected strain of returning to the community when subject to rigorous supervision after so many years of striving for release. Again, there is the suggestion that his emotional state – and thus his risk – was much more stable when he was given freedom to succeed as a 'normal' person, and there is no doubt that the immediate trigger to the offence was a belief – irrational and destructive – that he was condemned to be high risk indefinitely, and that if he was going to fail, he would do so in a way in which he had full control.

Clearly three examples can only provide a fleeting insight into some of the unpredictable and paradoxical responses of particularly risky and damaged men who try to live a 'good life' (Ward and Brown 2003). That there might be problems with the current political and social climate in relation to successful community management with a minority of individuals should not negate the considerable benefits that legislation and practice has brought in recent years to improving the consistency, communication and effectiveness of multi-agency arrangements to the majority. Furthermore, the case examples should not distort the picture that the majority of sex offenders do manage to return to the community and respond to risk management. Nevertheless, there are lessons to be learned, one of which must be that really thoughtful risk management does not always consist of rights and wrongs, but of dilemmas. Secondly, it is generally misleading to view success or failure as the outcome of a single – usually time limited – episode of care; rather it should be seen as a point on a much longer path to desistence from offending, which necessitates a sensitive collaboration with the offender over time.

It must also be clear from the case examples and the wider experience which they represent that there is a fine line between control and persecution, one that is difficult to detect at times, and that social exclusion – in the current climate – seems to be an unavoidable consequence of rigorous risk management. It seems to be counter-intuitive, and yet some of these higher-risk offenders appear to do better when left alone and given freedom, although judging just when that should happen seems impossibly difficult. However, such offenders are hypersensitive to perceived injustice and are unusually astute in recognising when stringent risk management has lost its focus and become a defensive institutional/agency measure. The possibility that stringent risk management approaches embodied within the MAPPA re-creates – for some offenders – the disturbing experiences of their early lives seems absolutely clear. That it may paradoxically result in triggering greater levels of offending is an uncomfortable idea, as is the suggestion that in order to reduce risk, sometimes professionals and agencies may need to take risks.

Part V
Pulling the threads together

Chapter 16

Pulling together the threads – public confidence and perceptions of fairness

Christine Glenn

I thought I would focus on public confidence as that is the real challenge for the Parole Board – that the public trust us to deal fairly with high-profile cases like that of Craig Sweeney. The nature of the Board's role means that the unpalatable truth is that risk assessment is not an exact science. Unfortunately some prisoners released will go on to reoffend. Our duty is to ensure that we have done everything possible to make our processes as tight as they can be to minimise this risk – and to have procedures in place to learn when things go wrong and to try and improve our decisions.

I posed four questions when I looked at this issue:

1. Where are we now?
2. What are the current issues?
3. How do we address them?
4. What will success look like?

Having listened to the contributors over the last two days, I fear that probably a bigger challenge is what Andrew Rutherford termed 'getting out of the NOMS mud' and I am looking forward to that journey and the final destination. However, I will keep to the four questions I want to address in this rather short paper as well as trying to pull in some of the themes we have had so far.

So where are we now? I don't think it's overstating the case to say that public confidence is probably at rock bottom with us at the moment. I think the impact of the two Bridges Reports has been fundamental largely because our role is so misunderstood. I had worked in the Criminal Justice service for 25 years before I joined the Parole Board and thought I knew the Board's role and what it did. I was wrong and many of our members who have great experience and expertise in the justice system say the same. One of the greatest misunderstandings seems to be the difference between what we do and what the Probation Service does, who is responsible for what, how our organisations fit together and how we must work well together to achieve good risk assessments and good risk management. I blame a lot of this – and I do use the word blame – on the set-up arrangements for the Board. Next year the Parole Board will be 40 but we are treated still rather as a troublesome child. The Board started as part of the Probation Unit in the Home Office when it was first set up. It moved to the Prison Service again as an integral unit there before finally several years ago achieving some status of independence as a non-departmental public body, first with the Prison Service as the sponsors and latterly the Home Office.

A major theme of this conference has been the lack of perceived independence caused by the sponsoring arrangements with the Home Office. It is not possible to justify a process where a tribunal has its members and its chairman appointed by one of the parties to the decisions it makes and in circumstances where that tribunal must follow directions set by that same party. It doesn't convey the impression of equality of arms. No matter that there has not been any attempt at any level to interfere in any individual case decision – the arrangements are not sustainable if we really want public confidence in the Board. The outcome of a move to the Department of Constitutional Affairs could also give us a ministerial champion. I listened with envy to the accounts of how human rights legislation had just not been an issue in Scotland – south of the Border, there are mixed messages about the proper balance between state and citizen and sometimes, as with the Rice report, we feel caught in the crossfire.

Another of our current issues is the review process and the need to respond to each such review. I know of five current reviews that concern us – these range from a review into our information needs to a Home Office-wide review of all non-departmental public bodies where our continued existence as a separate and discrete body is under active consideration. Action and change cost money so I am going to try to suggest where I think the action and the change could come.

I remember inviting two victims of crime to speak at a conference of the Board. They later came and observed a panel dealing with a number of cases. We have a number of visitors to panels and we ask them to write their comments in a visitors' book. One of them wrote how much he had valued lifting the veil on the 'black art' that had been his previous impression of how the Board worked. It does not help us that we are not able to explain to the public our reasons for making our decisions in individual cases. When the Board faced media scrutiny over our refusal to release Tony Martin early, I sought legal advice about whether we could publish all the reasons on our website, anonymising them as necessary. I am not suggesting that we look to name and shame or to give out personal details of where people are living. What I wanted to achieve was an ability to explain our decisions and the factors we have to weigh up in making them. I was disappointed that the advice we received was unequivocal – and negative. I am still of the view that if we were able to be more open here – as is the case certainly in many states of the USA – the public would have much better information and understanding of our role.

That said, I don't think the Board has been very good at giving out information about itself in the past. We are trying to get better and I am giving you an unashamed plug now for a series of three documentaries which are going out on BBC2 later this year. These have been two years in the making and tell the stories of eight prisoners and how their applications are dealt with. We hear the voice of the prisoners, of the members and most importantly of the victim. I hope the public will have a better understanding of the job that we do as a result of these programmes.

Our main practical problem is our reliance on others to provide us with timely and complete information on which we base our decisions. Good information is the oxygen of our business – and any risk assessment is only as good as the information on which it is based. The Board is both independent and interdependent. We depend on many other agencies for reports, risk assessments and the like and sometimes there is confusion about roles and remits here. I welcome the review on information needs and hope that minimum standards will be set about what reports must contain and a form of accreditation for those who make the risk assessments on which we base our decisions. This is something the public has a right to expect.

The Board has been working on its own quality agenda for over two years – setting standards for report writers, looking at research require-ments, improving the training of its members, tightening its member appraisal system and feeding lessons identified by its Review Committee into all aspects of member development. The next stage for us is implementing the scheme we have been developing to accredit our members in different types of Board work. The bottom line is that ultimately if we find a member just isn't delivering quality decisions then there must be an effective sanction mechanism and that is something we are working through. All of these necessary initiatives cost money and when 92 per cent of our current budget goes on staff and member costs just to deal with the current casework (which has gone up already 35 per cent this year) this is a challenge. Following a hugely rigorous selection process, Parole Board members receive a week's induction training. To put this in some international perspective, we have just hosted a visit from Renee Collette, the Executive Vice-President of the National Parole Board of Canada. Renee told me that in Canada new members get five weeks' induction training, where we get five days, and then 20 days a year development training, where we get only three or four. This is not a case of *vive la différence*!

Despite this lack of resources, the Board has made progress in implementing its quality agenda. Now is the time for the further step change needed so that the learning happens across the whole system. The Board is especially keen to start having some multi-agency case reviews – with the police, probation and prison services – in that small number of cases where someone released by us goes on to commit a further serious offence. We will of course have our own internal review but an honest and shared inquiry among the responsible agencies is necessary so that we can all be sure that our processes are really fit for purpose.

This brings me to another major issue for the Board – oral hearings. Over the past four or five years, the Board has changed quite fundamentally from an organisation that made most of its decisions on paper to what is effectively a tribunal with a large number of oral hearings conducted by panels in person. When I started at the Board four and a half years ago, we dealt with around 285 oral hearings a year. We are anticipating about 2,300 this year, and that doesn't include the ones that are deferred or adjourned and which have to be listed time and again. Currently, we are running at a deferral rate of about 30 per cent, which is just not on. It leads to delay in reviewing a prisoner's liberty and it is a waste of everyone's time and money. The single main cause here is that the dossiers are provided too late. The Board has set up a very detailed monitoring system now so we record every prison and every dossier. We could easily publish our own league table – so far we have not taken that step. We now receive about 40 per cent of lifer dossiers from prisons on time, but only 8 per cent are complete. When the whole system depends on this information being available at the right time, it is not surprising that the cases continue to be deferred.

The late dossier means that we are not able to use our sifting procedures and early case management reviews. It follows that our judges and panel chairs cannot make effective directions when the dossier comes in late. The fact that there are no sanctions to enforce our directions also means that they are less effective than could be the case. It seems that no one now really expects the hearing to go ahead first time and this has led to a culture of delay. Everyone has a responsibility to address this and the present position here is untenable.

One of our contributors yesterday said – and I wrote down the quote – that they were used to 'doing the Blue Peter job on the dossier'. The fact that sometimes hearings start and the panel members and the representatives etc. are all trying to get the pages in the right order and to check that everyone has all got the same contents is just not a way to run anything. We really did a lot of work two years ago on improving the oral process but it hasn't delivered the benefits that it should have done. Possibly part of that is that there is no clear accountability of who is responsible for the dossier. There really needs to be a senior person who is accountable for that being right and for everybody having the right one – and the same one in the same order. The fact is that this still doesn't happen.

Something that the Board does welcome is the Home Secretary's stated intention to enhance the role of the Secretary of State's representative at the hearing. It is just wrong to try and make a fair risk assessment that properly balances public safety and the correct reintegration of prisoners in the community when only one side of the table is adequately represented. So, improving representation really is a welcome step and should lead to real equality of arms here.

Another real problem issue is disclosure. Presently, there are two sorts of disclosure depending on the sort of case – one for the determinate sentence cases where the governor decides, the second for lifers where the Board makes the decision. This is a good example of difference without good reason – something that really cannot be satisfactorily explained. This in turn will not inspire confidence. Victims I know do not trust that information they give via the current process will be kept confidential and I worry that we are not getting information here sometimes that we should be getting in terms of risk relating to victims.

The government in its recent policy statement seeks to rebalance the criminal justice system so that much more regard is placed on victims. The Board welcomes this. We always seek to place the victim at the heart of our decisions, but there is a lack of understanding that the Board's role is not about punishment – rather we are looking to risk and the future. There is a lot of work to do to agree the right level of involvement of victims in parole decisions and I do have concerns that expectations might be raised too highly by what's coming out at the moment as it lacks so much detail. The Board is working with victim groups to manage and develop this policy together so that there is a real clarity and confidence about the Board's role and decision-making here.

Something else that would really make a huge difference is earlier involvement in policy development and better planning and impact assessment of new sentences.

I was surprised when Stephen Shute said the new recall system was an improvement on what it was because I don't think it is fit for purpose and I think the debate yesterday highlighted some of the problems. There are very tight deadlines for everyone – especially the Probation Service – and risk management plans are just not being provided for a very high number of people recalled to prison. This means that cases are churned and prisoners remain in custody sometimes even after their licence expiry date. The requirement for every one of these cases to be reviewed by the Board is just not necessary in my view. I am not suggesting for a moment that the process should be solely one for the Executive. But I don't think justice would suffer in the least for the Board only to consider cases where the prisoner was making representations against his or her recall. The requirement to consider all these cases is not adding any value in non-disputed recalls and is clogging up the system and causing unnecessary delay.

I turn to another of the new sentences, the indeterminate public protection sentence. There are now about 1,300 people in prison serving these sentences. So far, the shortest tariff I have heard is three months. The reality is that there is no possibility that people with short tariffs will have any real chance of release on or near tariff expiry. This was certainly not made clear to sentencers and the lack of forward planning here has put the system under pressure. Nick Sanderson, a senior civil servant, is conducting a review of the indeterminate public protection sentences to try and resolve the problems now being faced. This is welcome – but let's hope that we can learn from this and plan ahead in future when such major changes are proposed.

Probably the single biggest issue that has attracted media and public interest has been the debate about the impact of human rights on the work of the Parole Board. Much of this has stemmed from an apparent misinterpretation of some comments in the Rice report from Andrew Bridges. I was so grateful to Mark Elliott for his succinct and clear analysis here yesterday. Recent press coverage as a result has suggested how we are soft on human rights for prisoners. This is quite a contrast to what was in the press some months ago when we were described as Britain's answer to Guantanamo Bay. This was a very specific case where the Board decided that the interests of justice and the proper balancing of interests required that information should not be disclosed to the prisoner, Harry Roberts, or even to his own lawyer. Instead, we instructed a specially appointed advocate to deal with the sensitive material. There is rightly a public debate about fundamental and human rights and how these are balanced across the justice system. There do appear to be mixed messages going around Whitehall across the various departments and this misunderstanding is very soundly based on interpretations of what Andrew Bridges said. This is a priority that needs to be tackled head on.

236

I finish with a few thoughts about what success would look like for the Board. It would be a complete dossier received on time with risk assessments completed by accredited risk assessors. All cases would be listed by the Board in good time for the review decision to be made on time. Members would have more training and would be fully accredited. We would be able to publish decisions, properly anonymised. The public would have a good understanding of our role and have confidence that the processes were reasonable and properly and effectively reviewed with all responsible agencies where there were instances of serious reoffending. New sentences would be properly planned and resourced in advance so there was real transparency and fairness. And we would be perceived as a truly independent body by everyone.

Chapter 17

A personal overview

Hugh Southey

Introduction

This chapter is a reworking of a talk given at the end of the conference which attempted to identify some core themes. There are two preliminary points. Firstly, the breadth and depth of the other contributions to the conference meant that it was impossible to identify all the themes. I have inevitably focused on a few themes that appear to me to be important. Others who attended the conference will regard other themes as being more important. Secondly, this note inevitably contains my subjective views on the contributions of others. There may be contributors who feel that I have misrepresented them. If that is the case, I apologise.

As a lawyer who spends a lot of time representing prisoners before the Parole Board, it appears to me that at times it is suggested that lawyers representing prisoners have different objectives to others who participate in the parole system. However, what I hope to demonstrate is that actually there are common objectives and concerns that all participants share.

The objectives of the Parole Board

The first area of agreement may appear obvious. All the contributions to the conference proceeded on a key assumption. That assumption is that there are two key objectives that underlie the work of the Parole Board.

Prisoners who pose an unacceptable level of risk should not be released. However, prisoners who pose an acceptable level of risk should be released as soon as possible.

As a lawyer representing prisoners, it might be thought that I want to see a prisoner released whatever level of risk they pose. Obviously, my role in the process is to act as an advocate for my client whatever level of risk they pose. However, as someone concerned about penal justice and the interests of my clients, I do not want to see my clients released and then fail.

There are two reasons why it is important that prisoners are not released in circumstances in which they fail. Firstly, on an individual level failure is likely to delay eventual resettlement. A prisoner who fails is likely to be returned to conditions of higher security and so it will take them longer to progress towards release. In addition, on a wider level, each failure increases the political pressure to introduce policies that increase the unnecessary use of imprisonment.

Although there are good reasons to delay the release of a prisoner who poses an unacceptable risk, delaying the release of a prisoner who can be released is contrary to the interests of society. Firstly, as is well known, the continued imprisonment will cost tens of thousands of pounds. In addition, delaying the release of prisoners who know that they can be released will create a sense of unfairness and demoralisation. That sense of unfairness is likely to result in poor behaviour as the work of Professor Liebling demonstrates.

Although the objectives of the Parole Board are clear, it appears that there is agreement that it is almost impossible to achieve those objectives in every case. That is because both objectives depend upon an accurate assessment of risk. However, risk is not capable of accurate determination in every case. Practitioners know of cases where a prisoner has been released and then has committed a further offence that is so different to the index offence that it could not have been predicted. For example, I am aware of the case of an arsonist who was released and then committed a sexual offence despite the fact that he had no previous convictions for sexual offences.

The above analysis suggests that Terry McCarthy was wrong to state on behalf of the Parole Board that the unthinkable must not happen. The only way of preventing the unthinkable happening in all cases is to prevent prisoners being released in all cases. However, such an approach is obviously contrary to one objective of the Parole Board. That is, the release of prisoners who no longer need to be detained. It is more accurate to state that the unthinkable may happen and we must do what we can to minimise the possibility of it happening.

The fact that the unthinkable may happen has three consequences. Firstly, the problems of assessing risk mean that the Parole Board should only ever be seen as part of the system of risk management of offenders. However good the Parole Board is, it will be of little value if offenders are not properly supervised following release. That does not necessarily mean that prisoners should be subjected to excessively restrictive supervision. As Jackie Craissati pointed out, restrictive supervision can generate risk in the same way that inadequate supervision can. However, it does mean that there is a need to recognise that cuts in the budgets of the Probation Service are creating risk by meaning that few prisoners enjoy long-term relationships with their probation officers that result in trust and cooperation upon release.

Secondly, the blame culture that has been generated at times by the media is mistaken because it assumes that perfect decision-making is possible. We should acknowledge that the fact that a prisoner is released and then offends does not necessarily mean that anything has gone wrong. It may be that nobody could have foreseen the risk of further offending. The blame culture is damaging because it may result in defensive decision-making.

Finally, the need for accurate risk assessment requires the Parole Board to adopt the best possible decision-making process. A high-quality decision-making process can reduce the risk of a wrong decision.

Improving decision-making

Sir Duncan Nichol in his submission identified a number of ways in which the quality of decision-making can be significantly improved. However, it appears to me that there was one important matter missing. That is improved human rights.

Human rights are often portrayed in the media as meaning that prisoners are released when they would not otherwise be released. However, as Mark Elliott demonstrates, it has very little (if any) impact on who is released. It is almost entirely about the standards of procedural fairness that are adopted when the Parole Board takes decisions. As Professor Liebling commented, fairness is not the same thing as laxity.

The presentations to this conference and the chapters of this book make it clear that there are a number of ways in which procedural fairness can be improved. However, it is worth considering why these improvements matter. I hope that I can demonstrate that it is because it improves the quality of decision-making and hence assists the Parole Board to achieve its objectives.

The focus of many submissions was on independence and why the Parole Board lacks it. It was not just the representatives of prisoners who complained about inadequate independence. Sir Duncan Nichol and His

Honour Judge Thornton QC both made powerful submissions on a lack of independence. However, why does independence matter? Fundamentally, it is not because a prisoner has some right to independence. It is because independence improves decision-making.

If the Parole Board lacks independence from the Home Office, there is a risk that it will be unwilling to challenge material supplied by the Prison Service. Challenging material supplied by the Prison Service will not necessarily benefit the prisoner. As Professor Rutherford indicated, problems can arise where all the Prison Service reports support release. Challenging the reports in those circumstances may result in the prisoner being refused release. However, challenging the assumptions and logic underlying Prison Service reports is likely to improve the quality of decision-making. It may identify flaws in the reports.

The submission that independence will improve the quality of decision-making is supported by consideration of the ways in which independence can be improved.

His Honour Judge Thornton QC pointed out that independence would result in the Parole Board being able to summons witnesses. Such a power would improve decision-making as it would enable the Board to ensure that it heard from all relevant witnesses. However, it would not necessarily benefit prisoners. The power to summons witnesses would often be used in cases where a witness is afraid of a prisoner because they know that their evidence is hostile.

His Honour Judge Thornton QC also pointed out that independence would result in the Parole Board being able to determine its own procedural rules. Such a development would ensure that the Parole Board could use its experience to ensure that it had the powers necessary to achieve its objectives. However, while the Home Office makes procedural rules, there will be a legitimate concern that the rules will be influenced by the objectives of the Home Office such as the need to cut costs.

It is not just independence that demonstrates how procedural fairness can improve the quality of decision-making. It has been suggested in the media that legal representation of prisoners is unhelpful in some way. However, good quality legal representation improves the quality of decision-making by allowing evidence to be challenged and ensuring that all relevant evidence is presented. The problem that exists at present was identified by Jo Thompson. The Secretary of State needs to improve the quality of his representation so there is genuine equality of arms. If that happens then the quality of decision-making should improve as representatives will assist the Parole Board by ensuring that it has all relevant material.

Procedural improvements need not merely focus on oral hearings. Professor Shute made some very interesting points about Parole Board interviews that appeared to me to be misunderstood by some. I hope that I am not misrepresenting the views of Professor Shute when I say that his criticism was that the interview system was flawed in the manner that it operated in the past. For example, firstly he suggested that the role of the interview was unclear to prisoners. That limited their participation as they were on guard. In addition, the fact that the interviewer did not participate in the decision undermined its value.

The significance of Professor Shute's analysis is that it identifies clear ways in which decision-making can be improved. Plans to reintroduce interviews should not merely repeat the errors of the past. They should look at ways in which an interview system can be improved.

The analysis above hopefully demonstrates that, although people like Simon Creighton are correct to say that we have come a long way in improving the standards of fairness adopted by the Parole Board, there is a lot more that can be done in improving standards. If those steps are taken, it will assist the Parole Board to achieve its aim of taking reliable decisions.

Resources

The third area of agreement at the conference appeared to be that there have been significant problems caused by the increased workload faced by the Parole Board. This increase in workload was to a significant extent linked to the rise in the number of recalls.

The increase in workload has caused significant pressures for all the professionals involved in the Parole Board. Probation officers arranging recalls lack time to prepare recall reports. Parole Board staff arranging hearings find it difficult to arrange prompt hearings. Lawyers representing prisoners find their diaries full. As a consequence all complain about the pressures that they are under.

The pressure that professionals are under means that there is a risk that corners will be cut. One Parole Board member said during a coffee break that the Board cannot adjourn every case where they lack adequate reports. That may be an accurate statement of the realities faced by the Parole Board. However, it is not an acceptable state of affairs. Decisions taken on the basis of inadequate reports are likely to be poor decisions.

The pressures faced as a result of the increased workload may also result in the sort of problems described by both Gill Attrill and Professor Kemshall. There is a real risk that increased workload will result in a failure to consider the individual circumstances of a case. That is clearly contrary to basic fairness and will result in poor quality decision-making. There is also a risk that important risk management controls will not be applied correctly.

The answer to the problems caused by an increased workload is to ensure that greater resources are made available. Obviously all the participants in the Parole Board process receive public sector funding and there are limits on the funding that can be provided to the public sector. However, nobody can expect the public sector to cope with dramatic increases in workload without also increasing the resources available. In addition, account needs to be taken of the costs of poor decisions. As already indicated, detaining a prisoner who could be released is likely to cost tens of thousands of pounds every year. Releasing a prisoner who poses an unacceptable risk may result in harm that cannot be quantified in financial terms. As a consequence the costs of not adequately funding those involved in the parole process may well be higher than the costs of funding the process at a level that enables good quality decisions to be taken.

Conclusions

I hope that the analysis above demonstrates that there is substantial agreement about three matters:

- The objectives of the Parole Board appear clear. Essentially the Parole Board should seek to release prisoners who can be released but detain those who pose an unacceptable risk.

- The Parole Board can and should improve its decision-making process. That will enable more reliable decisions to be taken.

- There is a need for greater resources to cope with the increased workload.

I also hope that it is clear that when lawyers representing prisoners call for greater procedural fairness, they are not acting contrary to the objectives of the Parole Board. They are hoping to assist the Parole Board to achieve its objectives by ensuring that more reliable decisions are taken.

References

Adams, J. (1995) *Risk*. London: UCL.

Ahmad, S. (1996) *Fairness in Prison*. PhD thesis, University of Cambridge.

Allan, T. R. S. (1998) 'Procedural fairness and the duty of respect', *Oxford Journal of Legal Studies*, 18 (3): 497–515.

Arnott, H. and Creighton, S. (2006) *Parole Board Hearings*. London: Legal Action Group.

Barry, B. (1989) *Theories of Justice*. London: Harvester Wheatsheaf.

Beech, A., Friendship, C., Erikson, M. and Hanson, K. (2002) 'The relationship between static and dynamic risk factors and reconviction in a sample of UK child abusers', *Sexual Abuse: A Journal of Research and Treatment*, 14: 155–67.

Blair, A. (2005) Prime Minister's monthly press conference, August. Available at: http://www.pm.gov.uk/output/Page8041.asp.

Blair, A. (2006) *Our Nation's Future*. Lecture on the criminal justice system, 23 June. Available at: http://www.pm.gov.uk/output/Page9737.asp.

Blom-Cooper, L., Hally, H. and Murphy, E. (1995) *The Falling Shadow: One Patient's Mental Health Care*. London: Duckworth.

Bottoms, A. E. (1999) 'Interpersonal violence and social order in prisons', in M. Tonry and J. Persilia (eds), *Prisons, Crime and Justice: A Review of Research, 26*. Chicago: University of Chicago Press, pp. 205–82.

Bottoms, A. E. and Rose, G. (1998) 'The importance of staff–prisoner relationships: results from a study in three male prisons', in D. Price and A. Liebling (eds), 'Staff–Prisoner Relationships: A Review of the Literature'. Unpublished report submitted to the Prison Service.

Braithwaite, J. (2002) *Restorative Justice and Responsive Regulation*. New York: Oxford University Press.

Brennan, W. C. and Khunduka, S. K. (1970) 'Role discrepancies and professional socialization: the case of the juvenile probation officer', *Social Work*, 15: 87–94.

Bruce, R. (Assistant Chief Officer, Durham) (2003) Personal comment.

Carlisle Committee (1988) *The Parole System in England and Wales*, Cm 532. London: HMSO.

Clear, T. R., Harris, P. M. and Baird, S. C. (1992) 'Probationer violations and officer response', *Journal of Criminal Justice*, 20: 1–12.

Connelly, C. and Williamson, S. (2000) *Review of the Research Literature on Serious Violent and Sexual Offenders*, Crime and Criminal Justice Research Findings No. 44. Edinburgh: Scottish Executive Central Research Unit.

Cooke, D. J. and Hart, S. D. (2004) 'Personality disorders', in E. V. Johnstone et al. (eds), *Companion to Psychiatric Studies*, 8th edn. Edinburgh: Churchill Livingstone.

Copas, J. and Marshall, P. (1998) 'The Offender Group Reconviction Scale: the statistical reconviction score for use by probation officers', *Journal of the Royal Statistical Society*, Series C: 159–71.

Craig, P. (2003) *Administrative Law*, 5th edn. London: Sweet & Maxwell.

Craissati, J. and Beech, A. (2003) 'A review of dynamic variables and their relationship to risk prediction in sex offenders', *Journal of Sexual Aggression*, 9 (1): 41–55.

Craissati, J. and Beech, A. (2005) 'Risk prediction and failure in a complete urban sample of sex offenders', *Journal of Forensic Psychiatry and Psychology*, 16 (1): 24–40.

Craissati, J. and Beech, A. (2006) 'The role of key developmental variables in identifying sex offenders likely to fail in the community: An enhanced risk prediction model', *Child Abuse and Neglect*, 30: 327–39.

Craissati, J., Horne, L. and Taylor, R. (2003) 'Effective treatment models for personality disordered offenders', in NIMHE, *Personality Disorder: No Longer a Diagnosis of Exclusion*. London: HMSO.

Craissati, J., Webb, L. and Keen, S. (2006) 'The relationship between developmental variables, personality disorder and risk in an urban community sample of child molesters and rapists'. (Submitted)

Cullen, Lord (1990) *The Public Enquiry into the Piper Alpha Disaster*. London: HMSO.

Davies, R. (1996) 'The inter-disciplinary network and the internal world of the offender', in C. Cordess and M. Cox (eds), *Forensic Psychotherapy: Crime, Psychodynamics and the Offender Patient*. London: Jessica Kingsley.

Department for Constitutional Affairs (2006) *Review of the Implementation of the Human Rights Act*. London: Department for Constitutional Affairs.

Dicey, A. (1959) *An Introduction to the Study of the Law of the Constitution*, 10th edn. London: Macmillan.

Durham Police Authority (2005) *Annual Report 2004/2005*. Available at: http://www.durham-pa.gov.uk.

Elliott, C. (1999) *Locating the Energy for Change: A Practitioner's Guide to Appreciative Inquiry*. Winnipeg: International Institute for Sustainable Development.

Elliott, C., Liebling, A. and Arnold, H. (2001) 'Locating the energy for change: the use of appreciative inquiry in two local prisons', *Prison Service Journal*, 135: 3–10.

Ellis, A. J. (2005) *Psychological Torture by the Misuse of Long Term Solitary Confinement in New Zealand Prisons and the denial of Habeas Corpus: An International and Comparative Perspective*. MPhil, Essex University.

Eskridge, C. (1979) 'Education and training of probation officers: a critical assessment', *Fed Prob*, 43 (3): 41–8.

Feldman, D. (2006) 'Human rights, terrorism and risk: the roles of politicians and judges', *Public Law*, pp. 364–84.

Fennell, S. (1988) *Investigation into the Kings Cross Underground Fire*. London: Department of Transport.

Finn, P. (1997) *Sex Offender Community Notification*. Washington DC: National Institute of Justice, Office of Justice Programs, Research in Action.

Fletcher, H. (2003) 'Prison licence, community order breaches and the prison population', *Napo News*, 149: 1.

Fordham, M. (1998) 'Reasons: the third dimension', *Judicial Review*, pp. 158–64.

Friendship, C. and Thornton, D. (2000) 'Sexual reconviction for sexual offenders discharged from prison in England and Wales: implications for evaluating treatment', *British Journal of Criminology*, 41: 285–92.

Galligan, D. (1996) *Due Process and Fair Procedures: A Study of Administrative Procedures*. Oxford: Oxford University Press.

Garfinkel, H. (1967) *Studies in Ethnomethodology*. Englewood Cliffs, NJ: Prentice Hall.

Geiringer, C. (2005) 'Case note: *Rameka* v. *New Zealand*', *New Zealand Yearbook of International Law*, 2: 185–203.

Halliday, J. (2001) *Making Punishments Work: Report of a Review of the Sentencing Framework for England and Wales*. London: Home Office Communication Directorate.

Harris, D., Attrill, G. and Bush, J. (2004) 'Using choice as an aid to engagement and risk management with violent psychopathic offenders', in G. McPherson and L. Jones (eds), *Issues in Forensic Psychology*. Leicester: British Psychological Society, pp. 144–51.

Hart, S. D., Michie, C. and Cooke, D. (in press) 'The precision of actuarial risk assessment instruments: evaluating the "margins of error" of group versus individual predictions of violence', *British Journal of Psychiatry*.

Hawkins, K. (2003) 'Order, rationality and silence: some reflections on criminal justice decision-making', in L. Gelsthorpe and N. Padfield (eds), *Exercising Discretion: Decision-Making in the Criminal Justice System and Beyond*. Cullompton: Willan.

Health and Safety Executive (1988) *Blackspot Construction*. London: HMSO.

Heilbrun, K. (1997) 'Prediction versus management models relevant to risk assessment: the importance of legal decision-making context', *Law and Human Behaviour*, 21: 347–59.

Her Majesty's Government (2006) *A Five Year Strategy for Protecting the Public and Reducing Re-offending*, CM6717. London: Stationery Office.

Her Majesty's Inspectorate of Probation (2005a) *Realising the Potential: A Short Focused Inspection of the Offender Assessment System (OASys)*, Thematic Inspection Report. London: Home Office.

Her Majesty's Inspectorate of Probation (2005b) *Recalled Prisoners: A Short Review of Recalled Adult Male Determinate-Sentenced Prisoners*. London: Home Office.

Her Majesty's Inspectorate of Probation (2005c) *Management Reviews of Serious Incidents*. See: http://www.inspectorates.homeoffice.gov.uk.

Her Majesty's Inspectorate of Probation (2006a) *An Independent Review of a Serious Further Offence Case: Damien Hanson and Elliot White*. London: Home Office.

Her Majesty's Inspectorate of Probation (2006b) *An Independent Review of a Serious Further Offence Case: Anthony Rice*. London: HMIP. Available at: http://www.inspectorates.homeoffice.gov.uk.

Hewart, G. (1929) *The New Despotism*. London: Benn.

Hidden, A. (1989) *Investigation into the Clapham Junction Railway Accident*. London: HMSO.

Holloway, K. and Grounds, A. (2003) 'Discretion and the release of mentally disordered offenders' in L. Gelsthorpe and N. Padfield (eds), *Exercising Discretion: Decision-making in the Criminal Justice System and Beyond*. Cullompton: Willan.

Home Office (1979) *Prison Statistics England and Wales 1978*, Cmnd. 7626. London: HMSO.

Home Office (1990) *Crime, Justice and Protecting the Public: The Government's Proposals for Legislation* (White Paper), Cm 965. London: HMSO.

Home Office (1991a) *Prison Disturbances April 1990: Report of an Inquiry by the Rt. Hon. Lord Justice Woolf (Parts I and II) and his Honour Judge Stephen Tumim (Part II)*. London: HMSO.

Home Office (1991b) *Custody, Care and Justice: The Way Ahead for the Prison Service in England and Wales*. London: HMSO.

Home Office (1993) *Report of the Parole Board for 1992*, HC 712. London: HMSO.

Home Office (2004a) *Directions to the Parole Board on the Release of Determinate Sentence Prisoners*. London: Home Office.

Home Office (2004b) *Directions to the Parole Board on the Release and Recall of Life Sentence Prisoners*. London: Home Office.

Home Office (2004c) *MAPPA Guidance (Version 2)*. London: Home Office.

Home Office (2005) *National Standards 2005*, Probation Circular 15/2005. London: Home Office.

Home Office (2005/06) National Probation Service Performance Report 18 and Weighted Scorecard Q2.

Home Office (2006a) *Rebalancing the Criminal Justice System in Favour of the Law-abiding Majority: Cutting Crime, Reducing Reoffending and Protecting the Public*. London: Home Office.

Home Office (2006c) *Home Secretary Announces New Public Protection Measures*, Press Release 20 April. London: Home Office. See: http://www.press.home office.gov.uk (accessed 8 August 2006).

Home Office (2006d) *Home Secretary Pledges 8,000 New Prison Places – Putting Public Protection First*, Press Release 21 July. London: Home Office. See: http://www.press.homeoffice.gov.uk (accessed 8 August 2006).

Home Secretary (2006) *Annual Speech to the Parole Board, May 2006*. London: Home Office. See: http://www.press.homeoffice.gov.uk (accessed 8 August 2006).

Hood, C. and Jones, D. K. C. (1996) *Accident and Design: Contemporary Debates in Risk Management*. London: UDL Press.

Hood, R. (1992) *Race and Sentencing*. Oxford: Clarendon Press.

Hood, R. and Shute, S. (1994) *Parole in Transition: Evaluating the Impact and Effects of Changes in the Parole System – Phase One, Establishing the Base-Line*, Oxford

Centre for Criminological Research, Occasional Paper No. 13. Oxford: Oxford Centre for Criminological Research.

Hood, R. and Shute, S. (2000) *The Parole System at Work: A Study of Risk Based Decision-Making*, Home Office Research Study No. 202. London: Home Office.

Hood, R. and Shute, S. (2002) 'The changing face of parole in England and Wales: a story of some well-intentioned reforms and unintended consequences', in C. Prittwitz, M. Baurmann, K. Günther, L. Kuhlen, R. Merkel, C. Nestler and L. Schulz (eds), *Festschrift für Klaus Lüderssen*. Baden-Baden: Nomos Verlag, pp. 835–49.

Hood, R., Shute, S., Feilzer, M. and Wilcox, A. (2002) 'Sex offenders emerging from long-term imprisonment', *British Journal of Criminology*, [42]: 371–94.

Horlick-Jones, T. (1998) 'Meaning and contextualisation in risk assessment', *Reliability Engineering and System Safety*, 59: 79–89.

Howard, P. (2006) *The Offender Assessment System: An Evaluation of the Second Pilot*, Home Office Findings No. 278. London: Home Office.

Jones, T., Maclean, B. and Young, J. (1986) 'Crime, victimisation and policing in inner-city London', *The Islington Crime Survey*. Aldershot: Gower.

JUSTICE (1996) *Sentenced for Life*. London: JUSTICE.

Kemshall, H. (1998a) *Risk in Probation Practice*. Aldershot: Ashgate.

Kemshall, H. (1998b) 'Defensible decisions for risk: or "it's the doers wot get the blame"', *Probation Journal*, 45 (2): 67–72.

Kemshall, H. (2000) 'Conflicting knowledges on risk: the case of risk knowledge in the Probation Service', *Health, Risk and Society*, 2 (2): 143–58.

Kemshall, H. (2001) *Risk Assessment and Management of Known Sexual and Violent Offenders: A Review of Current Issues*, Police Research Series 140. London: Home Office.

Kemshall, H. (2003) *Understanding Risk in Criminal Justice*. London: Open University Press.

Kemshall, H., Mackenzie, G., Wilkinson, B. and Miller, J. (2006) *The Assessment and Management of the Risk of Harm*, Guidance and Training CD-ROM for NOMS. Leicester: De Montfort University with Home Office Public Protection Unit/NOMS.

Kemshall, H., Mackenzie, G., Wood, J., Bailey, R. and Yates, J. (2005) *Strengthening the Multi-Agency Public Protection Arrangements*, Practice and Development Report 45. London: Home Office.

Klofas, J. and Toch, H. (1982) 'The guard subculture myth', *Journal of Research in Crime and Delinquency* 19: 238-54.

Leggatt, Sir A. (2001) *Tribunals for Users: One System, One Service*, para. 2.20. See: http://www.tribunals-review.org.uk/leggatthtm/leg-00.htm.

Liebling, A. (2003) 'The late modern prison and the question of values', presentation to Australia and New Zealand Criminology Conference, Sydney, in Prison Reform Trust (2005) *Recycling Offenders Through Prison*. London: Prison Reform Trust.

Liebling, A. and Arnold, H. (2002) *Measuring the Quality of Prison Life*, Research Findings 174. London: Home Office.

Liebling, A. and Maruna, S. (eds) (2005) *The Effects of Imprisonment*. Cullompton: Willan.

Liebling, A. and Price, D. (2001) *The Prison Officer*. Winchester: Waterside Press.

Liebling, A. assisted by Arnold, H. (2004) *Prisons and Their Moral Performance: A Study of Values, Quality and Prison Life*. Oxford: Clarendon Press.

Liebling, A., Elliott, C. and Arnold, H. (2001) 'Transforming the prison: romantic optimism or appreciative realism?', *Criminal Justice*, 1 (1): 161–80.

Liebling, A., Elliott, C. and Price, D. (1999) 'Appreciative inquiry and relationships in prison', *Punishment and Society: The International Journal of Penology*, 1 (1): 71–98.

Liebling, A., Tait, S., Stiles, A. and Durie, L. (2005) 'Revisiting prison suicide: the role of fairness and distress', in A. Liebling and S. Maruna (eds), *The Effects of Imprisonment*. Cullompton: Willan.

Livingstone, S., Owen, T. and Macdonald, A. (2003) *Prison Law*, 3rd edn. Oxford: Oxford University Press.

Loader, I. and Sparks, R. (2002) 'Contemporary landscapes of crime, order, and control: governance, risk, and globalisation', in M. Maguire, R. Morgan, and R. Reiner (eds), *The Oxford Handbook of Criminology*. Oxford: Oxford University Press.

Logan, C. (2003) 'Ethical issues in risk assessment practice and research', in G. Ashead and C. Brown (eds), *Ethical issues in Forensic Research*. London: Jessica Kingsley.

London Probation (2005) *London MAPPA Annual Report 2004–2005*. London: London Probation. See: http://www.london-probation.org.uk.

Lord Chief Justice (2006) cited in 'Madness of dustbin jails' by Mary Riddell and Jamie Doward, *Observer*, 8 October.

Loughlin, M. (1978) 'Procedural fairness: a study of the crisis in administrative law theory', *University of Toronto Law Journal*, 28: 215–41.

Lucas, J. R. (1980) *On Justice*. Oxford: Clarendon Press.

Lupton, D. (1999) *Risk*. London: Routledge.

Lynch, M. (1998) 'Waste managers? The new penology, crime fighting, and parole agent identity', *Law and Society Review*, 32: 839–69.

Lynch, M. (2000) 'Rehabilitation and rhetoric: the ideal of reformation in contemporary parole discourse and practices', *Punishment and Society*, 2 (1): 40–65.

Macgill, S. (1989) 'Risk perception and the public: insights from research around Sellafield', in J. Brown (ed.), *Environmental Threats: Perception, Analysis and Management*. London: Belhaven Press, pp. 48–66.

McGuire, J. (1997) 'Ethical dilemmas in forensic clinical psychology', *Legal and Criminological Psychology*, 2: 177–92.

McMurran, M. and Ward, T. (2004) 'Motivating offenders to change in therapy: an organizing framework', *Legal and Criminological Psychology*, 9: 295–311.

Maguire, M., Kemshall, H., Noaks, L., Sharpe, K. and Wincup, E. (2000) *Risk Management of Sexual and Violent Offenders: The Work of Public Protection Panels*. London: Home Office.

Mair, G. (ed.) (2004) *What Matters in Probation*. Cullompton: Willan.

Marshall, P. (1997) *A Reconviction Study of HMP Grendon Therapeutic Community (No. 53)*. London: Home Office.

Maruna, S. (2004) '"California Dreamin'': are we heading toward a National Offender "Waste Management" Service?', *Criminal Justice Matters*, 56: 6–7.

Mate, P. (2006) 'The development of the Prison Service as a "Responsible Authority" within Multi Agency Public Protection Arrangements in England and Wales (2004–2005)', *Prison Service Journal*, 163: 50–4.

Maynard-Moody, S., Musheno, M. and Palumbo, D. (1990) 'Street wise social policy: resolving the dilemma of street-level influence and successful implementation', *Western Political Quarterly*, 43: 831–48.

Monahan, J. (1996) 'Violent storms and violent people: how meteorology can inform risk communication in mental health law', *American Psychologist*, 51: 931–8.

Moore, R., Howard, P. and Burns, M. (2006) 'The further development of OASys: realising the potential of the Offender Assessment System', *Prison Service Journal*, 167: 36–42.

Morgan, K. D. (1994) 'Factors associated with probation outcome', *Journal of Criminal Justice*, 22 (4): 342–53.

Morgan, R. (2004) 'Resettlement, the Criminal Justice Act 2003 and NOMS: prospects and problems', *Criminal Justice Matters*, 56: 4.

Nash, M. (1999) *Police, Probation and Protecting the Public*. London: Blackstone Press.

National Probation Service (2004) *The MAPPA Guidance*, Probation Circular 54/2004. London: NPS.

National Probation Service (2005) *Monitoring of Risk of Harm*, Probation Circular 82/2005. London: NPS.

O'Leary, V. and Glasser, D. (1972) 'The assessment of risk in parole decision making', in D. J. West (ed.), *The Future of Parole*. London: Duckworth, pp. 135–98.

O'Neill, O. (2002) *A Question of Trust*. Cambridge: Cambridge University Press.

Padfield, N. (2002) *Beyond the Tariff*. Cullompton: Willan.

Padfield, N. (2005) 'A critical perspective on private prisons in England and Wales', in N. Capus et al. (eds), *Public-Prive: vers un nouveau partage du contrôle de la criminalité?* Chur/Zürich: Verlag Rüegger.

Padfield, N. (2006) 'The Parole Board in transition', *Criminal Law Review*, p. 18.

Padfield, N. and Leibling, A. with Arnold, H. (2000) *An Exploration of Decision-making at Discretionary Lifer Panels*, Home Office Research Study No. 213. London: Home Office.

Padfield, N. and Maruna, S. (2006) 'The revolving door at the prison gate: exploring the dramatic increase in recalls to prison', *Criminology and Criminal Justice*, 6 (3): 329–52.

Paris, J. (1996) *Social Factors in the Personality Disorders: A Biopsychosocial Approach to Etiology and Treatment*. Cambridge: Cambridge University Press.

Parole Board (1993) *Annual Report 1992*. London: HMSO.

Parole Board (1998) *Report of the Parole Board for 1997–1998*, HC 1089. London: Stationery Office.

Parole Board (1999) *Annual Report 1998/99*. London: HMSO.

Parole Board (2003) *Annual Report and Accounts of the Parole Board for England and Wales 2002–2003*, HC 1182. London: Stationery Office.

Parole Board (2004a) *Annual Report and Accounts of the Parole Board for England and Wales 2003–2004*, HC 1100. London: Stationery Office.

Parole Board (2004b) *The Corporate Plan*. London: Home Office. See: http://www.paroleboard.gov.uk (accessed 8 August 2006).

Parole Board (2005) *Annual Report and Accounts of the Parole Board for England and Wales 2004–2005*, HC 518. London: Stationery Office.

Parole Board (2006a) *The Annual Business Plan*. London: Home Office. See: http://www.paroleboard.gov.uk (accessed 8 August 2006).

Parole Board (2006b) *Parole Board Responds to Home Secretary's Proposals for Reform*. London: Home Office. See: http://www.paroleboard.gov.uk (accessed 8 August 2006).

Parole Board (2006c) *Annual Report and Accounts of the Parole Board for England and Wales 2005–2006*, HC 1661. London: Stationery Office.

Parton, N. (1986) 'The Beckford Inquiry: a critical appraisal', *British Journal of Social Work*, 16 (5): 531–56.

Paternoster, R., Brame, R., Bachman, R. and Sherman, L. W. (1997) 'Do fair procedures matter? The effects of procedural justice on spouse assault', *Law and Society Review*, 31 (1): 163–204.

Perrow, C. (1984) *Normal Accidents: Living with High-Risk Technologies*. New York: Basic Books.

Petersilia, J. (1985) 'Community supervision: trends and critical issues', *Crime and Delinquency*, 36: 87–111.

Plotnikoff, J. and Woolfson, R. (2000) *Where Are They Now? An Evaluation of Sex Offender Registration in England and Wales*, Police Research Series No. 126. London: Home Office.

Prins, H. (1988) 'Dangerous clients: further observations on the limitations of mayhem', *British Journal of Social Work*, 18: 593–609.

Prison and Probation Ombudsman (PPO) (2004) *Report of the Inquiry into the Disturbance and Fire at Yarl's Wood Remand Centre*. London: HMSO.

Prison Reform Trust (2005) *Recycling Offenders Through Prison*. London: Prison Reform Trust.

Raphael, D. (2001) *Concepts of Justice*. Oxford: Clarendon Press.

Rawls, J. (1980) *A Theory of Justice*. Oxford: Oxford University Press; first published 1971.

Raynor, P. (2002) 'Community penalties: probation, punishment, and "What Works"', in M. Maguire, R. Morgan and R. Reiner (eds), *The Oxford Handbook of Criminology*, 3rd edn. Oxford: Oxford University Press.

Raynor, P. (2003) 'Research in probation: from "Nothing Works" to "What Works"', in W. H. Chui and M. Nellis (eds), *Moving Probation Forward: Evidence, Arguments and Practice*. Harlow: Pearson Longman.

RDS NOMS (2005) *Population in Custody*, November. London: Home Office.

Re-Entry Policy Council (2005) *Report of the Re-Entry Policy Council: Charting the Safe and Successful Return of Prisoners to the Community*. New York: Re-entry Policy Council, Council of State Governments.

Reid, J. (2006) Home Secretary's Annual Lecture to the Parole Board, 22 May. See: http://www.homeoffice.gov.uk.

Report of the Presidential Commission on the Space Shuttle Challenger Accident (1986) Washington, DC: Government Printing Agency.

Rex, S. (2001) 'Beyond cognitive-behaviouralism? Reflections on the effectiveness literature', in A. Bottoms, L. Gelsthorpe and S. Rex (eds), *Community Penalties: Change and Challenges*. Cullompton: Willan.

Risk Management Authority (2006a) *Risk Assessment Tools Evaluation Directory (RATED)*. Scotland: Risk Management Authority.

Risk Management Authority (2006b) *Standards for Guidelines for RMA Accredited Risk Assessors*. Scotland: Risk Management Authority.

Robson, C. (2002) *Real World Research*, 2nd edn. Oxford: Blackwell.

Runciman, W. B. (1993) 'System failure: an analysis of 2000 incident reports', *Anaesthesia and Intensive Care*, 21 (5): 684–95.

Satayamurti, C. (1981) *Occupational Survival*. Oxford: Blackwell.

Senjo, S. and Leip, L. A. (2001) 'Testing therapeutic jurisprudence theory: an empirical assessment of the drug court process', *Western Criminology Review*, 3 (1). Online at: http://wcr.sonoma.edu/v3n1/senjo.html.

Sentence Management Group (2001) *The Comprehensive Review of Parole and Lifer Processes*. London: Home Office.

Sheppard, D. (1996) *Learning the Lessons: Mental Health Inquiry Reports published in England and Wales between 1969–1996 and Their Recommendations for Improving Practice*, 2nd edn. London: Zito Trust.

Shingler, J. and Mann, R. E. (2005) 'Collaboration in clinical work with sexual offenders: treatment and risk assessment', in W. L. Marshall, Y. Fernandez, L. Marshall and G. Serran (eds), *Sexual Offender Treatment: Controversial Issues*. Chichester: Wiley.

Shute, S. (2003) 'The development of parole and the role of research in its reform' in L. Zedner and A. Ashworth (eds), *The Criminological Foundations of Penal Policy: Essays in Honour of Roger Hood*. Oxford: Oxford University Press, pp. 377–439.

Shute, S. (2004) 'Does parole work? The empirical evidence from England and Wales', *Ohio State Journal of Criminal Law*, 2: 315–31.

Shute, S. (2006) 'Sentencing "dangerous" offenders in England and Wales', in P. Tak and M. Jendly (eds), *The Implementation of Prison Sentences and Aspects of Security*. Nijmegen, Holland: Wolf Legal Publishers, pp. 75–95.

Siegal, M. (1982) *Fairness in Children: A Social-Cognitive Approach to the Study of Moral Development*. London: Academic Press.

Simon, J. (1993) *Poor Discipline: Parole and the Social Control of the Underclass, 1890–1990*. Chicago: University of Chicago Press.

Sims, B. and Jones, M. (1997) 'Predicting success or failure on probation: factors associated with felony probation outcomes', *Crime and Delinquency*, 43: 314–27.

South, N. (2002) 'Drugs, alcohol, and crime', in M. Maguire, R. Morgan and R. Reiner (eds), *The Oxford Handbook of Criminology*, 3rd edn. Oxford: Oxford University Press.

Sparks, R., Bottoms, A. E. and Hay, W. (1996) *Prisons and the Problem of Order*. Oxford: Clarendon Press.

Starbuck, W. H. and Milliken, J. (1988) 'Challenger: fine tuning the odds until something breaks', *Journal of Management Studies*, 25 (4): 319–40.

Stationery Office (2006) The Home Secretary's Five Year Strategy for Protecting the Public and Reducing Reoffending, Cm 6717. London: Home Office, announced 9 February.

Stephens, K. and Brown, I. (2001) 'OGRS2 in practice: an elastic ruler?', *Probation Journal*, 48: 179–87.

Thomas, T. (2005) *Sex Crime: Sex Offending and Society*. Cullompton: Willan.

Thornton, D. (2002) 'Constructing and testing a framework for dynamic risk assessment', *Sexual Abuse: A Journal of Research and Treatment*, 14: 139–53.

Thornton, D., Mann, R., Webster, S., Blud, L., Travers, R., Friendship, C. et al. (2003) 'Distinguishing and combining risks for sexual and violent recidivism', *Annals of the New York Academy of Science*, 989: 225–35.

Tuddenham, R. (2000) 'Beyond defensible decision-making: towards reflexive assessment of risk and dangerousness', *Probation Journal*, 47: 173–83.

Tyler, T. (1990) *Why People Obey the Law*. New Haven, CT: Yale University Press.

Tyler, T. and Blader, S. L. (2000) *Co-operation in Groups: Procedural Justice, Social Identity, and Behavioural Engagement*. Philadelphia: Taylor & Francis.

Tyler, T. and Huo, Y. J. (2002) *Trust in the Law: Encouraging Public Co-operation with the Police and Courts*. New York: Russell Sage.

USSR State Committee on the Utilization of Atomic Energy (1986) *The Accident at Chernobyl Nuclear Power Plant and Its Consequences*. Information compiled for the IAEA Experts' Meeting, 25–29 August, Vienna, IAEA.

Verheul, R., Van den Brink, W. and Koeter, M. W. (1998) 'Temporal stability of diagnostic criteria for antisocial personality disorder in male alcohol dependent patients', *Journal of Personality Disorders*, 12: 316–31.

Wade, W. and Forsyth, C. F. (2000) *Administrative Law*, 8th edn. Oxford: Oxford University Press.

Wade, W. and Forsyth, C. F. (2004) *Administrative Law*, 9th edn. Oxford: Oxford University Press.

Walmsley, R. (2005) *World Prison Population List*, 6th edn. London: Kings College London, International Centre for Prison Studies.

Ward, T. and Brown, M. (2004) 'The good lives model and conceptual issues in offender rehabilitation', *Psychology, Crime, and Law*, 10: 243–57.

Whitehead, J. T. and Lindquist, C. A. (1992) 'Determinants of probation and parole officer professional orientation', *Journal of Criminal Justice*, 20: 13–24.

Zevitz, R. and Farkas, M. (2000) 'Sex offender community notification: managing high risk criminals or exacting further vengeance?', *Behavioural Sciences and the Law*, 18: 375–91.

Index

Page numbers followed by 't' denote tables.